# OF GREED AND GLORY

# OF
# GREED
## and
# GLORY

In Pursuit
of Freedom
for All

DEBORAH G. PLANT

AMISTAD

*An Imprint of HarperCollinsPublishers*

HarperCollins books may be purchased for educational,
business, or sales promotional use. For information, please email
the Special Markets Department at SPsales@harpercollins.com.

FIRST EDITION

Library of Congress Cataloging-in-Publication Data has been
applied for.

ISBN 978-0-06-289849-4

23 24 25 26 27  LBC  5 4 3 2 1

For
my brother
Alfred Plant, Jr.

*In Honor of*
Saint Martín de Porres
Trees
The Ancestors
and
Foundational African Americans

# CONTENTS

# PROLOGUE

FIRST AND FOREMOST, THIS WORK is about universal, democratic freedom and personal sovereignty. It takes a comparative look at how the badges of slavery manifest in the relentless surveilling and policing of Black American citizens and communities; the ongoing deracination, dispossession, and disfranchisement of Black citizens; and the pernicious impoverishment of Black life. It is a meditation on the carceral system and the personal and collective calamity that it engenders within individual families and within the body politic of our nation.

Several hundred thousand Americans are caged in American jails *every single day*, not because they are necessarily guilty of a crime but because our wealth-based justice system targets those who don't have the money to post bail—if bail is set. And the vast majority of those caged are poor, Black, and brown.[1] Where popular discourse would have it that those entrapped in America's jails and prisons are paying their debt to society, the reality is that, like our Haitian cousins who were forced to pay reparations to France for its loss of Black "property" and slave labor after the 1791 Haitian Revolution,[2] African Americans have continued to pay a debt, a tax for our little eddy of freedom post-Emancipation.[3]

"Freedom" and "equality" are the watchwords of American democracy. But like justice, freedom and equality are meaningless when there is no corresponding practical application of the ideals they represent. Physical, bodily liberty lies at the core of an American's birthright of freedom and is fundamental to every

American's personal sovereignty. And yet millions of Americans are deprived of these basic freedoms every single day. We look the other way when the basic human rights of marginalized and stigmatized groups are violated and desecrated, not realizing that only the practice of justice everywhere secures justice for any of us anywhere.

In our society, liberty has been an ideal, but it has never been the practiced norm. Where America's "criminal punishment" system has systematically deprived millions of American citizens of their physical freedoms, so other oppressive and tyrannical institutions have trampled the basic freedoms, rights, and privileges of the American masses and have jeopardized our American democracy. "This freedom is a funny thing. . . . It ain't something permanent like rocks and hills. It's like manna; you just got to keep on gathering it fresh every day. If you don't, one day you're going to find you ain't got none no more."[4] An active vigilance is required of those who would be and remain free.

Until I began to think about what it might take to get my brother freed from Angola prison, I did not realize to what extent I myself was caught up in the American punishment system and its prison-industrial complex.[5] What I comprehended about "the system" before that moment was superficial at best. I never understood to what extent I and my family have unconsciously contributed to the maintenance and continuance of this wretched and barbaric institution every time, over the past twenty-plus years, that we have communicated or visited with my brother— money orders, phone calls, emails; food and drink purchases to enjoy with him during our visits; purchases of instant photos in some vague attempt to memorialize our brief reunions; leaving him cash money with the commissary clerk on our way out.

Because my brother was locked up and *we visited him*, I didn't realize how I was also locked up with him—like anyone or any family who insists on maintaining a relationship with an incarcerated loved one. Your life is strangely there, too. I gradually came to know intimately the truth that "judges and prosecutors don't think about the fact that when they incarcerate a man or woman, that they're locking a family up with them."[6] In their haste to convict and incarcerate, America's judges and prosecutors overlook or ignore the fact that "the defendant" is also someone's brother, son, father, somebody's child—a human being. The complex character of the person captured is reduced to one dimension: *criminal*. Tried and "duly convicted,"[7] the defendant's sovereign human life doesn't factor into the punishment imposed. It doesn't factor into the decision "to put a person away for 20, 30, 40, 50 years, because they're afraid of them."[8] It didn't factor into their decision to put away, to "disappear," my brother—for life.

&#10070; &#10070; &#10070;

Having taught African American and African Diasporan history and culture for most of my professional career, I know how the history of "slavery" informs and shapes American social and cultural institutions, particularly American penal institutions. But my brother's life imprisonment in Angola is not academic. Nor are the lives of millions of other detained and incarcerated human beings and their families. And yet as I looked into the possibility of my brother's freedom and began to ask the question "How did we get here?" I felt as though I was experiencing some version of *The Truman Show*, where I was a character already

cast and playing her role in a national narrative—weren't we all?[9]
I was living the *history*, the official American "*master* narrative"
that I had been researching and teaching.

My folks had finally been able to move from renting a house
to home ownership in 1970. The street on which we lived intersected with Fuqua Street. Other than its curiosity, I never gave
the name of that street a second thought. But in researching the
history of Angola, the place that I was condemned to visit and
sustain for the duration of my life or my brother's life, I learned
that Fuqua Street was named for Louisiana governor Henry Luse
Fuqua, who, before he became governor, was the first general
manager of the Louisiana State Penitentiary in Angola. And in
researching the roots of Angola prison, I found myself retracing
the routes of the European transatlantic "slave trade."

Angola state prison was originally a "slave plantation." Many
believe that the plantation and the prison were named to com-
memorate the place of origin of those who had been enslaved
there. Others state that the timeline of the United States' 1807
abolition of the international trafficking of Africans and Isaac
Franklin's purchase of Angola Plantation in the 1830s doesn't
support this popular belief.[10]

While the name "Angola" did refer to the region from which
millions of Africans were extracted and forced into an abominable history, the plantation was not named by Franklin as "a
nod" to enslaved Angolans. Rather, "slave trader" and "slave-
plantation" owner Isaac Franklin named the estate "Angola" to
laud his success and his prominence in the commerce of the international trafficking of Africans. Proof of his business prowess,
the naming was a testament to his greed for excess wealth and
fame. It was a trophy that symbolized his prerogative "to take

the ancestral languages and words" of those subjugated; a flaunting of the glory he gained in holding dominion over the bodies of human beings that he ventured to claim as his property.[11]

Though the naming of Angola Plantation was an act of hubris and the appropriation of the name correlates with the historical and the contemporary seizure and subjugation of Black human bodies, the reclamation of the name "Angola" nevertheless underscores the reality of the historical Angola, in southwest and central Africa, as the matrix of struggles for freedom and national sovereignty. "Angola" held symbolic meaning for those formerly enslaved on the Angola Plantation and holds symbolic meaning for those who have been incarcerated in Angola prison, in a "slavery by another name."

The word "Angola" is derived from the Kimbundu-Bantu word *ngola*. It refers to an iron object that symbolized a leader or king and was the title accorded to the leader of Ndongo (Angola).[12] The name recalls Angola's warrior queen Njinga, who waged a fierce and relentless battle against Portuguese colonizers and their African allies in the seventeenth century. And "Angola" conjures the spirit of enslaved and nominally free Africans who escaped from North and South Carolina and Georgia and joined with the Seminoles to form one of the largest maroon societies in Spanish Florida. Known as the "Angola community," the establishment of this settlement of six hundred to seven hundred fifty maroons coincided with the ending of the War of 1812 between the US and Britain.

Their story documents a quest for freedom, a *refusal* to be circumscribed and defined by external controlling narratives and oppressive individuals and the systems that enable them.[13] It demonstrates a people's expressed self-determination, power, and sovereignty, and their will to live on their own terms, practicing their own self-affirming rituals and cultural traditions. Theirs is also a story of tragedy, as US general Andrew Jackson, who was told "to take no immediate action," nonetheless commanded their destruction in 1821, just prior to Florida becoming a US territory in 1822, and later a "slave state" in 1845.[14] Under orders from Jackson, the Angola settlement was raided, and houses and fields were burned to the ground.[15] Some who survived the assault were re-enslaved. Some escaped to other maroon communities. And others escaped to Andros Island in the Bahamas.

The Angola maroon community thrived a little more than sixty miles from the Tampa Bay area, where I live in Florida. The history of this settlement, however, had been burned to ashes and "buried under three feet and two centuries of earth." But excavations initiated in 2006 retrieved Angola from oblivion and reconnected its narrative with the Underground Railroad Network to Freedom. The story of Angola maroons in Florida documents this "stirring in the soul for freedom."[16] And the soul's stirring for freedom is a *human* story, an utterly important point that cannot be overemphasized, for fundamental to the administration and functioning of America's Peculiar Institution was the attitude and perception that Black people were not quite human, but indeed, that we were *chattel*, a word derived from the Latin *capitalis*, meaning "capital," i.e., movable real estate.

And so it was okay to hunt and capture Africans, to cage us in *barracoons*, to pile us into the holds of ships like so much lumber, to auction us off to the highest bidder—to commodify our and our children's entire existence as property, as merchandise. It was okay to patrol and surveil African Americans within and outside the perimeters of our communities; to racially profile us; to randomly frisk and harass us; to break into our bedrooms, on purpose and by accident, with and without warrants—knock-knock or no-knock; to indiscriminately arrest us, intentionally and by mistaken identity and racialized glitches in digitized systems of facial recognition; to indifferently kill us or cage our bodies because most of us are too poor to post bail, let alone hire lawyers who are not aligned with America's punishment bureaucracy of mass incarceration.

In examining the roots of the Louisiana State Penitentiary at Angola, I retraced its historical and political routes to the nexus of US constitutional law. Just as the 1793 Fugitive Slave Clause in Article IV had criminalized freedom-seeking Angola maroons, who were hunted, re-enslaved, killed, or scattered, so the Thirteenth Amendment's Criminal Punishment Clause had criminalized free African Americans, who were terrorized, exploited, and legally re-enslaved within state and federal prison systems. The designation "criminal" became synonymous with "slave," and both terms reduced Black human beings to the status of objects, of chattel, to be used and economically exploited for the profit and benefit of individuals and states alike and by both state and federal governments.

The process of the criminalization of individual Black Americans is simultaneously the process of the dehumanization of all Black Americans. As US congresspersons and state legislators work to pass abolition amendments to end the "legalized slavery" that fuels mass incarceration, and activists, lawyers, and politicians move to decarcerate America and abolish the prison-industrial complex,[17] we are reminded that ending the systematic caging of America's vulnerable citizens of color and poor whites is both a radical stand for democracy and "a deeply human project."[18]

The official, political spin that portrays African Americans and people of color as suspect and objectifies the "duly con-victed" as a danger and a threat to white American society has the effect of both locating people of color beyond the pro-tections of the Constitution and undermining their humanity. These controlling "master" narratives are designed to ease and soothe the conscience of the masses of Americans while they mute the voices and void the histories and stories of those killed, caged, and incarcerated for life, and thereby rewrite the story of *how we got here.*

Our histories and our stories humanize us. This fact is what confounded Thomas Jefferson in his reaction to the poetry of the enslaved woman Phillis Wheatley. After all, stories—myths, legends, tales, histories, orature, *and* literature—are at the core of human civilization and culture. Thus, disappearing a people, erasing a people's history, burying their stories, and silencing their voices are means of denying and dismantling their human-ity. Keeping their stories buried facilitates keeping their bodies caged. As Alec Karakatsanis notes in *Usual Cruelty: The Com-plicity of Lawyers in the Criminal Injustice System*, the success of mass incarceration enterprises and the American punishment bureaucracy "depends on erasing people and their stories."[19]

Movements to end "slavery" in all its forms and to end the injustice of systems of punishment include rethinking how we per-ceive and talk about "slavery" and the meaning, method, and ob-jective of the Punishment Clause, the harm it causes, and those it harms. Does it actually achieve public safety, or does it, in reality, facilitate private and corporate profit?[20] Included in the processes of thinking and talking about the "criminal injustice system" is the development of empathy and compassion and the capacity to see the "othered" as the self. And inside of that, the capacity to allow ourselves to be touched by the humanity of other human beings and see that what is happening to some of us is actually happening to all of us, whether we realize it or not. And yet the work is that we come to realize it. "Injustice anywhere is a threat to justice everywhere" is not just a neat phrase.[21]

Vital to these processes are the remembered histories and resurrected stories of marginalized and criminalized Americans. Vital, also, is the courage to reclaim American stories that have been outlawed by gubernatorial fiat or "anti-woke" laws passed by legislative bodies that are aligned with the American punishment bureaucracy. Instrumental to these processes is the developing language of freedom, personal sovereignty, inclusive democracy, and justice for all.

The details and aspects of my brother's story resound in every story of separation and unfairness and inhumanity. Thus, my brother's story speaks to unity, justice, and humanity. And at the intersection of the history of Angola prison and the story of Angola maroons is a crossroads, a space in which we can envision an unfolding story of an America where all Americans are perceived as human beings and as equal citizens, an America that protects the civil rights of historically marginalized and mainstreamed Americans alike, that honors "the people" and our sovereign and constitutional authority, an America where freedom is understood and respected as both a human and holy right, and a democratic America that embraces justice for all. Such an America requires a new vision. And a new vision requires a "jailbreak of the imagination."[22] We will never evolve beyond the controlling and punishing historical narratives of the past until we imagine a future to evolve into.

Ultimately, to talk about "slavery" and the Slavery Clause is to talk about freedom and personal sovereignty, for "slavery" is unnatural to the human spirit, and therefore, it is an impossible idea. No amount of rationalization, justification, historical and biblical points of reference, or prosecutorial arguments will ever still the "stirring in the soul for freedom." Those of us who believe in freedom cannot rest until freedom is our practical reality, as Sweet Honey in the Rock teaches.[23]

I am imagining my brother free.

## NOTES

1. Alec Karakatsanis, *Usual Cruelty: The Complicity of Lawyers in the Criminal Injustice System* (New York: The New Press, 2019), 15, 157.

2. In 1825, more than twenty years after national sovereignty had been established in Haiti, French king Charles X sent a flotilla of warships into the Caribbean waters to extract from Haitian president Jean-Pierre Boyer an agreement to pay 150 million francs to France as reparations or be subject to more war and re-enslavement. Haiti was forced into taking out a high-interest loan from a French bank in order to pay the extorted reparations. In the 122 years that it would take to pay off the loan, the Haitian people would pay French enslavers and their descendants "between $20 and $30 billion in today's dollars."

Having staged several political and military interventions in Haiti and having violently occupied the island nation for nineteen years, from 1915 to 1934, the United States had also taken control of Haiti's public finances, "siphoning away around 40% of Haiti's national income to service debt repayments to the U.S. and France." The scholar Marlene Daut proclaims this economic disaster imposed on Haiti as "the greatest heist in history."

Prized as "the most lucrative colony" of the French empire, Haiti, today, is described as one of the poorest nations in the world. Though Haitians declared their independence after defeating the French in the 1791 Haitian Revolution, France forced Haiti into economic enslavement, and both France and the United States would work to undermine Haitian freedom, democracy, and sovereignty over the ensuing centuries. Western popular media has effectively cast the Haitian government as politically corrupt and Haitian peoples as incapable of self-government; however, that media never speaks to the role of Western powers in keeping Haiti destabilized and Haitians insecure and impoverished.

(Greg Rosalsky, "'The Greatest Heist in History': How Haiti Was Forced to Pay Reparations for Freedom," NPR, October 5, 2021, https://www.npr.org/sections/money/2021/10/05/1042518732/-the-greatest-heist-in-history-how-haiti-was-forced-to-pay-reparations-for-freed; and Marlene Daut, "When France Extorted Haiti—the Greatest Heist in History," *The Conversation,*

June 30, 2020, https://theconversation.com/when-france-extorted-haiti-the
-greatest-heist-in-history-137949.)

3. Paraphrase of excerpt from Colson Whitehead, *The Underground Railroad*
(New York: Doubleday, 2016), 29: "Sometimes a slave will be lost in a brief
eddy of liberation."

4. Zora Neale Hurston, *Moses, Man of the Mountain*, in *Zora Neale Hurston:
Novels and Stories*, ed. Cheryl A. Wall (New York: Library of America,
1995), 577.

5. This concept of the "American punishment system" is informed by Alec
Karakatsanis's essay "The Punishment Bureaucracy," which discusses civil
rights cases he and his organization brought to challenge "widespread
injustices in the punishment system" and the deception of "criminal justice
reform," in Karakatsanis, *Usual Cruelty*, 2.

6. Reuben Jonathan Miller, "Out of Prison but Still Trapped: Examining the
'Afterlife' of Incarceration," interview by Terry Gross, *Fresh Air*, NPR,
March 24, 2021, https://www.npr.org/2021/03/24/980671402/out-of-prison
-but-still-trapped-examining-the-afterlife-of-incarceration.

7. Thirteenth Amendment: Article XIII, Section 1, in "The Constitution," in *The
Debate on the Constitution: Federalist and Antifederalist Speeches, Articles,
and Letters During the Struggle over Ratification, Part One: September 1787 to
February 1788*, ed. Bernard Bailyn (New York: Library of America, 1993), 985.

8. Miller, "Out of Prison but Still Trapped."

9. For an insightful analysis that demonstrates how objectification of people
exploits and undermines their humanity as it simultaneously diminishes our
human capacity for empathy, see Susannah McCullough and Debra Minof,
"The Truman Show Tried to Warn Us," The Take, posted July 30, 2020,
YouTube video, https://www.youtube.com/watch?v=gRb7illNciw.

10. Marianne Fisher-Giorlando and Chris Turner-Neal, "Angola: Fact and
Fiction," *64 Parishes*, https://64parishes.org/angola-fact-and-fiction.

11. Joshua D. Rothman, *The Ledger and the Chain: How Domestic Slave Traders
Shaped America* (New York: Basic Books, 2021), 303.

12. *Ngola* was an iron object that symbolized kingship: see "Angola," South
African History Online, https://www.sahistory.org.za/place/angola.

13. I use the term "refusal" in contradistinction to "resistance." As defined by
Professor Lindsey Stewart, "refusal *withholds* recognition of the oppressor's
power or authority to define our lives." (*The Politics of Black Joy: Zora Neale
Hurston and Neo-Abolitionism* [Evanston, Illinois: Northwestern University
Press, 2021], 33.)

14. "Destruction of Angola - 1821," Reflections of Manatee, https://
reflectionsofmanatee.org/freedom-seekers/.

15. Isaac Eger, "Angola's Ashes: A Newly Excavated Settlement Highlights
Florida's History as a Haven for Escaped Slaves," *Sarasota Magazine*, June 27,
2018, https://www.sarasotamagazine.com/news-and-profiles/2018/06/a-newly
-excavated-settlement-highlights-florida-s-history-as-a-haven-for-escaped-slaves.

16. Eger, "Angola's Ashes."

17. Jeff Merkley, "The Abolition Amendment," https://www.merkley.senate.gov

/imo/media/doc/The%20Abolition%20Amendment%20One%20Pager%20
-%20117th_.pdf.

18. Karakatsanis, *Usual Cruelty*, 10.

19. Karakatsanis, *Usual Cruelty*, 10.

20. Karakatsanis discusses "the punishment bureaucracy as a tool of power in service of white supremacy and profit." (*Usual Cruelty*, 18.)

21. Martin Luther King, Jr., "Letter from a Birmingham Jail (1963)," in *I Have A Dream: Writings and Speeches That Changed the World*, ed. James Melvin Washington (San Francisco: HarperSanFrancisco, 1992), 85.

22. Mariame Kaba, *We Do This 'Til We Free Us: Abolitionist Organizing and Transforming Justice* (Chicago: Haymarket Books, 2021), 25.

23. This statement is inspired by the Freedom Day Rally speech (1964) of Ella Baker that was memorialized in "Ella's Song" (1988) by Sweet Honey in the Rock.

# CHAPTER 1

# THE ENTERPRISE OF FREEDOM

Is AMERICA EXPERIENCING A PERIOD of reckoning? A paradigm shift? Are we poised to realize the vision of a more perfect union that embraces all equally? Are we ready to look honestly at the consequences of reckless imbalances of illegitimate power and illegal privilege? Are American politics at a tipping point?

Juneteenth, a day commemorating the end of enslavement, became a national holiday on June 17, 2021. While the National Independence Day Act was signed into law, lawmakers also reintroduced legislation to strike the "punishment clause" loophole from the US Constitution's Thirteenth Amendment. A joint resolution of the US House and Senate, the proposed Abolition Amendment would close the loophole that has perpetuated mass incarceration for a century and a half and allowed private and public officials and industries and corporations, alike, to profit from the forced labor of convicted prisoners, disproportionately African Americans and people of color.[1]

Slavery and involuntary servitude were formally abolished by the Thirteenth Amendment, except as punishment for those "duly convicted" of a crime.[2] A consequence of this "criminal-exception" loophole is that millions of politically vulnerable Americans have been criminalized and unduly deprived of their freedom, robbed of a sense of personal sovereignty, dispossessed of the fruits of their labor, and stripped of their citizenship rights—*for life*.

A consequence of the Punishment Clause is legalized slavery. A consequence of legalized slavery is the proliferation of corrupt state and federal policies that sanctioned and continue to sanction arrests and convictions for minor infractions, mandatory minimum sentencing, and excessive, life imprisonment sentences. A consequence of legalized slavery and corrupt public policy is a rigged and racialized judicial system that imposes fines and sets bails that most folk cannot pay, a judicial system that employs prosecutors and public defenders to negotiate plea deals that are simply legal catch-22s, and a judicial system that cloaks America's antidemocratic legal processes in robes of justice.

The proposed Abolition Amendment, cosponsored by Senator Jeffrey Merkley and Congresswoman Nikema Williams, underscores and advances the abolitionist work of activists, lawyers, and lawmakers, that began in the antebellum era and has continued into twenty-first-century America. As Merkley and Williams state, "The *Abolition Amendment* would finally finish the job started by the Civil War, Emancipation Proclamation, and 13th Amendment and end the morally reprehensible practice of slavery and forced labor in America, and send a clear message: in this country, no person will be stripped of their basic humanity and forced to toil for someone else's profit."[3]

The pursuit of profit, like an addiction, was the driving force that sustained America's Peculiar Institution of slavery. That same greed for profit that was fed by the forced labor of Black people continued unabated. This pattern of destroying Black lives for the profit and benefit of private individuals, public officials, and corporate enterprises was apparent in the convict-leasing system that re-enslaved thousands of Black men, women, and children across the American South. It was apparent in the rule of lynch law during the era of Reconstruction and Jim Crow, a time when Black businesses and Black communities and towns were indiscriminately terrorized, burned, and looted. And that pattern has persisted into the modern age of the prison-industrial complex that facilitates the detention, incarceration, and post-incarceration enthrallment of Black people, people of color, and poor white people across the nation.

In 2018, Colorado became the first state to repeal the criminal-exception clause from its constitution, thereby abolishing slavery and involuntary servitude "in all circumstances."[4] In the following two years, the states of Nebraska and Colorado removed from their constitutions the clause that continued the preservation of slavery as punishment for crime. In 2022, Alabama, Louisiana, Oregon, Tennessee, and Vermont held referendums on repealing or reforming the "Slavery Clause" in their constitutions. Louisiana, alone, elected to preserve slavery.

The controversial vote in Louisiana was nonetheless historic and perhaps even propitious.[5] The initiative to amend Louisiana's Slavery Clause entailed a revision to the latter part of Article I, Section 3 of the state constitution, titled "Right to Individual Dignity": "Slavery and involuntary servitude are prohibited."[6] That the state of Louisiana recognized in its proposed legislation that individual dignity is a right that the State should not abrogate, even as that right pertains to incarcerated persons, is important.

For, since the Civil War, Black Louisianians have been forced to endure "badges and incidents of slavery,"[7] both in the sphere of the general public and within the walls of the state's prison system. Louisiana is home to the Louisiana State Penitentiary called Angola, one of the most infamous plantation prison systems in America. Angola was built with "convict" labor on a former slave plantation, and Louisiana was among the first Southern states to re-enslave newly freed Black people within the state's equally infamous convict-leasing system.

"Louisiana! Louisiana! That dear old state of ours"[8] is also my home. When my family visited relatives "across the river," in Bayou Plaquemine, Bayou Goula, Caddo, the Pointe, and White Castle, my siblings and I would sometimes race up and down the levees, some distance away from the cows grazing there. At the summit of the hill, you could see the Mississippi waters through stands of trees and brush. It never occurred to me that our "playground" was the living testimony of Black men, prisoners of Angola whom the state of Louisiana had re-enslaved in the convict-leasing system. I was unaware of the horrendous, humiliating, and inhumane conditions under which these men were forced to perform the deadly work of raising levees, digging canals, and laying a latticework of railroad tracks across the state.

Louisiana is home, and Angola would become familiar ground to me and my family after my brother was condemned to life imprisonment at Angola in 2000. So, both the proposed US amendment and the unsuccessful Louisiana referendum to repeal the "Slavery Clause" are important to me as a US and world citizen, as a native of Louisiana, and as a sister whose brother has been "taken up" and imprisoned for life. As Representative Edmond Jordan of Louisiana (quoted in Paterson 2021) proposed the amendment to abolish legalized slavery "in all cases," Congresswoman Nikema Williams proclaimed that the federal Abolition

Amendment would take us "one step closer to achieving true justice and equality for all."[9]

"States are amending their constitutions to finally abolish slavery in all forms, and Congress will lead the way and finally abolish involuntary servitude in America," Williams assures us. "We are in a period of reckoning with our country's history and a lot of that history is marked with racism and systems of oppression. Eliminating the loophole in the 13th Amendment that allows for slavery is another opportunity to do that."[10]

"Indisputably racist" is how Williams and Merkley describe the Punishment Clause, which is also dubbed the Slavery Clause. This exception clause in federal and state constitutions is also indisputably antidemocratic, elitist, and patriarchal. In addition to the practice of racism, the clause allows for the practice of other -isms that Williams broadly identifies as "systems of oppression."[11] As systems of oppression tend to be intersecting, one form of oppression can easily conceal another more fundamental and pernicious form of oppression. Such is the case with the "indisputable" racism associated with America's race-based Peculiar Institution of slavery, as it obscures and distracts us from recognizing other systems that function to maintain slavery in its relentless and virulent reformulations in modern American society.

*Of Greed and Glory* looks at the apparent and concealed systems of oppression that are inherent in the "Slavery Clause" of our Constitution. Through my brother's letters about his experiences of arrest, detention, and eventual incarceration at Angola prison, *Of Greed and Glory* addresses the indisputable system of racial oppression. In context of the history of Angola prison and my brother's lived experiences there, this work explores the increasingly more apparent intersecting system of economic oppression.

Less apparent but fundamental to both racial and economic oppression is patriarchal oppression. The system of American patriarchy has as much to do with the police killing and over-incarceration of Black men and boys as it has to do with sexism, heterosexism, the repression and subjugation of women and girls, and the US Supreme Court's recent overturning of *Roe v. Wade*.

Many bemoan the fact that "we are still working to abolish slavery more than 155 years after the passage of the Thirteenth Amendment."[12] One of the reasons that the movement to abolish slavery is ongoing is that slavery in America is associated with Black people. And the post–Civil War political and social con-structions of Black people as inferior, uncivilized, brutish, and innately criminal served to justify our incarceration. Like the Peculiar Institution of slavery, penal institutions are seen as a fit environment for a purportedly dangerous and unruly people. Indeed, the discourse of generations of scholars and historians has served to justify, and thus normalize, racial slavery.

The trafficking in Africans and continued exploitation of people of African descent within America's Peculiar Institution has long been justified by many historians and economists as *necessary*. And such spurious claims about how the land *needed* "develop-ment," thus prompting a "demand for cheap labor,"[13] and how "the demands of the sugar crop" *required* slave gang labor[14] pro-vide a refrain for the historical and contemporary justifications for reducing millions of Black human beings to chattel (i.e., cattle). So, no less than slavery, itself, the mass incarceration of Black people is perceived as neither cruel nor unusual, but *necessary*. And if a profit can be made from their imprisonment, all the better.

Certainly, the politics of extracting the labor, intelligence, creativity, and resources of Black people has remained a key element in the political economy of America. Thus, in addition to the Slavery Clause in the Thirteenth Amendment that permitted the convict-leasing system, African Americans were forced into the oppressive economic systems of sharecropping, tenant farming, and debt peonage—some of slavery's other names.

Scholars, over time, have detailed how America's practice of enslavement *became* race based and how racialized social and economic disparities and inequities became systemic and structural across institutions. However, though racism became integral to the institution of enslavement, nationally, globally, and historically, racism was not an essential aspect of *slavery* as an enterprise. And even as the Reconstruction era ushered in neo-slavery economics and the Jim Crow era spoke to "the nadir of the Negro's status in American society,"[15] both eras also bespoke the brutality of the social system of Western patriarchy.

So, basically, even though those of us who suffer the direct impacts of the criminal-punishment loophole are "disproportionately Black Americans and people of color," this fact accounts, only in part, for the slow pace of change.[16] And yet America must wake up to the fact that slavery and involuntary servitude, in any form, have no place in a democratic republic. The badges of slavery that subjugate, exploit, and humiliate are anathema to the creed of freedom and justice for all. Injustice is not "a Black thing," and locking up (white) police officers, celebrities, corrupt and misogynistic politicians, and corporate moguls/tycoons—female and male alike—doesn't make America's corrupted justice system less corrupt, nor does it make the country's carceral status more acceptable. Making orange the new black doesn't make any of it right.

Another, and perhaps more fundamental, reason that the abolition movement is continuing is that the intersecting and interlocking systems of oppression work in sync to keep America's Peculiar Institution viable and transmissible—in one form or another, and through the subjugation of one vulnerable group or another, regardless of citizenship status. So when we and our civic and political leadership talk about engaging in acts "to end slavery, once and for all," then we all are compelled to search out the root causes of this disgraceful and repugnant chapter in our common history.[17]

We need to understand deeply, in the real time of abolitionist movements to amend loopholes and envision justice and freedom for all, that injustice anywhere never ceases to be a threat to justice everywhere. Otherwise, like the proverbial weed, injustice crops up elsewhere, in other forms, criminalizing folk and taking prisoners. Ending slavery in America *once and for all* is a radical idea. If we are to eradicate the practices and politics of the Peculiar Institution of slavery from American soil, society, and culture, it is not enough to recognize the insidious forms enslavement takes as they pertain to African Americans. We must also become intimately familiar with and knowledgeable of *slavery's essence*, the essence of slavery, of that which generates and informs slavery's political incarnations and institutional reformulations.

At the core of each of the main interlocking systems of American slavery—racism, monopoly capitalism, and patriarchy, and their *vade mecum*, elitism—is a "master-slave" dynamic. Individuals and groups whose ideology and worldview are inflected with this dynamic assume themselves superior, privileged, deserving, and entitled. The "master-slave" dynamic did not remain on Southern plantations, and it did not die on American Civil War battlefields. More in retreat than in defeat, this dynamic reasserted itself at every opportunity in postbellum America. The Criminal Punishment or Slavery Clause, represents just one opportunity in a history of such opportunities that we can trace back to the 1787 US Constitutional Convention and its three-fifths compromise that empowered an American slavocracy within a bourgeoning American democracy.

An elitist "master-slave" dynamic is incompatible with the principles of democracy, freedom, and equality. This dynamic, as reflected in the systems that cohered into America's Peculiar Institution, was and is—in addition to being racist, economically oppressive, elitist, and patriarchal at its core—an inheritance of European old-world tyranny and is naturally antidemocratic and un-American. As Senator Merkley affirmed, "This country was founded on the beautiful principles of equality and justice— principles that have never been compatible with the horrific realities of slavery and white supremacy."[18]

In Merkley's reference to "this country," certain assumptions are implied about a unified America. And yet, there are two Americas. Though the United States was proclaimed "one nation, indivisible,"[19] two distinct ideologies developed simultaneously in the new republic: One ideology declared liberty, freedom, and justice for all, and the other insisted on aristocratic rule sustained by a slave-based economy. The former was oriented toward ideals of individual freedom and self-government, and the latter was oriented toward extravagant wealth and tyrannical power. Where the first ideology was rooted in the ideals set forth in the Declaration of Independence and the broader ideals expressed in the US Constitution, the latter was rooted in the narrow, old-world schemata of the Fundamental Constitutions of Carolina.

Some founders were compelled by the dream of a democratic society and the principles of individual sovereignty, equality, and universal freedom. Others, inspired by a greed for expeditious and excessive wealth and the desire for a glory derived from elitist and tyrannical power, were driven by this "master-slave" dynamic. Greed is a strain that is intricately woven into the American Dream. The essential theme here is that one is driven to having more than one could ever need. And, like a virus, this insatiable greed has wormed its way into the soul of America.[20]

If America is "in a period of reckoning with our country's history," as Congresswoman Williams states,[21] if we are at a tipping point and poised for a shift into a more perfect union, then it behooves us to inquire into the contending ideologies that have resulted in a house that has remained divided. Supposedly, the Civil War dismantled the politics that pitted "slave states" against "free states." And yet the effect of the punishment-exception clause in the Thirteenth Amendment was to not only sanction the preservation of slavery and involuntary servitude, but also to extend it nationwide. We have been told and we want to believe that there are no red states and blue states—but there are. Further, in 2022, we have also witnessed the partitioning of the country into states where women's personal sovereignty is recognized and those states where motherhood is again politicized, with the consequences that women and the people who love and care for them are criminalized and thus subject to treatment as chattel.

The absence of choice is the absence of voice. And whether one is disfranchised because one has been "duly convicted," or because the Voting Rights Act has been gutted, or because Supreme

Courts decide that the masses of women have no rights that ty-rannical and patriarchal justices are bound to respect, the fact is that tyrants demand that their subjects be voiceless and that the personal sovereignty of their subjects be annulled. This essential element of the systems of oppression that preserved the institution of slavery has permeated *all* American institutions and has left no facet of American life and society untouched.

Racialized political and social propaganda has taught main-stream America *not to see* the fundamentally antidemocratic, anti-American roots of "legalized slavery." Importantly, Americans have been indoctrinated to have so little empathy or compas-sion for one another—except during acute moments of national crisis—that we cannot see our similarities or how our experi-ences as "we the people" mirror rather than rival one another's. In those rare moments, when most of us see eye-to-eye and we breathe in rhythm as we did when George Perry Floyd, Jr., drew his last breath, we then understand something about our common humanity and American identity.

In his book *From Generosity to Justice: A New Gospel of Wealth*, businessman, philanthropist, and civic leader Darren Walker maintains that the journey to justice requires us to "raise the roots" of the issues or problems that impede our progress "by addressing causes, not consequences." As we work in the meantime to mollify and mitigate consequences, fundamental so-cietal change requires us to also search beyond the consequential into the layered causes and circumstances of issues that obstruct and undermine structural change. "We constantly have to push ourselves to dig deeper, to excavate more," Walker writes. "The root causes of injustice are often obscured—buried deep in our history, our institutions, and our cultural practices."[22]

Mass incarceration is a consequence. Systemic racism is a consequence. Economic marginalization and poverty are consequences. Sexism and misogyny are consequences of a network of oppressive systems deeply rooted in an ideology of greed and glory, of excess and tyrannical power. Monopoly capitalism, patriarchy, and "'white' supremacy" number among the oppressive systems in which the "master-slave" dynamic operates. Elitism, signifying superiority, is their crowning feature. The taproot of this network of interconnected, mutually reinforcing systems of oppression is unconsciousness.

Many Americans adopt the position that, when the unthinking decisions were made that generated the racial and social disparities and structural economic gaps that we experience today, they weren't the ones who made them. Yet as each successive generation unquestioningly continues the practices established through custom or law and the attitudes that galvanized them, said practices become normalized as "tradition" and as "our way of life." If nothing interrupts the habitual sociocultural loop, then we unconsciously repeat historical patterns. Even as we might consciously distance ourselves from the oppressive dogma of "the past," unconsciously, we continue it, as some are privileged and others are disparaged in accordance with the established dispensation of colonial American society.

Encoded into laws and loopholes like the Slavery Clause are the prejudices, politics, and propaganda of the colonial "master class." Far from being past history, the belief that Black people should be enslaved *ad vitam*, for life, informs the harsh and excessive sentencing of Black people and people of color in the modern era of mass incarceration. The life of my "duly convicted" brother and the consequent enthrallment of our family are a testament to James Baldwin's insight that we have yet to fully appreciate the nature and function of history:

> History, as nearly no one seems to know, is not merely something to be read. And it does not refer merely, or even principally, to the past. On the contrary, the great force of history comes from the fact that we carry it within us, are unconsciously controlled by it in many ways, and history is literally *present* in all that we do.[23]

"It could scarcely be otherwise," Baldwin wrote, "since it is to history that we owe our frames of reference, our identities, and our aspirations."[24]

What aspirations are reflected in the Criminal Punishment Clause that has kept the institution of slavery "alive and well in Louisiana's prison system" and in state and federal prison systems throughout America?[25] To effectively end slavery *once and for all*, it is necessary that we identify, deconstruct, and abolish the incidents and badges that continue to bind us to the past of slavery. This entails that we must also have the courage to identify, deconstruct, and abolish the incidents and badges that empower the continued reign of the "master class" in modern American society. For it stands to reason that when the Thirteenth Amendment preserved slavery, it also preserved the enslaver. We must all account for the history that we carry within us. For we are our history, as Baldwin would have us understand, and further, "if we pretend otherwise, we literally are criminals."[26]

Race-based, intergenerational chattel slavery is peculiar to America. But, of course, *slavery* is not. And the ideological underpinnings of this Peculiar Institution began neither in America nor with Americans, but in the Atlantic world of the fifteenth century and with European imperialist ideas about "Doctrines of Discovery" and "perpetual slavery." There was no American republic at that point in time. But as Americans, we have inherited this legacy of greed and glory that has enthralled us all in one way or another. And this moment in history is ours to be the difference necessary to evolve our society. What if the proverbial "buck" literally stopped, here and now, with us, "the people"?

The relentless assault on Indigenous peoples, the debasement and enslavement of Africans, the imperialist war against Mexicans, and the exploitation and exclusion of Asians are difficult stories to weave into the narrative of America the beautiful, and they trouble the dreaming of the American Dream. Yet, as demonstrated by activist-artist and shaman Alice Walker, we must honor the difficult, just as we must consider, nonetheless, that we all have a stake in the Dream. We are fortified to the extent that we embrace the dishonorable and allow admission of hard truths to do their transformative work. Thus, we galvanize and elevate the American spirit.

America is not alone in its efforts to acknowledge the difficult history of slavery. Private citizens and public officials alike have recognized the consequences of historical enslavement in our nation and have been moved to disrupt and dismantle the new forms that slavery takes and that obscure the "master-slave" dynamic that continually regenerates human oppression. The story of slavery in America reflects the global history of *slavery*. And abolitionist efforts at home intersect with initiatives abroad that seek to bring awareness to, and work to bring an end to, the scourge of slavery.

In 1985, for instance, the United Nations proclaimed December 2 as the World Day for the Abolishment of Slavery. In 1995, this date was established and observed as the International Day for the Abolition of Slavery. On this day, governments, institutions, organizations, and individuals are called on to denounce and proactively work to eradicate modern-day slavery "in all its forms"[27]: forced labor (prison labor, child labor, coerced industrial labor), forced marriage, military impressment of children, human trafficking, sex trafficking, and debt bondage.[28] We are called on to recognize modern manifestations of slavery in all unequal, exploitative, objectifying, and dehumanizing situations involving coercion, violence, intimidation, and deception, those situations wherein compliance is forced, a person's power to say "no" is nullified—denied, compromised, punished, or outlawed—all human relations that, in one configuration or another, re-produce the "master-slave" dynamic.

The December 2 date was chosen in order that we remember the December 2, 1949, UN Convention for the Suppression of the Traffic in Persons and of the Exploitation of the Prostitution of Others. In 1998, the UN established August 23 as the International Day for the Remembrance of the Slave Trade and its Abolition. The August 23 date was chosen in order that we remember the 1791 revolution in Santo Domingo (Haiti and the Dominican Republic). The day commemorates the Haitian struggle for freedom and independence and acknowledges Haiti's critical role in the abolition of transatlantic trafficking, in the dismantling of the formal system of slavery, and in stemming the tide of European imperialism and colonialism.[29]

Where the International Day for the Remembrance of the Slave Trade and its Abolition highlights the historic causes of the trafficking of Africans, the International Day of Remembrance of the

Victims of Slavery and the Transatlantic Slave Trade emphasizes
the consequences. Established in 2007 on March 25, this day of remembrance observes the human cost of the business of trafficking.
The day is a time to commune with the souls of millions of African
men and women and boys and girls and babies and lives in utero
who died in the atrocities of capture and who suffered the horrors
of the Middle Passage and forced labor in the Americas.

The day pays tribute, as well, to the legion of enslaved rebels,
abolitionists, allies, and the sung and unsung heroes and heroines
who were slain as they took action to prevent or end trafficking
and enslavement. Importantly, in addition to helping to educate
the global community about the victimization of millions, the day
is also an occasion to help people the world over to see and understand the dangers and consequences of racism and prejudice.

At the 2015 ceremonies at the United Nations Headquarters
in New York, *The Ark of Return* was unveiled. This sculpture,
designed by Haitian American architect Rodney Leon and constructed by an international team of artists and artisans from the
Caribbean and various parts of Africa and Europe, was created
as a permanent physical marker to create a sacred space of remembrance. The sculpture features three triangular marble pan-
els that document the "slave routes" from Africa to destinations
in the Caribbean and South, Central, and North America.[30]

In creating the design of *The Ark of Return*, Rodney Leon
was moved by the maps that traced "the triangular slave trade"
and inspired by the history and lore surrounding the Door of
No Return, at *La Maison des Esclaves* (The House of Slaves) on
Gorée Island in Senegal. In evoking the image of the Door of No
Return and the tragedy it symbolized, Leon memorialized the
experiences of the human beings who "were held in these slave

castles or prisons awaiting to be taken out, stripped away from their lives and their families and everything they knew through this Door of No Return, never to return."[31]

He and his team "were also interested in the idea of the slave ships and these vessels that carried people through tragic conditions to the new world," Leon reflected. "So we felt it would be a good counterpoint to establish a spiritual space of return, an 'Ark of Return,' a vessel where we can begin to create a counter-narrative and undo some of that experience."[32] A study in alchemy, the sculpture transforms hundreds of trafficking vessels into an Ark of Return that plows through a turbulent history toward a future of just societies. The site of *The Ark of Return* is intended as a point of pilgrimage, a destination where we can individually and collectively commune, reflect, communicate, and galvanize our courage and strengthen our resolve to heal the world body politic, evolve human consciousness, and elevate the human spirit.

The refrain to "end slavery once and for all" resounds in the calls and declarations emanating from the United Nations Head-quarters, and it echoes through the corridors of the US Congress. And yet the United States of America, a UN member state and permanent member of the UN Security Council, still sanctions slavery. Our country's inconsistency regarding slavery, in the form of forced prison labor, compromises America's leadership and moral authority on the global stage.

The United States has outwardly shunned autocratic, author-itarian, and tyrannical governments and has banned imports of goods produced in certain countries that utilize forced labor. At the same time, in the US, slavery and involuntary servitude are retained as fit punishment for crime, prison inmates are subjected to uncompensated or undercompensated forced labor, their labor is still being leased to American corporations, and unwitting American citizens consume the items and services they produce.[33] Seeing daylight between America's domestic policy and international politics on human rights abuses, Senator Jeffrey Merkley issued this statement:

> The use of forced labor in American prison systems undermines our international human rights leadership and gives our foreign adversaries propaganda that they can use to challenge the legitimacy of American leadership abroad and Americans' trust in their government at home.[34]

The question of slavery has always been a major fault line in American history and society. The American colonists had come to the point of revolution with England and then the establishment of a new government precisely because they felt themselves to be "slaves." Plantocrats and merchants saw the imposition of trade restrictions and taxation, without their voice in the matter, to be acts of tyranny that reduced them to a condition of white slavery.

Where pro-slavery delegates to the Constitutional Convention in 1787 saw their own resistance to tyranny as legitimate and their own lives as worthy of freedom's cause, their capacity to recognize the unconditional dignity due each and every human being[35] was blighted by greed, ambition, and the pursuit of aristocratic glory. They insisted on the continued enslavement of Black people while they celebrated their own freedom. And they jealously guarded their right to political representation while denying unpropertied adult white men any vote at all.

Though fully aware that "white freedom" was secured with the support of both enslaved Blacks who built fortifications and "free" Blacks who fought on the front lines of the Revolution—even as many white "elites" withdrew to the Carolinian and Virginian backcountry during the Revolutionary War—delegates, like those from South Carolina and Georgia, debated against universal freedom and insisted on provisions in the Constitution for the continuation of slavery and the continued importation of Africans. Informing Thomas Jefferson on some points of the ongoing debates over sticking points in drafting the Constitution, James Madison wrote, "Some contended for an unlimited power over trade including exports as well as imports, and over slaves as well as other imports. . . . The result is seen in the Constitution. S. Carolina & Georgia were inflexible on the point of the slaves."[36]

Benjamin Franklin perceived the Constitution that was drafted as a faulty document, as it reflected his own fallibilities as well as the prejudices, passions, erroneous opinions, self-interest, and provincialism of all the delegates gathered. He confessed that he did not entirely approve of the new Constitution, but that he would agree to adopt it and to recommend it "with all its Faults."[37] The question of Black slavery was reconciled, compromises concerning representation and taxation of "slave states" were agreed to, and the Constitution was adopted. Adopting a constitution averted the potential consequences that some delegates, like Alexander Hamilton, feared as imminent, had a consensus not been brokered: immediate dissolution of the confederation, reformulation of polities, or civil war.[38] However, the fault lines of Black slavery remained, and they deepened and widened.

America's Peculiar Institution remained intact and those who argued for the continued importation of Africans were awarded with an extension of ten years of international trafficking. Having incorporated slavery and enslavers into the US Constitution and the American body politic, defenders of America's "original sin"[39] continued with the body of lies constructed to fix the narrative of Black inferiority and servility and undermine Black humanity in the hearts and minds of the masses of white Americans. Yet, as there is often misconception and a good deal of injustice in "a generally admitted idea," abolitionist Harriet Beecher Stowe contested the false narratives justifying Black degradation.[40]

In prefatory remarks written for William Cooper Nell's *The Colored Patriots of the American Revolution*, Stowe commented on the incidents of "generosity, disinterested courage and bravery" among Black revolutionary soldiers and contended with the prejudices that impugned the character of "the colored race" and condemned their dark skin as "a badge of disgrace." She hoped that in reading the ignored, dismissed, devalued, and otherwise little-known history of the "Colored Patriots," that "their white brothers" would recognize that valor was not the attribute of a "particular race and complexion."[41] Stowe urged readers to be considerate in their assessments of the contributions of Black patriots:

> We are to reflect upon them as far more magnanimous, because rendered to a nation which did not acknowledge them as citizens and equals, and in whose interests and prosperity they had less at stake. It was not for their own land they fought, not even for a land which had adopted them, but for a land which had enslaved them, and whose laws, even in freedom, oftener oppressed than protected. Bravery under such circumstances has a peculiar beauty and merit.[42]

To interrogate the history—full of facts and faults—that we embody, carry within us, and transmit to our children is to bring the unconscious to conscious awareness and increase our capacity for higher perception, empathy, and the elevation of our individual and collective conscience.[43] From this vantage point, we can better see the daylight between our principles and our practice. To do so is absolutely courageous and brave.

In discussing the ethnographic research she carried out for her book *Barracoon: The Story of the Last "Black Cargo,"* cultural anthropologist Zora Neale Hurston discovered that the history of race, race relations, and slavery was far more complex and nuanced than the "generally admitted idea" she had been taught. She was taken aback to learn that white people didn't just wave a red handkerchief to lure Africans on a ship and then sail away with them. "The white people had held my people in slavery here in America. They had bought us, it is true and exploited us. But the inescapable fact that stuck in my craw was: my people had sold me and the white people had bought me. . . . I know that civilized money stirred up African greed. That wars between tribes were often stirred up by white traders to provide more slaves in the barracoons and all that," she continued. "But, if the African princes had been as pure and as innocent as I would like to think, it could not have happened."[44]

Hurston's realization is further complicated by the fact that there were no "my people" on the continent that came to be called Africa, and there were no "Africans." The identity of the Indigenous peoples on the African continent was not based on skin pigmentation but on kinship determined by familial, ethnic, cultural, and geographic affiliations. Ideology and worldview also informed the basis of kinship and political alliances. Thus, some

African leaders collaborated with their "European" kin and captured and sold those belonging to ethnic groups with whom they
did not identify. The same politics of collaboration held true for
the Portuguese, Dutch, French, and British, who waged wars
against one another, on land and sea, to control the so-called
trade and form alliances with African leaders.

   Hurston found it sobering to learn that "Africans" "had butch-
ered and killed, exterminated whole nations and torn families
apart, for a profit before the strangers got their chance at a cut."
In a sobering tone, she wrote, "It impressed upon me the universal nature of greed and glory." She contemplated how what is
"right and just" is often contorted to serve a human being's base
desires and how ambition, outfitted in "the cloak of Justice" is
sent out "a-whoring after conquests."[45]

&#9752; &#9752; &#9752;

From Gorée Island to Manhattan Island, from the colonial and
antebellum eras to contemporary American society, there is an
arc of consequences resulting from humanity's bane of greed and
glory and its abiding "master-slave" impetus. An outgrowth of
slavery, the criminal-punishment system which was sanctioned
by the Criminal Punishment Clause, has been normalized in the
American psyche as right and just and has grown deep roots in
American society. Ending the slavery loophole is essential to the
enterprise of freedom. It is essential to the work of dismantling
legalized injustice and uprooting systemic racism. And it is critical to the work of exposing and reckoning with the oppressive
systems that intersect and interconnect to keep slavery "alive and
well" and keep Americans deceived and in danger of losing our

democracy and the liberty that only some are still permitted to enjoy.

The critical step required to abolish slavery once and for all requires our capacity to engage in critical thought—something that many antidemocratic political and corporate "elites" are working relentlessly to prevent. We must be able to recognize tyranny when we see it—when we are victimized by it and when we perpetrate it. We must be consciously aware that among America's framers and founders were those who maintained a "master-slave" mentality, not only those who believed in liberty. We ignore that reality to our peril.

We must be willing to hold all of America's stories—those overshadowed, those buried and banned, those marginalized, those disfranchised, and those locked away. We must develop the audacity to give these stories honest reflection and contemplation. As we develop the courage to see clearly and to discern when practices don't align with principles, we must muster the fortitude to grow our integrity and close the gap. It behooves us to cultivate creativity and the optimism essential to evolving a society that is not a prison state but a promise that is ever moving toward greater expressions of freedom and justice and equality.

George Washington described the nascent American government as "the last great experiment, for promoting human happiness." While he praised what had been accomplished and what it portended, he conceded that the government was "not absolutely perfect."[46] The operative idea inherent in "revolution" is evolution. The American Revolution is our collective inheritance, and it compels us to evolve our individual and social consciousness. When "we the people" of the United States and "we the people" of the United Nations have difficult dialogues and do the work of recognizing and closing contradictory gaps, we are empowered to commit to the ongoing work that supports freedom's cause of human dignity and sovereignty. We are then empowered to move from the egocentric, fear-based logic of a little eddy of freedom for me[47] to universal freedom for all; from privilege for a self-proclaimed precious few to justice for everywoman, everyman, everychild; from the stealth of wealth to a generosity of spirit that supports and advances the American pursuit of human happiness.

No matter how long we've been lulled into the oblivion of unconsciousness, at the end of the day or the dawn of new beginnings, we are conscious beings and we are all accountable to one another and the larger society.

## NOTES

1. Jeff Merkley, "The Abolition Amendment," https://www.merkley.senate.gov/imo /media/doc/The%20Abolition%20Amendment%20One%20Pager%20-%20 117th_.pdf.

2. Thirteenth Amendment: "Article XIII, Section1, The Constitution," from *The Debate on the Constitution, Part One*, ed. Bernard Bailyn (New York: Library of America, 1993), 985.

3. "Ahead of Juneteenth, Merkley, Williams Propose Constitutional Amendment to Close Slavery Loophole in 13th Amendment," Jeff Merkley, June 18, 2021, https://www.merkley.senate.gov/news/press-releases/ahead-of-juneteenth-merkley -williams-propose-constitutional-amendment-to-close-slavery-loophole-in-13th -amendment-2021.

     Merkley and Williams reintroduced the Abolition Amendment proposal initiated in 2020 and cosponsored by Merkley and Representative William Lacy Clay: "Democratic Lawmakers Introduce a Resolution to Amend the 13th Amendment to End Forced Prison Labor," Jeff Merkley, December 4, 2020, https://www.merkley.senate.gov/news/in-the-news/democratic-lawmakers -introduce-a-resolution-to-amend-the-13th-amendment-to-end-forced-prison -labor.

4. "Repeal Exception to Constitutional Ban on Slavery," H.C.R. 18-1002, Colorado General Assembly (2018), https://leg.colorado.gov/bills/hcr18 -1002.

5. Louisiana lawmakers were described as having torpedoed their own efforts to end forced prison labor. "They told voters to reject it because the ballot measure

included ambiguous language that did not prohibit involuntary servitude in the criminal justice system." (Aaron Morrison, "Slavery, Involuntary Servitude Rejected by 4 States' Voters," Associated Press, November 9, 2022, https://apnews.com /article/2022-midterm-elections-slavery-on-ballot-561268e344f17d8562939cde 301d2cbf.)

6. Edmond Jordan, "House Bill No. 196," H.L.S. 21RS-188, Louisiana State Legislature (2021), https://www.legis.la.gov/legis/ViewDocument.aspx?d=1206408.

7. In the Civil Rights Cases of 1883, the US Supreme Court ruled that African American citizens were not protected from private or public race-based discrimination, segregation, and exclusion, as a majority of justices decided that such practices did not constitute "badges and incidents of slavery." In his dissenting opinion, Justice John Marshall Harlan argued for a more substantive interpretation of the Thirteenth Amendment and the authority of Congress to enforce the amendment through legislation "for the eradication, not simply of the institution, but of its badges and incidents." (Supreme Court of the United States, "US Reports: Civil Rights Cases," 109 U.S. 3 [1883], Library of Congress, https://tile.loc.gov/storage-services/service/ll/usrep/usrep109/usrep 109003/usrep109003.pdf.) Justice Harlan would later argue against the "separate but equal" doctrine that was sanctioned in *Plessy v. Ferguson* (1896), a case originating in the courts of Louisiana.

8. Vashti R. Stopher, "Song of Louisiana," NETSTATE, last modified August 10, 2017, https://www.netstate.com/states/symb/songs/la_song_of_louisiana.

9. Blake Paterson, "Slavery in Louisiana's Prisons? This Lawmaker Wants Voters to Outlaw Forced Labor for Good," *The Advocate*, April 7, 2021, https://www .theadvocate.com/baton_rouge/news/politics/legislature/article_e2c56dba-97e1 -11eb-af3f-dbbbc78da12b.html; and "Ahead of Juneteenth."

10. "Ahead of Juneteenth."

11. "Ahead of Juneteenth."

12. "Ahead of Juneteenth."

13. Kenneth M. Stampp addresses these claims in *The Peculiar Institution: Slavery in the Ante-Bellum South* (New York: Vintage Books, 1956), 4–5, 22.

14. Eugene D. Genovese, *Roll, Jordan, Roll: The World the Slaves Made* (New York: Vintage Books, 1976), 321.

15. Rayford W. Logan, *The Betrayal of the Negro: From Rutherford B. Hayes to Woodrow Wilson* (New York: Da Capo Press, 1997), 52.

16. Merkley, "The Abolition Amendment."

17. "Ahead of Juneteenth."

18. "Ahead of Juneteenth."

19. Francis Bellamy, "The Pledge of Allegiance," USHistory.org, https://www.ushistory .org/documents/pledge.htm.

20. Ideas here are inspired by Sweet Honey in the Rock, "Greed," track 6 on *Twenty-Five*, Rykodisc, 1998.

21. "Ahead of Juneteenth."

22. Darren Walker, *From Generosity to Justice: A New Gospel of Wealth* (New York: Disruption Books, 2023), 93, 159.

23. James Baldwin, "The White Man's Guilt," in *James Baldwin: Collected Essays*, ed. Toni Morrison (New York, Library of America, 1998), 722–23.

24. Baldwin, "The White Man's Guilt," 723.

25. Paterson, "Slavery in Louisiana's Prisons?"

26. Baldwin, *I Am Not Your Negro* (France: Velvet Film, 2017).

27. "International Day for the Abolition of Slavery," Time and Date, accessed July 3, 2022, https://www.timeanddate.com/holidays/un/international-day-abolish -slavery.

28. António Guterres, "Secretary-General's Message - 2021," United Nations, December 2, 2021, https://web.archive.org/web/20211223140747/https://www .un.org/en/observances/slavery-abolition-day/messages.

29. "International Day for the Remembrance of the Slave Trade and Its Abolition," UNESCO, https://www.unesco.org/en/days/slave-trade-remembrance-day.

30. "FEATURE: Architect of UN Slavery Memorial Explains 'The Ark of Return,'" UN News, March 25, 2015, https://news.un.org/en/story/2015/03/494402 -feature-architect-un-slavery-memorial-explains-ark-return.

31. Mary Ferreira, "Rodney's Journey: Making the Ark of Return," United Nations, posted April 10, 2015, YouTube video, https://www.youtube.com/watch?v=Dx -gnst3mC8. See also "FEATURE: Architect of UN Slavery Memorial Explains 'The Ark of Return.'"

32. "FEATURE: Architect of UN Slavery Memorial Explains 'The Ark of Return.'"

33. Merkley, "The Abolition Amendment."

34. Merkley, "The Abolition Amendment."

35. Paraphrase of statement from UNESCO Director-General Audrey Azoulay: "It is time to abolish human exploitation once and for all, and to recognize the equal and unconditional dignity of each and every individual." ("International Day for the Remembrance of the Slave Trade and Its Abolition.")

36. James Madison, "James Madison to Thomas Jefferson, October 24, 1787: *The Constitution Explained and Justified, with an 'Immoderate Digression' on a Defeated Proposal*," in Bailyn, *Debate on the Constitution*, 202.

37. Benjamin Franklin, "Benjamin Franklin's Speech at the Conclusion of the Constitutional Convention, September 17, 1787: *'I Agree to This Constitution, with All Its Faults,'*" in Bailyn, *Debate on the Constitution*, 3.

38. Alexander Hamilton, "Alexander Hamilton's Conjectures About the New Constitution, September 1787," in Bailyn, *Debate on the Constitution*, 9–10.

39. Jeff Merkley: "Slavery is our nation's original sin and this loophole has been exploited for far too long to criminalize Black and Brown Americans." (Brakkton Booker, "Democrats Push 'Abolition Amendment' to Fully Erase Slavery from U.S. Constitution," *NPR*, December 3, 2020, https://www.npr .org/2020/12/03/942413221/democrats-push-abolition-amendment-to-fully -erase-slavery-from-u-s-constitution.)

40. Harriet Beecher Stowe, "Preface," in *The Colored Patriots of the American Revolution*, by William Cooper Nell, 2017 Edition (Boston: Robert F. Wallcut, 1855; Coppell, Texas: n.p., 2017), 5.

41. Stowe, "Preface," 5.

42. Stowe, "Preface," 5.

43. G. Vithoulkas and D. F. Muresanu, "Conscience and Consciousness: A Definition," *Journal of Medicine and Life* 7, no. 1 (March 15, 2014): 104–8, https://www.ncbi.nlm.nih.gov/pmc/articles/PMC3956087/.

44. Zora Neale Hurston, *Dust Tracks on a Road*, in *Hurston: Folklore, Memoirs, and Other Writings*, ed. Cheryl A. Wall (New York: Library of America, 1995), 708.

45. Hurston, *Dust Tracks on a Road*, 708.

46. Letter from George Washington to Catharine Sawbridge Macaulay Graham, The National Archives and Records Administration, Founders Online, "From George Washington to Catharine Sawbridge Macaulay Graham, 9 January 1790": https://founders.archives.gov/documents/Washington/05-04-02-0363.

47. Paraphrase of excerpt from Whitehead, *The Underground Railroad*, 29: "Sometimes a slave will be lost in a brief eddy of liberation."

# CHAPTER 2

# RECKONINGS

THE MOMENT I SAW TWO suited white men get out of a car and look in the direction of our house, I intuitively knew that their appearance signified some kind of trouble. Some kind of unimagined change.

I instinctively responded to the unarticulated fear that arose in me by alerting my brother about the advancing men and instructing him to "go out the patio door and stay outside until I come get you." The detectives—as they would soon identify themselves—had reached the steps that led to the screened porch door where I had been standing, noticing their approach. They were poised to knock as I was returning. They had their rote questions and I had impromptu answers because this was anything but routine for me. Being stopped by uniformed traffic cops was one thing. But I had only seen suited detectives on television, not at my door. *Yes, I'm his sister. He doesn't live here. No, I don't know where he lives. I don't live here either, just visiting. Sure, if I see him. Sure. I'll tell him that you're looking for him. Of course.*

In fact, my brother didn't live there because my dad had put him out. I lived, I think, in Nebraska at the time, or Tennessee, and was making one of my frequent visits home to Louisiana, Baton Rouge. And I had already told my brother that the suited

men were looking for him, even before one of them handed me
his card with the expressed request to contact them should I . . .

⚔ ⚔ ⚔

These men were the first signs of a situation I was unaware that
we were in, much less that we were already deeply entangled in it.
At the time, I didn't even realize that what we were in *was*, indeed,
a situation—an ordinarily *peculiar* one at that. A situation that
would later have me personally see how the historical reality of
America's Peculiar Institution was "literally *present*" in my life.[1]

Tracking my brother through time, recalling visits home and
events wherein I remembered him free and laughing, I try to pin-
point the moment when it was apparent that he was in danger of
losing his freedom. At what point, exactly, were we vulnerable to
having him "taken up" and separated from the family—*forever*. In
my reflections, I recalled learning about my brother's chronically
abusive relationships and his use of drugs. Some other members of
the family were privy to this. I was perplexed by it all, and also by
my not knowing about these aspects of his life. But weren't there
ways to treat addiction? Weren't there interventions to address
and nurture behavioral changes—interventions that would not
result in a life sentence *without the possibility of parole*?

Looming like a menacing shadow just behind my helter-skelter
inquiries was the reality that my brother was always in danger
of losing his "eddy of liberty."[2] We all were. As I scrutinized
what my brother may have or may not have done that brought
these suited men to the steps of our family home, what came
into full relief out of the shadowy distance was *the system*.
What revealed itself was the system that these men—uniformed

in muted tones of authority, white and white-shirted with tie, and deceptively cordial—represented, reinforced, and reproduced: America's carceral system, its "punishment bureaucracy" or "prison-industrial complex."

Many of the prisons in this system were once "slave plantations." The state penitentiary of Louisiana at Angola is such a place. The enslaved gang labor that was utilized to mass-produce cotton, sugarcane, and corn on this former slave plantation is now performed by farm work details of incarcerated men. Where mounted overseers with whips once surveilled enslaved workers, armed prison guards now sit astride horses monitoring prison inmates. Seventy-five percent of the inmates in Angola prison are Black men. And like the Black people before them who were held in bondage for life, a majority of the Black inmates at Angola are sentenced to life imprisonment. This Louisiana State Penitentiary, called Angola, is where my brother is being held.

## THE "PUNISHMENT CLAUSE"

America's system of mass incarceration has depended on and continues to depend on a steady supply of the bodies of Black men and women and children since the nineteenth century. On the back of opened envelopes containing letters mailed to me from my brother, the stamped imprint indicates the date the letter was received and it notes that Angola is "AN ALL MALE PENAL INSTITUTE." Six thousand and three hundred males. More or less. The average population of a small town.

The system of mass incarceration is the result of incarcerating Black people, *en masse*, just as they had gained their citizenship and birthright of freedom. The major hallmark of this system that has expanded and entrenched itself in American society is that it reproduces the incidents and bears the badges of America's Peculiar Institution of slavery from which Black people had been freed. This system—mass incarceration—is *slavery's evolution* in contemporary America.

Literally in the middle of the constitutional declaration that "slavery" and "involuntary servitude" shall not exist in the United States or any place under its jurisdiction is the parenthetical clause that—in practice if not in intentionality—contradicted the expressed declaration that slavery and any form of forced servitude had been abolished. For this parenthetical clause allowed enslavement and other forms of bondage to continue: **as a punishment for crime,** "whereof the party shall have been duly convicted."[3]

This exception, often described as a loophole, provided the political rationale and established the legal grounding that facilitated the development of post-emancipation penal institutions like the convict-leasing system, prison labor camps, and debt peonage that effectively re-enslaved African American *citizens* and gave rise to the mass incarceration of Black people. Black men were primary targets of local and state officials. Black women and boys and girls were indirectly affected by the extraction of Black men, and they, too, were directly victimized by the system of forced labor and servitude that was intent on undermining Black economic security, breaking up Black families, and destabilizing Black communities.

Callously separating Black family members is a practice of expedience and social control in "freedom" no less than it was in "slavery." Black families today are living this so-called past history. Constant and systematic destabilization of Black families and communities engendered and structured Black dependency. Many Black men who might have financially supported or otherwise contributed to the viability of their families, once incarcerated, instead found themselves relying on their family members for support. This is the situation in which my brother, a father of three, found himself.

## "THE-NEGRO-AS-CRIMINAL"

Ratified in 1865, the language of the Thirteenth Amendment parroted the language of the Northwest Ordinance of 1787: "There shall be neither slavery nor involuntary servitude in the said territory, otherwise than in the punishment of crimes whereof the party shall have been duly convicted."[4] In establishing governance for the Northwest Territory that was claimed by the United States, the authors of the ordinance provided for the reclamation of any enslaved fugitive escaping into the territory. The "criminal-exception loophole"[5] and the provisions regarding fugitives provided proslavery advocates—then, and later, after the Civil War—with the political framework in which to preserve a slavocracy in the midst of a purportedly free and democratic republic.

In postbellum America, the kind of "crimes" of which a person might be "duly convicted," and therefore subject to (re-)enslavement, were enshrined in state statutes called "Black Codes." Vagrancy, unemployment, possession of a firearm, walking beside a railroad, theft, "taking" of livestock,[6] and speaking loudly in public (in the presence of whites, particularly white females), were among the crimes for which Black people would be arrested and jailed or imprisoned.

Enactment of these so-called statutes or laws reflected the same codification of prejudice and privilege sanctioned by colonial American lawmakers, and they mimic the English sumptuary laws that were pervasive in antebellum America. Sumptuary laws were intended to distinguish the "aristocracy" from the peasantry and to demand deference from the poor toward their presumed superiors. In postbellum America, they also became a legal means to extort wealth from Black Americans and the legal basis used to deprive them, once again, of their freedom.

Black Codes, Code Noir, and Black Laws existed in America before the Civil War, in the North as well as the South. Instituted by English, Spanish, and French colonists, these earlier codes derived from and were comparable to the "slave codes" that governed both enslaved and nominally free Black persons. Similar codes or laws were also legislated in reaction to the 1787 ordinance governing states developed in the Northwest Territory. But after the passage of the Thirteenth Amendment in 1865—with its legacy loophole—the class of codes established during this period were designed to *re*-establish white political and economic domination and social control over Black life.

These postbellum black codes racialized state statutes throughout the South. Capitalizing on the Punishment Clause in the Thirteenth Amendment, Southern planters, merchants, and financial "elites" renewed their pursuit of greed and excessive profit at the expense of both criminalized Black persons and the exploited and terrorized "free" Black population. These statutes legalized the racial hierarchy in the South and codified its glorification of "whiteness."

Black codes were inaugurated in the state of Mississippi in 1865. Mississippi did not ratify the Thirteenth Amendment until 1995 and only signed it into law officially in 2013, nearly a century and a half later.[7] South Carolina, Alabama, and Louisiana followed Mississippi's lead in establishing black codes. These penal codes became the basis of Jim Crow laws and the separate-but-equal doctrine that was sanctioned by the US Supreme Court in the 1896 *Plessy v. Ferguson* decision.

The Thirteenth Amendment's criminal-exception loophole set the conditions under which Southern lawmakers assumed the authority to contradict the Constitution's declaration of the independence and social and political parity of Black Americans. It permitted their authority to criminalize the newly freed Black citizenry and to return control of their persons and their labor to the State. That is, racialized Southern lawmakers assumed the authority to once again treat African Americans *peculiarly*, as chattel. "This paved the way for the country's burgeoning prison labor system and the world's largest prison population at 2.3 million."[8]

The criminal-exception loophole provided in the Thirteenth Amendment only proved that many racialized whites believed that they were "endowed by their Creator" with the unalienable right to rule over Black people forever. These racialized government officials and private citizens had no commitment to the sanctity of life, the unalienable right to liberty, nor the pursuit of happiness when accorded to their Black fellow and sister Americans. When a stated or implied "but" is introduced into a statement, it radically limits, undermines, or nullifies *all* that precedes it. As in: "*Well, I believe in life, liberty, happiness, and justice for all, but . . .*"

The crafters of the Thirteenth Amendment made Black freedom a tenuous thing. The freedom of Black people that was recognized by virtue of the declaration that slavery shall not exist was confounded by the internal clause that retained the institution of "slavery" and "involuntary servitude" and conflated "slavery" with criminal punishment. Because black codes were derived from slave codes, they had the effect of simultaneously casting Black people as both criminals and slaves. These codes ensured that

Black Americans, despite their citizenship status, would be criminalized and imprisoned, subjected to one sort of bondage or another. The Criminal Punishment Clause formalized and legalized this conflation. Indeed, codifications and systems that facilitated the imprisonment and enslavement of Black people have long existed side by side, the one operating in conjunction with the other.

## FROM "SLAVE PENS" TO PLANTATIONS TO PRISONS

During the four hundred years of European trafficking of Africans, structures described as holding pens, *barracoons*, "slave houses," or "slave castles" functioned something like contemporary holding cells that are used to confine prisoners awaiting some judicial procedure or determination. In *La Maison des Esclaves* ("The House of Slaves") on Senegal's Gorée Island, for example, captured Africans were confined in cells and held there until the Europeans—whose accommodations were upstairs above the cells, like ship captains on deck above the hold—negotiated the value and the destinations of their lives.

A prelude of things to come, during daylight, the captives at Gorée supplied the labor that maintained the island, loading or unloading cargo ships, crushing the shells that would be made into lime, or cutting basalt rocks into building material.[9] Once captains of trafficking vessels were assured of a full load, the captives, now treated as cargo themselves, were herded aboard and into the ship's hold, condemned to a life of forced labor, subjugation, and all the indignities heaped upon human persons adjudged to be both chattel and capital.

Occupied by the Portuguese in 1444, Gorée Island was considered a maritime prize as a natural fortress with a coastline that allowed for easy anchorage and protection from ocean swells. The Portuguese, Dutch, British, and French continually fought one another for control of the island. In the eighteenth century, the French and British were in constant battle. To better defend the island, the British had mandated that the ground-floor walls of newly erected buildings be constructed with loopholes—narrow openings in the walls through which to shoot or fire upon attackers while remaining protected from counterattacks.[10]

The term "loophole" originally described a narrow splayed or beveled slit in the wall of a medieval fortress or castle through which to shoot arrows. Figuratively, the term came to mean a small opening or an outlet of escape, a means by which to evade or escape an enemy or to run away. In modern usage, "loophole" is understood as an ambiguity, omission, technicality, or error in a statute or contract which can be used to circumvent or avoid adhering to the expressed or implied intention of the statute or contract. In the context of the Thirteenth Amendment, "loophole" identifies how some public officials chose to conceptualize the Punishment Clause proviso and the lens through which they chose to interpret it: as an escape route that looped back to oppression and tyranny, as a means to evade honoring the freedom and sovereign rights of African Americans, and as the political scaffold on which to reconstruct America's "House of Slaves" and continue the interminable pursuit of greed and glory at the expense of Black humanity.

❌ ❌ ❌

The house proclaimed as *La Maison des Esclaves* was built in 1776 by Nicolas Pépin, the brother of Anne Pépin. An African

French *signaré*, Anne Pépin owned *La Maison*, several houses among an estimated fifteen other houses built for similar purposes, and several trafficking vessels.[11] *La Maison des Esclaves* still stands and has since become a museum and a memorial to those whose social reality as sovereign persons ended there, as elsewhere along the so-called slave coast: at Badagry, for instance, in the *barracoons* along the Bight of Benin at Ouidah; also Elmina and the Cape Coast castles that lace the Gulf of Guinea; and at Bunce Island, a castle that splits the Sierra Leone River.

As a "Site of Conscience," *La Maison des Esclaves* is also a witness to humanity's proclivity to engage in unconscious and unfeeling *business*.[12] It is a commentary on the inhumanity and cruelty of Europeans and Africans—men and women alike—whose greed for silver, gold, pounds, francs, dollars, stock options, power, and the glory of *la dolce vita* had them conspire and collaborate in extracting from captured Africans that which only the Divine Creator gave them—their life breath.

In 1989 and again in 1993, during the tenure of Boubacar Joseph Ndiaye, the celebrated curator and docent of *La Maison des Esclaves* museum, I journeyed to Gorée Island and stood in the cells said to have imprisoned thousands of Africans. My journal reflections from that time don't quite capture the poignancy of what our ancestors likely experienced or of what I felt:

Having disembarked the ferry, we wandered about the island. I was in awe of majestic baobabs, wide of girth, dignified and stout against time, stalwart guardian spirits. It seems all of Senegal closes at eleven a.m. and opens again at 2:00 or 2:30. We were waiting for the opening of *La Maison des Esclaves*. It is the place where Africans were held before being shipped to all parts of the world. There are messages, explanations, sayings, explications written in French, on paper and cardboard, all about the walls *de la maison*. We photographed most of them. We looked at and photographed the small cells into which people were packed. Some cells that were only for children. Some only for *les jeunes filles* (young girls), who, too, were at the mercy of the Europeans who lived above these quarters.

I could see them. Packed. In there. Confused. Fearing. Half-crazed with the unbelievable, unconceivable tragedy that they—we—were living. Imagine a child crying; the grunt and groan of a man; a mother's wail. . . . And this but the beginning of centuries of tragedy waiting for them—us—beyond that "door of no return."

If my senses did not deceive me—and my companions said they did not—I smelled the must, the stale must of millennia of sweating bodies, sweat mingled with other secretions of the body. I wanted to cry, and I did—inside.

Our guide through *la maison*, Joseph Ndiaye, told us so well about this monstrous tragedy. It was all in French. I did not understand perfectly all that was said. But between reading the posters and comprehending what I could, then sensing what he said, I was able to give my companions the gist of his talk. Like the baobab, he was a man very firm. Eloquent in his speech. Afterwards, at the end, he pointed us out as actual living evidence of the sordid history he had just recounted, and asked, *"Vous connaissez l'histoire?"* I said, *"Oui."*

My people were there, in darkness, screaming, in pain, in fear of the unknown, and in grief over the last known—there, and in countless other cells in other "slave houses." But it is all one. And there I was and there were my companions, surrounded by Europeans, surrounded by the terrible "remem-ory" of our mothers and fathers there, in those holding cells.

*"Oui, nous la connaissons"* ("Yes, we know this story"). It is something, *non?*

※ ※ ※

The large, wide doors of *La Maison des Esclaves* open onto a horseshoe-shaped staircase flanked by a number of small hold-ing cells. Beneath the stairs is the cell for "the recalcitrant(s)."[13] Those deemed intractable would be shut into this airless chamber. The imprisoned Africans who survived the trek, the conditions at Gorée, the forced labor, the sexual violence, the depression, and the fear-laden atmosphere were then marshalled down the dank, dark passageway, Ndiaye tells us, and through the Door of No Return and loaded onto waiting ships.

### IN THE WAKE

I stood there in the Door of No Return, looking across the At-lantic in the direction of America. I pondered one of the placards on the wall of the prison called *La Maison des Esclaves*: *"Serait-elle l'Amérique sans le peuple noir?"* ("What would America be without Black people?"—or "Would America *be* without Black people?") Walking through many doors of no return, perhaps sun-blinded, my ancestors did not see the future into which they gazed. As I stood in the Door of No Return, I had also stood on my back porch, looking through the screened door. My vision was no better.

Thousands of Africans were exported out of Gorée into a diaspora of bondage of one kind or another. In *"l'Amérique,"* by the mid-seventeenth century, colonial officials in Virginia had reduced Black people to chattel and established race-based slavery. A. Leon Higginbotham, Jr., writes in his classic work, *In the Matter of Color: Race and the American Legal Process: The Colonial Period*, that the justice system established in Virginia more than three hundred fifty years ago enshrined the white male's prerogative to oppress, exploit, and dominate Africans, Indigenous peoples, and "white" women.[14]

"Whiteness" as a social identity was codified in statutes like the 1681 Maryland law that used "the terms *Christian, free, English,* and *white*" interchangeably "as metonyms."[15] Winthrop Jordan's *White Over Black* and Higginbotham's *In the Matter of Color* document the colonial era's legal and political constructions of whiteness and the codification of white privilege. The first racially discriminatory law enacted in Jamestown, Virginia, in 1639, provided the right to bear arms to "all persons except Negroes."[16] Ensuing laws in Virginia and throughout the colonies provided legal rights and protections for white servants while simultaneously depriving Black servants "of all basic human rights."[17]

Laws like those that penalized "any English servant" who ran away "in company with any negroes," and those that penalized "Christians" who committed "Fornication with a negro man or woman" also functioned to elevate the dignity of white persons and to adjudicate the "cycle of Negro debasement."[18] Within the matrix of colonial law lies the basis of economic, racial, and social disparities and the origins of *"white* privilege" in America.

It may be unimaginable, but there was no Peculiar Institution of racial slavery awaiting the Africans who disembarked at Jamestown, Virginia, in 1619. The castigation of Africans as chattel and their condemnation to serve as slaves "'Durante Vita'—for life," was not an inevitable evolution, but the result of a series of decisions made by colonial officials and enshrined in the statutes on which they voted their agreement.[19] Their votes and judgments reflect the movement of greed, like a virus, through the minds and hearts of early colonial leaders.

By the early eighteenth century, "racial slavery and the necessary police powers had been written into law."[20] Virginia's judicial process and the prejudices and biases encoded within it became the example other colonies followed, informing the legislative procedure and actions throughout antebellum and postbellum America and into the America of Jim Crow.[21]

So habituated to consuming the bone and blood and issue of Black people, the planters and their class could not fathom a labor pool that was not at their disposal and under their direct control. A 1903 Alabama journal article (quoted in Blackmon 2008) depicted the Negro as the "inheritance" of the white South and bemoaned the bygone days *when he was the faithful servant, the willing worker and the protector of the family of his master.*[22] As racialized Southerners resisted the intention of the Thirteenth Amendment, they could not conceive of the Tenth Amendment and the sovereignty it provided as having application to people whom they had erstwhile reduced to chattel. Those like Ben "Pitchfork" Tillman, the US senator from South Carolina, for example, were incensed that Booker T. Washington advised and dined with President Theodore Roosevelt: "Now that Roosevelt has eaten with that n[———] Washington, we shall have to kill a thousand n[———] to get them back to their places."[23]

The position of racialized Southern political and financial

"elites" was that Black people were without personhood and, *ipso facto*, they had no personal sovereignty that white people were bound to acknowledge, let alone honor. The Tenth Amendment recognized the power of the federal government and the states, and it also recognized the power of "the people." Accordingly, it states: "The powers not delegated to the United States by the Constitution, nor prohibited by it to the States, are reserved to the States respectively, or to the people."[24]

As the legal scholar Elizabeth Anne Reese has written, "Primarily, the Tenth Amendment protects that power which is at the heart of popular sovereignty as well as the foundation of our democracy, the power of the people to choose their government." However, she notes, this portion of the Tenth Amendment is grossly overlooked. "By ignoring the people in the Tenth Amendment, American jurisprudence has ignored a vital structural protection against federal and state tyranny and risked government-driven erosion of democracy in America."[25] In the same way that contemporary efforts to amend the Thirteenth Amendment pertain to the freedom of all Americans, so appropriate attention to provisions in the Tenth Amendment pertain to the sovereignty of the nation itself.

That power which is at the heart of popular sovereignty is the very power that pro-slavery advocates wished to obliterate among the Black electorate. The ruling class of the former Confederacy feared and resented the political power of newly freed Blacks who were eager to participate in local and national life, *as free persons*. This fear and resentment informed the Black codes and the rule of lynch law.

Very much in sympathy with the Confederate South, President Andrew Johnson pardoned Confederate leaders and returned confiscated land (including the "forty acres" granted to some freedmen) and sovereignty to the seditious states. Having regained their political autonomy, the leadership of the former Confederacy would deny the sovereignty of African Americans, though they swore an oath to honor laws and proclamations "with reference to the emancipation of slaves."[26]

As the loopholes in the fortifications on Gorée Island allowed for the defense of the island and its protection from invaders, so the criminal-punishment loophole in the Thirteenth Amendment allowed the former Confederacy to defend the South's Peculiar Institution of slavery and to protect the institution and plantation society from Northern "invaders." The loophole provided treasonous Southerners with an escape from their oath of allegiance to the US Constitution and "the Union of the States," and it provided them with a means to legally nullify their vow to relinquish their claims to Black people as "property" and to honor the status of Black persons as American citizens.

Repaired and restored to their former positions of power, racialized and avaricious Southern leaders were given authority to negotiate the South's transition from a slavocracy to democracy. However, they used their authority to enthrall a people and to impose on them, again, the badges of slavery that were intended to signify Black inferiority and servility while also reinforcing the mythic fiction of so-called white supremacy.

Mass incarceration bolstered the political economy upon which the Southern oligarchy was dependent. Lynching and white mob rule ensured social control of Black people, while silencing the voices of millions of African Americans by undermining their freedom of speech, their freedom to protest, and their right to vote, ensured their political disempowerment. Given that in most states, citizens convicted of a felony lose their voting privileges, the mass incarceration of Black people has functioned as a tool of

Black disfranchisement. Thus, those against the abolition of slavery and forced servitude and in defiance of universal freedom cir-
cumvented the intentions of the Constitution, thereby preserving
the spirit of tyranny and mocking the principles of democracy.

## IN THE AWAKENING

After nearly two hundred fifty years in bondage, African Americans could finally proclaim their freedom as heralded by the
victory of the Union Army and the Reconstruction Amendments.
However, once Johnson restored autonomy to the South in 1865,
ushering in the "Presidential Reconstruction," and President
Rutherford Hayes removed federal troops from the South in 1877,
the sovereignty of Black citizens was no longer protected. They
were engulfed in what the historian Rayford Logan described as
the nadir of the Black experience in America. Between 1865 and
1876—during Johnson's "Presidential Reconstruction"—that
nadir saw upwards of two thousand racial terror lynchings, including rape, of African American men, women, boys, and girls.
And between 1877 and 1950, racialized white individuals and
mobs lynched over four thousand American citizens.[27]

Even though racialized and hate-filled white Americans continued to terrorize and lynch Black Americans throughout the twen-
tieth and into the twenty-first century, it wasn't until 2022, in the
first quarter of our twenty-first century, that the federal government would declare lynching a federal crime and sign the Emmett
Till Antilynching bill into law. The Antilynching Act is named
to honor the life of Emmett Till, the fourteen-year-old African
American boy who, in 1955, was kidnapped, tortured, mutilated,

shot, lynched, and drowned in the Tallahatchie River that runs through Money, Mississippi, where Till was visiting relatives for the summer. So named, the act also memorializes the lives of the more than six thousand lynched African Americans whose deaths were documented and the countless others whose deaths remain undocumented.[28] So named, the act speaks to the terror and emotional and spiritual devastation suffered by the families and communities of those murdered.

The March 2022 Emmett Till Antilynching Act specified lynching as a federal hate crime. In 1900, Congressman George Henry White had introduced into Congress the first proposal to outlaw lynching. It was never voted on. Over the span of 120 years, over two hundred proposals met a similar fate. Preceding White's initiative were the efforts of investigative journalist Ida B. Wells. In 1889, Wells and eight Illinois congressmen met with President William McKinley. Addressing McKinley, Wells stated, "Nowhere in the civilized world save the U.S. of America do men, possessing all civil and political power, go out in bands of 50 and 5,000 to hunt down, shoot, hang or burn to death a single individual, unarmed and absolutely powerless."[29]

In her firsthand experience of investigating lynching scenes and her research into the white terrorization of Black communities, Wells glimpsed both the economic incentives and political motivations of ruling white "elites." Importantly, Wells would discover that the reasons presented by the white community to justify the wholesale lynching of African Americans were lies— false narratives. One of the more inflammatory charges against lynched Black men was the charge of rape. Wells learned that more often than not, the charge of rape that justified the lynching of Black men was a "threadbare lie."[30] And even where Black people had committed some offense, they had been denied their due process of the law.

Frederick Douglass had joined forces with Ida B. Wells in her crusade against lynching. He had observed that the stereotyped constructions of "the Negro" that were published in news articles had a point of origin, a phase, and a purpose. Manufactured during the antebellum years, the Negro-as-insurrectionist construction portrayed Black people as full of "schemes to murder all the white people."[31] This narrative justified the cruel and repressive measures perpetuated against Blacks as a means to assuage white fear. In the aftermath of the Civil War, the Negro-as-supremacist construction ironically portrayed Black people as inferior savages keen on dominating and ruling whites. This narrative, reflected in D. W. Griffith's *The Birth of a Nation*, rationalized the violent repression of Black people in the public sphere and in the political life of the war-torn nation. The Jim Crow years of mob rule gave birth to the Negro-as-rapist construction, which justified the theft of Black property, the desecration of Black political sovereignty, and the violence and barbarity of racialized white Americans.[32]

The three controlling narratives delineated by Wells and Douglass closely correlate with the charges on which most of the inmates at Angola prison have been convicted: murder, assault, and rape. And one can see the Negro-as-criminal narrative as the latest stereotyped construction of "the Negro," a permutation designed to harness the strength and life force of African American bodies and to justify the modern era of mass and perpetual incarceration. The journalist Jeffrey Goldberg reports that of the six thousand three hundred men imprisoned at Angola in 2015, 75 percent of them were serving life sentences without the possibility of parole. Eighty percent were African American. These facts reflect the old colonial law of condemning Black people to bondage *durante vita*—for life.

"Louisiana has some of the toughest sentencing laws in the country," says Goldberg, "and these guys are not going home."[33]

Behind all of these numbers and percentages and dire thoughts are sovereign human beings with families and friends and supporters. My brother among them. His family among them. My brother is guilty of assault. But he was convicted of rape. Due process of the law, in his case, was not duly respected, which was the case for so many Black and poor prisoners. Ninety-seven percent of incarcerated people never have their day in court. They are typically coerced into plea deals, which are significantly harsher for Blacks and people of color than for whites.[34]

The majority of criminal cases in the US are resolved through the plea-bargaining process. These deals determine the crime and the sentence a defendant faces. In "Criminalizing Race: Racial Disparities in Plea-Bargaining," Carlos Berdejó reports that where white defendants "are twenty-five percent more likely than Black defendants to have their most serious initial charge dropped or reduced to a less severe charge," African American defendants "are more likely than white defendants to be convicted of their highest initial charge. . . . As a result, white defendants who face initial felony charges are approximately fifteen percent more likely than black defendants to end up being convicted of a misdemeanor instead."[35] Low-income people of color and whites who literally cannot afford to await trial outside of jail or who have been denied bail are subject to being pressured into making a plea deal. My brother was pressured and then proffered one of those plea deals. He said, "No."

The will to disregard the sovereign rights of African Americans and exploit the loophole in the Thirteenth Amendment has led to a failed justice system that has been described by members of Congress as "legalized slavery." As activists and civil rights organizations have long protested the prison-industrial complex and have worked to find alternatives to America's "punishment bureaucracy," the US Congress has moved to address the long-standing injustice of mass incarceration and the violation of the sovereign rights of those incarcerated.

## JUSTICE FOR US ALL

The proposed Abolition Amendment seeks "to prohibit the use of slavery and involuntary servitude as a punishment for a crime."[36] Cosponsors of the 2021 bill, Senator Merkley and Representative Williams decry the "Punishment Clause" as "indisputably racist in origin and in impact." They argue that "there should be no exceptions to a ban on slavery," and they declare that the loophole, in its concept, purpose, and consequences, does not reflect the nation's values. "The Abolition Amendment," they have resolved, "would close this loophole that has been used for a century and a half to perpetuate mass incarceration and allow others to profit from the forced labor of their fellow Americans, disproportionately Black Americans and people of color."[37]

After a century and a half, the federal government officially acknowledged mass incarceration as *de facto* slavery and is moving to "end slavery once and for all."[38] This is a bold and welcome resolution, for the prison-industrial complex is but one form that slavery takes in America; it is but one means by which Black people are re-enslaved and plundered of their material and financial resources and deprived of their human rights, their citizenship rights as Americans, and their constitutionally recognized personal sovereignty.

Mass incarceration, from post–Civil War penal institutions to the contemporary prison-industrial complex, is one of the more recognizable forms that re-enslavement of Black Americans takes. The rattle and clank of chains in which the enslaved were bound and transported resound in the chains that bind coffles of prison inmates. Links in those same chains bind the life force of Black people beyond prison walls. Where there is money to be made through the exploitation of Black people, one can hear the muffled clanking. The economic imperative that has always been touted as an excuse for trafficking and enslaving Black people must be given constant and vigilant attention because, like a virus, it mutates. And as it mutates, the means and methods of re-enslavement are reconfigured, and are thinly disguised as "racial disparities," "economic inequities," "the market."

The nation's prison policies that have generated billion-dollar profits through forced labor underscore the capacity of public officials to objectify and commodify Black life. In this industry, the incidents and badges of slavery are more readily apparent. One more easily sees how the trope of the "Black criminal" simply supplants "Black cargo" and how the flow of money and the heady intoxication of tyrannical authoritarianism have continued unabated.

For every badge of slavery experienced by imprisoned African Americans, there are comparable experiences among those of us who move about in the larger society. For instance, many inmates are forced into a state of dependency as they are forced to work without pay or, like fifty-three million other Americans, they are forced to work for pay that does not constitute "a living wage."[39] A majority of inmates and former inmates cannot vote, just as Black, activist, and progressive voices are being stifled through suppression of First Amendment rights, gerrymandering, and restrictive voting measures.[40] And the humiliation of being confined and constantly observed is felt whether one is racially profiled while shopping, driving, gardening, or jogging, or whether one works on the floor of corporate factories or in corporate offices or on company-required laptop computers that track keystrokes and site visits to compile and report stats of the user to management.

And so we see how the badges of slavery manifest in the relentless surveilling and policing of Black people and communities. Where popular discourse would have it that prisoners are paying their debt to society, the reality is that, like our Haitian cousins before us, the masses of African Americans continue to pay a debt without ever having committed a crime.

The Abolition Amendment proposed in 2020 and reintroduced in 2021 is hailed as a potential victory for Black American citizens. But we are mistaken if we don't understand this move as a potential victory for all Americans and for the viability of this evolving democratic republic. There is the presumption that the incidents and badges of American slavery are suffered only by Black people, that economic nooses tighten only around Black and brown necks. That the loss of personal sovereignty is an unfortunate inconvenience visited on people of color and the luckless white poor.

There is the assumption by the masses of mainstreamed white Americans that the greed that compelled plantation and prison politics is not a threat to them or that it has not already reached them. But even a superficial glance at the structure and bottom-line operations of corporate America will show the skeletal framework of slavery. The most cursory inquiry into the American legal system will reveal that the same colonial legal processes that trapped Black people in perpetual slavery, also codified a social, economic, and political hierarchy that disadvantaged and disempowered white women.

From the beginning, American colonial law was codified to control and regulate the reproductive life of Black, Indigenous, and white women. And the same overreach of government into the sovereign rights of "the people"—which includes all women—has been reformulated and reactivated. So, *Of Greed and Glory* also looks at how the badges of slavery manifest in the corporate realm *and* in America's patriarchal social system, both of which are reinforced and sustained by the political and legal establishment.

In a speech that marked the occasion of his acceptance of a US Senate nomination, Abraham Lincoln addressed the critical task "of putting an end to slavery agitation. Under the operation of that policy," he said, referencing the Supreme Court's Dred Scott decision, "that agitation has not only, *not ceased*, but has *constantly augmented*." He opined that only a crisis, reached and passed, would bring the Peculiar Institution to an end. A crisis, he said, was necessary; for the government, the nation, would not endure "permanently half *slave* and half *free*":[41]

> "A house divided against itself cannot stand." . . . It will become *all* one thing, or *all* the other. Either the *opponents* of slavery, will arrest the further spread of it, and place it where the public mind shall rest in the belief that it is in course of ultimate extinction; or its *advocates* will push it forward, till it shall become alike lawful in *all* the States, *old* as well as *new—North* as well as *South*.[42]

"Have we no *tendency* to the latter condition?" he asked. As I write, I imagine Lincoln, a brow raised, head slightly angled to one side, a piercing look compelling the conscience of each one present, allowing his question to sink in. I ponder his question about our tendencies as well. Did not the Thirteenth Amendment's criminal-exception loophole make slavery legal "in *all* the States," old and new, North and South? Has not the network of public and private prisons, juvenile and immigrant detention centers, and colonized communities across the American landscape demonstrated our tendency to become complacent as millions of human beings suffer under conditions of slavery and forced servitude? The ascendency of autocratic governors across America, whose government overreach impinge upon protected speech, academic freedom, the right to protest, voting rights, and the political sovereignty of "the people," is a glaring example of antidemocratic tendencies among us. And the use of mob violence to halt the certification of a presidential election and still the democratic process speaks volumes of our tendency to acquiesce before tyranny.

The crisis to which Lincoln alluded, like slavery itself, has been perpetual in America. And the 2022 Antilynching Act and the 2021 Abolition Amendment proposal attest to the fact that we are still reckoning with this crisis.

## "A JAILBREAK OF THE IMAGINATION"

Once my brother was "duly convicted," he was transferred by bus from the East Baton Rouge Parish Prison to the Louisiana State Penitentiary in Angola, Louisiana. Like chattel, condemned to a fate from which no return would be permitted, my brother, like many others, was ushered into a Middle Passage kind of existence. Entering through one barbed wire gate and past the next, my brother and millions of brothers and fathers and uncles and sons were swallowed up by the looped hole in the edifice of democracy. Unconscionably, the guardians of our Constitution left the door open to return Black people back to holding cells on this side of the Atlantic. From sea to shining sea.

As I am putting pen to paper, I am struck by my brother's innocent tenacity in holding on to his personal sovereignty and his unflinching commitment to his Self, to his will to stand in and for the truth of his Being. More than willing to assume responsibility for actions he did commit, he refused to plead guilty to those he did not—even when "failing to comply" with the charges against him meant life—*durante vita.*

On Gorée Island, my companions and I walked the Rue Saint-Germain that leads to The House of Slaves. In Louisiana, my family members and I follow the winding 19.9-mile Tunica Trace Byway that dead-ends at the gates of Angola. "Gorée" is Dutch for "good road." Rue Saint-Germain and Tunica Trace are the same ironical road. What was remarkable about walking the dark corridor that led to the Door of No Return was that the light beyond that door was radiant. In that light, I imagine my brother free. I imagine "the people" sovereign. I imagine America past our crisis.

## NOTES

1. James Baldwin, "The White Man's Guilt," in *James Baldwin: Collected Essays,* ed. Toni Morrison (New York, Library of America, 1998), 723.
2. Paraphrase of excerpt from Whitehead, *The Underground Railroad,* 29: "Sometimes a slave will be lost in a brief eddy of liberation."
3. Thirteenth Amendment: "Article XIII, Section1, The Constitution," from *The Debate on the Constitution, Part One,* ed. Bernard Bailyn (New York: Library of America, 1993), 985.
4. "Northwest Ordinance (1787)," National Archives, last modified May 10, 2022, https://www.archives.gov/milestone-documents/northwest-ordinance.

5. Caroline M. Kisiel, "Loopholes Have Preserved Slavery for More than 150 Years After Abolition," *The Washington Post*, January 27, 2021, https://www.washingtonpost.com/outlook/2021/01/27/loopholes-have-preserved-slavery-more-than-150-years-after-abolition/.

6. The class of Black codes called "pig laws" changed the penalty for the taking of livestock from a misdemeanor to a felony. Oftentimes Blacks so charged were defiantly reclaiming what they were entitled to, but had been cheated out of. The pig laws subjected them to prosecution for felony offenses. ("Black Codes and Pig Laws," PBS, https://www.pbs.org/tpt/slavery-by-another-name/themes/black-codes-and-pig-laws/.)

7. Sam Blum, "Mississippi Ratifies 13th Amendment Abolishing Slavery . . . 147 Years Late," February 18, 2013: https://www.theguardian.com/world/2013/feb/18/mississippi-us-constitution-and-civil-liberties. Accessed June 18, 2023.

8. Kisiel, "Loopholes Have Preserved Slavery for More than 150 Years After Abolition."

9. Jean-Claude Blachère and Michel Renaudeau, *GOREE* (Paris: Richer Hoa-Qui, 1992), 17.

10. Blachère and Renaudeau, *GOREE*, 5, 8–9.

11. Blachère and Renaudeau, *GOREE*, 16–17; and Caroline Newman, "Preserving Senegal's 'House of the Slaves,'" *UVA Today*, June 29, 2016, https://news.virginia.edu/content/preserving-senegals-house-slaves.

12. A "Site of Conscience" is a historic site, a place-based museum or memorial that is purposed with preventing historical erasure, preserving "even the most traumatic memories," and enabling visitors to make connections between the past and present-day human rights issues. ("About Us," International Coalition of Sites of Conscience, https://www.sitesofconscience.org/about-us/about-us/.)
    See also "Maison Des Esclaves – Senegal," International Coalition of Sites of Conscience, https://www.sitesofconscience.org/membership/maison-des-esclaves/.

13. Blachère and Renaudeau, *GOREE*, 17.

14. A. Leon Higginbotham, Jr., *In the Matter of Color: Race and the American Legal Process: The Colonial Period* (New York: Oxford University Press, 1978), 42.

15. Winthrop D. Jordan, *White Over Black: American Attitudes Toward the Negro, 1550–1812* (Chapel Hill, North Carolina: The University of North Carolina Press, 1968), 7, 97.

16. Higginbotham, *In the Matter of Color*, 32; and Jordan, *White Over Black*, 78.

17. Higginbotham, *In the Matter of Color*, 38.

18. Jordan, *White Over Black*, 44, 79, 81.

19. Winthrop D. Jordan, *The White Man's Burden: Historical Origins of Racism in the United States* (New York: Oxford University Press, 1974), 45.

20. Jordan, *The White Man's Burden*, 46.

21. Higginbotham, *In the Matter of Color*, 19, 32.

22. Douglas A. Blackmon, *Slavery by Another Name: The Re-Enslavement of Black Americans from the Civil War to World War II* (New York: Doubleday, 2008), 200.

23. Blackmon, *Slavery by Another Name*, 166.

24. Thirteenth Amendment: "Article XIII, Section1, The Constitution," from *The Debate on the Constitution, Part One*, ed. Bernard Bailyn (New York: Library of America, 1993), 983-984.

25. Elizabeth Anne Reese, "Or to the People: Popular Sovereignty and the Power to Choose a Government," *Cardozo Law Review* 39, no. 6 (2018): 2051, http://cardozolawreview.com/wp-content/uploads/2018/08/REESE.39.6.2-1.pdf.

26. "Prest. Johnson Amnesty Proclamation," Library of Congress, https://www.loc.gov/resource/rbpe.23502500/?st=text.

27. "Reconstruction in America: Racial Violence After the Civil War, 1865–1876," Equal Justice Initiative, 2020, https://eji.org/report/reconstruction-in-america/.

28. "Reconstruction in America."

29. Tianna Mobley, "Ida B. Wells-Barnett: Anti-lynching and the White House," The White House Historical Association, April 9, 2021, https://www.whitehousehistory.org/ida-b-wells-barnett-anti-lynching-and-the-white-house.

30. Ida B. Wells-Barnett, *The Red Record: Tabulated Statistics and Alleged Causes of Lynching in the United States* (1895; Cavalier Classics, 2015), 14.

31. Frederick Douglass, "Why Is the Negro Lynched? *The Lesson of the Hour*, 1894," in *Frederick Douglass: Selected Speeches and Writings*, ed. Philip S. Foner (Chicago: Lawrence Hill Books, 1999), 758.

32. Douglass, "Why Is the Negro Lynched?," 759.

33. *Angola for Life: Rehabilitation and Reform Inside the Louisiana Penitentiary*, produced by Jeffrey Goldberg, Sam Price-Waldman, and Kasia Cieplak-Mayr von Baldegg, posted September 9, 2015, on *The Atlantic*, https://www.theatlantic.com/video/index/404305/angola-prison-documentary/.

34. Jeff Merkley, "The Abolition Amendment," https://www.merkley.senate.gov/imo/media/doc/The%20Abolition%20Amendment%20One%20Pager%20-%20117th_.pdf.

35. Carlos Berdejó, "Criminalizing Race: Racial Disparities in Plea-Bargaining," *Boston College Law Review* 59, no. 4 (2018): 1191, https://lira.bc.edu/work/ns/8911a8f4-41d6-4fee-9f70-9b0e7a01daa1/reader/3bd4b627-6b42-468d-b07b-0a85e8e141e1.

36. "Proposing an Amendment to the Constitution of the United States to Prohibit the Use of Slavery and Involuntary Servitude as a Punishment for a Crime," H.J. Res. 53, 117th Cong. (2021–2022), accessed April 25, 2022, https://www.congress.gov/bill/117th-congress/house-joint-resolution/53.

37. Merkley, "The Abolition Amendment."

38. Merkley, "The Abolition Amendment."

39. A living wage in the US in 2021 was calculated to be $24.16 per hour or $100,498.60 per year for a family of four. (Stephanie Moser and Chet Swalina, "A Calculation of the Living Wage," MIT Living Wage Calculator, May 19, 2022, https://livingwage.mit.edu/articles/99-a-calculation-of-the-living-wage.)
    However, a Brookings Institution report indicates that 53 million Americans, 44 percent of all workers, are "low-wage" workers who earn a median wage of $10.22 per hour or about $18,000 per year, $10,000 below the official poverty line of about $28,000 per year for a family of four. (Martha Ross and Nicole Bateman, "Low-Wage Work Is More Pervasive than You Think, and There Aren't Enough 'Good Jobs' to Go Around," Brookings Institution,

November 21, 2019, https://www.brookings.edu/blog/the-avenue/2019/11/21
/low-wage-work-is-more-pervasive-than-you-think-and-there-arent-enough
-good-jobs-to-go-around/; and "Poverty Guidelines," Office of the Assistant
Secretary for Planning and Evaluation, January 12, 2022, https://aspe.hhs.gov
/topics/poverty-economic-mobility/poverty-guidelines.)

40. In the aftermath of Black Lives Matter protests and demonstrations against the
police murder of George Perry Floyd, Jr., the Florida legislature, for instance,
passed "anti-protest" legislation that fosters and sanctions "mass arrests, illegal
force, the criminalization of protest, and other means intended to thwart the
right to free public expression, assembly, and association." This antidemocratic
sentiment has also informed voter repression tactics in Florida, like the creation
of the "election police unit." ("Demonstrations and Protests," ACLU Florida,
https://www.aclufl.org/sites/default/files/field_documents/kyr_demonstrations
_and_protests_-_aclu_of_florida_final.pdf, accessed June 2023; and Anthony
Izaguirre, "Florida Governor Signs Bill Creating Election Police Unit," PBS,
April 25, 2022, https://www.pbs.org/newshour/politics/florida-governor-signs
-bill-creating-election-police-unit.)

Antidemocratic sentiment has also prompted "election integrity legislation"
in Texas, generating obstacles to voting, such as the ban on "drive-thru" voting,
the ban on twenty-four-hour voting, and new ID requirements. Assisting elderly
or differently abled voters is subject to criminal penalties, and poll watchers are
allowed to function as instruments of surveillance. Georgia's Election Integrity
Act has prohibited the distribution of food or water near polling places or within
twenty-five feet of anyone waiting in line to vote. And the US Supreme Court
voted to allow states to use unlawfully gerrymandered congressional maps in the
midterm elections of 2022. (Alexa Ura, "Gov. Greg Abbott Signs Texas Voting
Bill into Law, Overcoming Democratic Quorum Breaks," *The Texas Tribune*,
September 7, 2021, https://www.texastribune.org/2021/09/01/texas-voting-bill
-greg-abbott/; Michael Bartiromo and Nexstar Media Wire, "Is It Illegal to Hand
Out Water or Food Outside Your Polling Place?," *The Hill*, November 1, 2022,
https://thehill.com/homenews/Nexstar_media_wire/3709676-is-it-illegal-to-hand
-out-water-or-food-outside-your-polling-place/; and Henry L. Chambers, Jr.,
"Supreme Court Allows States to Use Unlawfully Gerrymandered Congressional
Maps in the 2022 Midterm Elections," University of Richmond School of Law,
June 2, 2022, https://law.richmond.edu/features/article/-/21904/supreme-court
-allows-states-to-use-unlawfully-gerrymandered-congressional-maps-in-the-2022
-midterm-elections.)

41. Abraham Lincoln, "June 16, 1858: 'A House Divided' Speech," June 16, 1858,
Miller Center, transcript, https://millercenter.org/the-presidency/presidential
-speeches/june-16-1858-house-divided-speech.

42. Lincoln, "June 16, 1858: 'A House Divided' Speech."

## CHAPTER 3

## MY BROTHER

*This is a call from an incarcerated individual at the Louisiana State Penitentiary. This call is not private. It will be recorded and may be monitored. If you believe this should be a private call, please hang up and follow facility instructions to register this number as a private number. Fund an inmate's calling account to make sure a call is never missed. You can fund an inmate's account without setting up a calling account of your own. Simply visit www.securustech.net or call 1-800-844-6591 and select the option to fund an inmate debit account today. To accept this free call, press one. Thank you for using Securus. You may start the conversation now.*

✖ ✖ ✖

BOBBY, HEY, BOBBY, I'M HERE. . . ."
I don't have the luxury of time to respectfully, patiently wait until my brother speaks, and during our conversation, I am prone to interrupt him before he finishes what he is saying to me. It is a rush of words with us. In everyday conversations, I try to practice actually listening to all of what someone is saying to me and then, in my turn, responding accordingly. This practice sometimes entails spaces of silence—between the listening and the responding.

But when I'm talking with my brother, the silences seem an absolute luxury I can't afford, once I've "pressed one."

Because of the COVID-19 pandemic, incarcerated persons at Angola, perhaps like the incarcerated around the world, could not receive visitors. And because of that and the long-term presence of the virus and likely, also, because of a modicum of human compassion, those confined at Angola were allowed free biweekly, ten-minute calls. Bobby called me. I was so glad to be able to hear from him, especially when I learned that he was experiencing COVID-like symptoms. Even family who live in Louisiana who might have been able to visit and check on him in person, could not.

The whole place was on lockdown, and no relatives or friends were allowed in to see about their loved ones. But I had to know, and during the time he was experiencing symptoms, the incarcerated there had not yet been allotted the free calls. But I kept calling the prison, and from one operator to the next and one receptionist to the next, I finally managed to speak with a nurse who had seen him. But I wasn't listed as the "relative of record" who would be privy to information about my brother's health.

My dad, Alfred Plant, Sr., was listed as the family member who could have access to this type of information. But our dad had died in 2018, and it apparently had not crossed my brother's mind to update the record. I was in a bit of a panic. I couldn't be there with my brother—no one could—and this prudent technicality was proving to be an impediment. Still, I needed to know his condition. We had learned through an email from Bobby to another brother that Bobby had lost his sense of taste and smell. He had lost his appetite and was losing weight. And I was afraid for my brother and for us and for me. Bobby is my heart. I could not be okay with not knowing.

So I pressed my case with the nurse. Under the circumstances and out of compassion for a sister's need to know about her baby brother, the nurse let me know that Bobby had just been released from the infirmary. That he was okay. The doctors seemed to think that he didn't have COVID. That he was experiencing seasonal allergies. We were still in the early days of the virus, when the nature of the virus and its effects were still largely unknown. I suspected that my brother had contracted the virus but that the more dire effects had not expressed in him. In any case, he was assessed as healthy enough to be released from the infirmary. I was relieved. And I could stop holding *my* breath.

So we began our accelerated, ten-minute minuet that the automated operator invariably breaks into to remind me that I am speaking with "an offender at a Louisiana Department of Corrections facility" and then again to inform us that "you have one minute left." One minute. To say what had been left unsaid. Remaining messages, details, queries are hurriedly merged with I-love-yous and take-cares and final bye-byes.

⌘ ⌘ ⌘

I have five brothers. The personality of each one is singular, and my relationship with each one has its own specialness. Bobby was the fourth of five boys in a two-parent family of eight siblings (three girls). He was "the baby" for ten years before the last boy child was born. Bobby, before he was taken from me, was the kind of brother who would wash and wax your car for you with no expectation of receiving anything in return. Not payment, nor a return favor. Not permission to use the car, nor the presumption of an earned entitlement to be driven somewhere. He just cleaned it, waxed it to a new-car shine, and gave me my keys.

When our mother had to go back into the Charity Hospital in New Orleans in 1978, I had to figure out how to make sure she was all right. I needed to see to her welfare while I also continued to "take care of the house," which included cooking, cleaning, shopping, looking after my then eight-year-old youngest brother, and generally helping out my dad, who was still working full-time as a mechanic. Momma had stopped eating. No matter what I cooked for her, she didn't want it. Which also meant that she had stopped taking her medications. Trying to mix her distasteful medicine in with the few dishes she still enjoyed eating didn't help the situation. Because she had stopped eating, my dad and I had to get her readmitted. It broke my heart to think of her alone in the hospital. She would be in a ward with others and not that far from the nurses' station. But still, no one was going to take care of her the way I wanted her to be taken care of.

I had begun taking care of my mother during my last year at Southern University when we learned that my mom had been diagnosed with multiple myeloma, a cancer of the bone marrow. By the time we, the siblings, found out about her condition, the cancer had already progressed into the last stages. So I turned down a teaching assistantship at Atlanta University to be with my mom and help her to get better. "Get better" because I had no experience of "terminal." And I had no clue of what "fatal" meant, not really, not like I was about to learn.

When she was at home, I would sit by my mother's bedside, watching her sleep. During the times she had to be admitted, I half slept in hospital chairs, listening for her requests for a sip of water or an extra blanket. Later on, I drove her to chemotherapy treatments on Tuesdays, Thursdays, Saturdays. And then Tuesdays and Thursdays. And then not even just Tuesdays. And so I

# Sell your books at sellbackyourBook.com!

Go to sellbackyourBook.com and get an instant price quote. We even pay the shipping - see what your old books are worth today!

00066159956

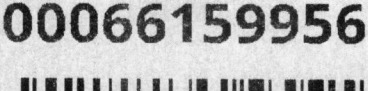

explained to Bobby that we had to take Momma back to the hospital, and that she couldn't be there alone, but that I had to look after our little brother and get him ready for school and be there when he got out and so, would he, Bobby, let me take him up to the hospital to stay with Momma until I could get back up there to see after her. Bobby was the kind of brother who said yes.

Momma was glad to see us. It was the last time I would see her alive. I was grateful my brother could come and be with her, be her comfort. Now she wouldn't be alone, without us. And I reasoned, too, that it was fitting. In the previous days when she was still lucid, my mom had shared with me her concern for Bobby and her last child. She was worried about Bobby's future and concerned about my youngest brother's presently problematic character. He was haughty, self-centered. Conceited. But then, they, my parents, had spoiled him with their he's-the-last-one logic. She wanted to rectify this error, do some kind of intervention.

I promised her that I would see to both my brothers, that she didn't have to worry about them, that she should focus on getting better. I wanted to put her mind at ease, but I also meant what I said. So having Bobby with her, she knew, for the moment anyway, that he was okay. And because I was at home and not there with her, she also knew that I was looking after her youngest child.

It was about four or five the next morning when Bobby awoke. He was lying on the floor, next to Momma's bed. He opened his eyes to find himself embraced in her last breath of sight. He called to tell me that Momma was gone. I knew her last wishes. I made the arrangements. I was busy until I wasn't. And then I had to be with what all the business was about. The ushers at New Jerusalem had taken me to one of the auxiliary rooms off from the main congregation. I had just kinda lost it when the attendants were closing the lid of the casket and I realized I would no longer be able to see my mother's face. I would understand this ceremonial detail later as established funereal ritual. But no one had told me, and it was so unexpected. In that anguished space where suspended belief bows to what is so, I understood "terminal" and something of the meaning of "fatal." And it was too much.

It was Bobby who came to get me and walked me back to rejoin the family. In his turn, he would have me be present before our mother, present to the unstoppable ceremonies of closing lids and closing doors and changing worlds and changed lives. He would be my comfort, and all my mother's children would be around her, present and accounted for, like each of the gems on the birthstone ring we had given her one Mother's Day. This ring that complemented the blue dress in which she was buried. This ring that would be a keepsake for her eternal journey.

Atlanta University had written to inform me that the teaching assistant position was still open and inquired about my availability. I accepted the position. I left home because I couldn't stay. Elouise Porter Plant died and changed my world. When I returned on visits from school, Bobby was the kind of brother who would cook me some red beans and rice or gumbo. Sometimes he'd throw me a party and gather family and friends so we'd have some fun together and catch up. Other times, me and my own Bobby McGee would be all the party we needed. We'd go to a restaurant and sit and eat and drink and talk and laugh for hours until one of us remembered something we were supposed to be doing or somewhere else we were supposed to be being. We'd head off to whatever that was with the glee from our communion still warm and smiling within us.

So on one visit, when I spied two white men in suits—detectives,

I seem to recall—making their way toward our house, I told my brother to leave immediately through the patio doors on the opposite side of the house. I only delayed the inevitable.

✠ ✠ ✠

My brother has been locked up for over twenty years. He spent two years in East Baton Rouge Parish Prison awaiting trial. In February of 2000, a Louisiana grand jury indicted my brother with "aggravated rape, simple kidnaping, aggravated battery and second degree battery." His trial began April 19, 2000. "One day later, on April 20, 2000, a 12-person jury returned unanimous guilty verdicts on all charges." Post-trial motions filed on August 31, 2000, were denied. Sentencing was handed down September 7, 2000: "life at hard labor for the aggravated [rape], 5 years hard labor (concurrent) for the simple kidnaping, 10 years hard labor (concurrent) for the aggravated battery and 5 years hard labor (concurrent) for the second degree battery." As though he were in some kind of army, he was "given credit for time served," but no provision was made for the possibility of parole.[1]

His motion for appeal was denied September 19, 2000, and the "criminal appeal with a request for oral argument," filed on January 24, 2001, by the lawyers my dad hired, was also denied.[2] Because the prosecutor brought felony charges against my brother, his case had to go before a grand jury. I contemplated the fact that the charges a grand jury considers are brought by the prosecutor and that prosecutors are given a great deal of authority in judicial processes. Until 1993, they enjoyed "absolute immunity."[3]

Qualified or relative immunity notwithstanding, they still wield a great deal of power and "have more power over sentences than judges do" since prosecutors determine the starting point for plea negotiations.[4] Prosecutors decide what charges will be filed initially, and just as they have the power to reduce serious charges to less serious ones, they have the power to "overcharge" a defendant and file more severe charges.[5] And this latter power is often applied prejudicially: "black defendants are more likely than white defendants to be convicted of their highest initial charge."[6]

The appeal brief written and filed by my brother's lawyers challenged the logic and legality of the lesser "second degree battery" charge that was "subsumed in the aggravated battery charge." It questioned a charge of "aggravated battery" in the absence of "a dangerous weapon." And it found that the charges of "simple kidnaping" and "aggravated rape," like the aggravated battery charge, were made despite insufficient evidence.[7]

An eyewitness account contradicted the kidnapping charge, and the medical testimony of "the state's own witness," the physician "who performed a rape kit at Earl K. Long [hospital] the night of the alleged attack," refuted that a rape had occurred. After having performed requisite examinations and analyses, the physician "could not say [that the fiancée] was raped or even that sexual intercourse occurred. . . . [In] establishing the facts of the offense," the testimony of a survivor of rape is sufficient "to prove sexual penetration and the other elements of the offense." Such testimony, however, stands only when it is "absent irresolvable conflict with the physical evidence."[8] During court proceedings, this "irresolvable conflict" was not resolved but ignored. And it is the charge, indictment, and conviction of aggravated rape that had underwritten my brother's life sentence at Angola prison.

Given the errors in the findings of the grand jury and the verdicts reached by the trial court in the absence of sufficient evidence, my brother's lawyers asserted in the appeal brief that "the law and evidence does not support a guilty finding beyond a reasonable doubt." They cited the "insufficient and inadequate" counsel of the public defender who represented my brother and the public defender's "unprofessional errors" as factors contributing to my brother's conviction. Since the trial judge articulated no reason for imposing the "extreme" sentences, though a statement of reason is required by law, they argued further that my brother's sentences be reviewed "for excessiveness" and that his sentences be either reduced or remanded for further consideration.[9]

Even as checks and balances, theoretically, are integral to America's criminal justice system, these counterbalancing calculations apparently do not factor in the differential treatment to which Black people have been subjected consequent to the Criminal Punishment Clause in the Thirteenth Amendment and which drives ongoing racial disparities in the dispensation of justice in America. "The end result of these disparities is a pair of dispiriting statistics that are well-known to many—black males are incarcerated at a rate that is five times that of white males, and one third of black males can expect to be imprisoned at some point in their lives."[10] Thus, the almost inevitable imprisonment of my brother.

In addition to the presumption of the guilt of Black people generally, as a justification for the Black Codes of the post-Reconstruction South, was the presumption of "dangerousness"—particularly regarding Black men. Such presumptions underscore the implicit bias inherent in the justice system, then and now. Court officials, including defense attorneys, are subject to "using a defendant's race (an observable attribute) as a proxy for the defendant's inherent criminality (an unobservable attribute). . . . If judges perceive black defendants as being more dangerous and more likely to recidivate than white defendants, then judges may (consciously or subconsciously) punish black defendants more severely than similar white defendants."[11]

My brother Bobby admitted to the charge of battery against his fiancée. "In as much as he admitted striking the defendant," the lawyers stated in the appeal brief, "he is guilty of second degree battery."[12] But how did the prosecutor enter a felony charge of rape with no evidence of rape? How did the grand jury indict him for "aggravated rape" with no evidence that a rape or sexual intercourse had occurred? How could the trial court find him guilty of "aggravated rape" when conflicting physical evidence was not resolved? How could the trial judge impose the maximum sentence for a conviction that ignored the evidence that pertained to "reasonable doubt"?

Historically, the Black-male-as-rapist was among the first stereotypes constructed of newly freed Black men during the Reconstruction era. As Ida B. Wells's investigations revealed, innocent or guilty, the charge of aggravated rape against a Black man was justification enough to lynch him. Where a Black man was permitted to live long enough to stand trial, evidence in his defense was irrelevant. Thus, due process was denied to the innocent and guilty alike. Inherent in the *charge* of rape was the indictment, the conviction, and the sentence of death. Or in my brother's case—life.

A grand jury is perceived as a check on the extensive power of the prosecutor. The deliberations of a trial court are presumed to leverage inconsistencies in the findings of a grand jury. The trial judge is presumed to be the one to balance the scales of justice in context of charges brought and the range of sentencing associated with those charges. However, historically, there has been no effective way to counterbalance subconscious perceptions of the guilt of Black people or subconscious beliefs that all Black men are innately dangerous and sexually violent.[13]

Advocates of criminal justice reform have criticized policy that dismisses a Black defendant's claim of the violation of his or her Fourteenth Amendment protection of due process. In such cases, courts have historically chosen to ignore "statistical evidence showing patterns of racial discrimination" and have placed the burden of proof upon a plaintiff to demonstrate "racially discriminatory intent or purpose. . . . If subconscious racial biases do contribute to racial disparities," as studies show that they do, and if courts are reluctant to accept the statistical evidence, then "there would be no constitutional means to address these [disparities] under the evidentiary requirements articulated by the courts."[14]

How does one reveal subconscious racial bias or disrobe consciously cloaked racism? How does one sound and make manifest the subconscious racialized beliefs that dictate the actions and nonactions of court officials and civilian participants? How does one account for systemic historical amnesia or the discounting of the influence of the "past"? Whether conscious or subconscious, expressed or repressed, activated or latent, the politics of racial *difference* that individuals bring to judicial processes have very real consequences for defendants and their families.

It was my brother's opinion that jurors could think and feel more deeply, not only about the cases with which they are presented but also about their own predisposition and subjectivity. His experience was that his trial was less about the evidence than it was about who told the more impressive story. And from where he sat, the jurors were enthralled by the version of events narrated by the prosecution. And the story the prosecutor told was a variation on the theme of the Negro-as-rapist.

✕ ✕ ✕

It must have seemed like *déjà vu* to him. The very same day of the parole board meeting, with the briefest of deliberations—if their headshakes and eye glances could be called that—the officials of the board denied my brother a pardon. After twenty years of imprisonment, my brother petitioned for clemency. He was notified on January 19, 2021, that a hearing would be granted. He sought clemency so that he might become eligible for parole. The hearing was scheduled for March 22, 2021.

I was one of the three people he was allowed to select to speak on his behalf. Speakers who opposed his bid for clemency would be present as well. Given the COVID-19 pandemic, there would be no in-person meeting. At the appointed time, we were to gather, as it were, in the virtual realm of Zoom. The surreal effect of this telescoping of the years and the anxious confluence of feelings of anger and pain, loss and grief, and hope and possibility, into the rectangular frame of a computer screen was about as absurd as the notion that the State could take my brother away from me and keep him forever.

My brother's former fiancée and their daughter were present to argue that his petition be denied. The prosecutor rounded out the trio of opposition. The prosecutor, the agent of the State, was there to ensure that the State's intention, as the prosecutor had interpreted, crafted, and presented it, would not be thwarted—that my brother would not escape.

As the board had ruled that the State's will would continue to be done, I had begun to wonder what else might our family do. What other steps we might take to get my brother back. I knew that resuming the counsel of lawyers would require money. In the aftermath of the denied appeal that was filed by the lawyers my dad had hired, there was the sense that there was no real chance of success. At that time, none of us understood the appeals process and that sometimes cases can be won if one has the stamina, time, optimism, and money to keep appealing.

Early on, my dad wanted to mortgage our home in order to pay a private lawyer to handle my brother's case during the initial trial, rather than leave it in the hands of a public defender. "But I told him, 'No,'" my brother informed me. My brother actually believed that justice would prevail. He knew he had not committed rape, and he believed that the evidence would prove his innocence. "But what I didn't know," he wrote, "is that the court system is not a place for a black man or woman or poor people. So I went with a public defender and he was not on my side because of the D. A. I didn't know that the courts play the give and take game, meaning, 'Give me him and I let you take the next one.'"[15]

Public defenders, like prosecutors and judges, are paid by the government—federal, state, city, county, or parish government. Their purpose is to represent those who cannot afford an attorney, thus fulfilling a constitutional mandate. Theoretically, a public defender is tasked with serving the best interests of that demographic of the American public who are economically marginalized. However, my brother's experiences had him understand this ironic twist: "The court will appoint you [a P. D.] which is a public [defender]. Now, most people don't know when you are [locked] up, you are no longer a part of the public. So, it's the D. A. [District Attorney] and the P. D. [Public Defender] against you."[16]

How is justice served when justice is politicized? When certain prosecutors are compelled by conviction rates and certain public defenders choose to collaborate with those prosecutors and accept plea deals that sacrifice the lives of their clients? How are we to understand justice when the government that provides prosecutors and public defenders is the same government that sanctioned the Criminal Punishment Clause in the Thirteenth Amendment?

How do we overcome systemic injustice when the Thirteenth Amendment's criminal-exception clause effectively criminalized Black people, rendering us enemies of the public good, but the US Supreme Court, in *Alexander v. Sandoval* (2001), decides to ignore the statistical evidence of the disparate impact of racial bias and discrimination in criminal justice processes?[17] This ruling "closed the courthouse doors to claims of racial bias at every stage of the criminal justice process, from stops and searches to plea bargaining and sentencing," thus flouting the Fourteenth Amendment's provisions for due process and equal protection.[18] How do we evolve our way out of a house divided when the Supreme Court continues to close the courthouse doors on our legal pathway to justice?

&#9187;  &#9187;  &#9187;

And so I began to calculate. And it dawned on me that I was, no doubt, having the same feelings and thoughts and experiences of ancestors who plotted on stealing loved ones and escaping with them or who scraped together and saved what monies they came by in order to buy their loved ones back. To pay their ransom. To make reparations for "merchandise" relinquished.

It dawned on me, too, that as I must make these calculations, thousands of other African Americans have had to make these same calculations—in "freedom" as in "slavery." They have had to contemplate this same sordid bargaining and *purchase*. And as I reflected on the money that I and my family have spent to support and sustain my brother for more than two decades, I fathomed on a deeper level the unfathomable bottom-line economics of maintaining the "Punishment Clause" that sanctioned a continuation of "slavery and involuntary servitude" in America.

I began to understand, viscerally, the meaning of "prison-industrial complex." It's not a concept. It is the reification of racialized resentment, hate, greed, and cunning. It reflects the same abominable (that is, inhuman *and* inhumane) spirit that infused the minds of the architects of America's Peculiar Institution and the plantation society that cultivated and celebrated it. I paused to feel what it feels like to be trapped alive within the hold of the *history* of "slavery."

As my mother's death had me know the meaning of the cessation of life, my brother's life sentence had me know the meaning of protracted death in "life." I didn't quite know what I felt after the officials so summarily dismissed the efforts that my brother and our family put forth to seek even the possibility of his freedom. I was by turns perplexed, quietly enraged, indifferent, contemplative, philosophical, outdone, and resigned—but not really. When we all—siblings and relations—called to check on one another after this event that was so momentous to us but seemed so trivial to the appeals officials, I said I was all right. But I wasn't.

On a drive to the store on the day after the hearing, I just happened to catch the tail end of a radio interview with the sociologist, criminologist, and social worker Reuben Jonathan Miller. He was discussing his new book, *Halfway Home: Race, Punishment, and the Afterlife of Mass Incarceration.* What he was saying about his experiences in relation to his incarcerated brother resonated with me. He had put a word to what I was feeling: shame. What was it like for Miller, the interviewer wanted to know, when he was negotiating the legal and practical aspects of his brother's pending release from jail, while also maintaining other commitments in his personal and professional life?

"The feeling that I came to, often," responded Miller, "was a feeling of shame. And it was a feeling of shame of being alone." He had felt "isolated." And though he would discover that it was not true that others in his professional circle had not had similar experiences, he felt "profoundly" the shame of being alone. And yet one in two people in America has a loved one who has been jailed or imprisoned, Miller went on. "This is where we live. . . . This is so many people's experiences."[19]

Peering at others through Zoom windows, I, like Miller, had felt alone, isolated in my Florida silo. I was able to see my brother by virtue of computer cameras and bytes, but the decision of the board made poignant our separation. In 2018, after twenty years of confinement in Louisiana penal institutions, my brother had begun preparing his request for clemency. We all contributed to his application packet, submitting letters of support, requisite copies of official documents, information pertaining to work and housing that would be in place should my brother, at some point in time, be released. In January of 2021, my brother was informed that he had been granted a hearing. So, by March 22, 2021, we all had come a long way.

In less than thirty minutes, parole board officials—all white, one female—had dismissed my brother's appeal. The patronizing and perfunctory manner in which the board considered my brother's appeal underscored my sense that not only would my brother and our family remain separate but also that we were separate from the goodwill of the State.

I saw the light go out of my brother's eyes. His nervous optimism dimmed. They wouldn't even listen to him speak about the rehabilitation efforts he had made over the years: the anger management classes he had taken; the certificates received in Bible study; activities as church pianist and musical director; and importantly, his remorse for the violence against his then fiancée. These activities may have redressed the charges of battery and kidnapping for which he had already served, concurrently, five years for second degree battery, ten for aggravated battery, and five for simple kidnapping. He was now doing time—for life—for rape. So it didn't matter what he had done if his actions and activities did not correlate with the required rehabilitation protocols prescribed for "rapists." Not only would that include specific rape-charge-related classes but also the admission of guilt of the act of rape.

The words and body language of board officials seemed to say:

*You were convicted. Therefore, you are guilty of kidnapping and aggravated rape as well as the battery you do admit to. Don't insult us and don't lie and further demean yourself by contesting the verdict, saying that you "didn't rape her." Besides, you've only been here twenty years.*

Twenty years of my brother's laboring. Two and a half years

of the family's listening for the parole board's response. A day of pacing in our separate homes across three states, in a virtual prison waiting room before our brother's case even appeared on the docket. Registration for the Zoomed hearing began at 7:15 a.m. (Central time), and the hearing was to begin at 8:30 a.m. In the information sent to us, there was no indication that my brother's hearing would be but one of many. His case wouldn't come up until late afternoon.

In between cases, the board would chat like family members during a TV commercial break. During one of these chat sessions, the one female board official expressed how much she admired "inmates" who had never denied their crime. They were so unlike all those others who deny their crimes, resist taking responsibility, and try to avoid paying their debt to society.

Yet the idea that all persons are guilty of the crimes of which they are convicted is contradicted, for example, by the 375 DNA exonerations in this country as of January 2020. "The vast majority (97%) of these people were wrongfully convicted of committing sexual assault and/or murder. Although these individuals were innocent of these crimes, approximately 25% had confessed and 11% had pleaded guilty." Two hundred and twenty-five (60 percent) of the 375 people wrongfully convicted were African American.[20]

Nonetheless, the board member's admiration for inmates who professed guilt and her annoyance with those who did not seemed to be the tenets of a personal as well as a professional and official credo. And so my brother and his family got short shrift. Certainly, if my brother were a guilty liar, listening to his family served what purpose? The board related to our family as though we were taking up too much of their time. I had typed the statement of support I wanted to make. I timed it to make sure it didn't go over the allotted time. I had gotten a little choked up as I was nearing the end of my statement, reading the part about how my brother, through all the years of his incarceration, never stopped being a brother to me.

I had taken a moment to calm myself. This pause in the reading of my testimony seemed a convenient moment for one of the board members to rush me along in finishing up because they had other cases on the docket. She had rushed none of the grieving family members of the previous proceedings, whether they were offering testimonials of support or petitions in opposition to a pardon or parole appeal.

I was embarrassed for myself, my brother, and for all of us. These authorities, these agents of the state of Louisiana, related to my brother as though he were some reconfiguration of Dred Scott, who was perceived by Justice Taney as "an ordinary article of merchandise and traffic, whenever profit could be made by it."[21] Resonant with the spirit of a Justice Taney, the sentiment of the members of the parole board toward my brother and the rest of us was that we had no sovereign rights which they were bound to respect—no sovereign right to an honest *hearing*, no sovereign right to dignity nor respect.

I was mortified by my own sense of humiliation. The indignation. The shame of being treated as though the decades of my family's separation and our efforts to restore our union didn't matter. There was the shame of being separate and isolated, as Miller had described it. And there was also the shame that speaks to the incident of being treated disdainfully, a shame that is, itself, a badge of slavery. Just as "slavery" did not end with the Thirteenth Amendment, the trauma and shame associated with enslavement has continued within those situations, circumstances, and institutions that reproduce "slavery and involuntary servitude" and "slave-plantation" politics in America.

In "The Name of the Game Is Shame: The Effects of Slavery and Its Aftermath," the psychotherapist Gilda Graff writes that "slavery was traumatic, and that shame accompanies trauma." She references the capture of African peoples, the deracination from their land and language, the disruption of their community and customs, the disconnection from a sense of place, security in the continuity of the past, and confidence in "an expectable future" as ground zero for the individual and collective trauma that continues to haunt African Americans.[22]

The anthropologist Marimba Ani conceptualized this trauma, this disaster, as the "Maafa."[23] This Maafa that unfolded in "slave houses" along the coastline of West Africa would be reproduced in the courthouses of America. The strike of the "slave auctioneer's" gavel separated and displaced Black family members who had been reduced to merchandise and condemned to "perpetual slavery." That same strike would resound in the judge's gavel that separated and separates Black family members who have been reduced to criminals and condemned to excessive sentencing, "life" and death punishment, and a post-incarceration afterlife controlled by forty-five thousand federal and state laws, policies, and administrative sanctions—each one a variation of the country's "fugitive slave" laws.[24]

The resulting shame and "severe anxiety" consequent to relentless victimization and circumscribed freedom undermine personal identity and selfhood. "In addition to the shame and trauma of being enslaved itself, [the clinical psychologist Janice] Gump states that to be the victim of human induced trauma is the ultimate mortification, for there is no shame as profound as that which destroys subjectivity, 'which says through word or action, "What you need, what you desire, and what you feel are of complete and utter insignificance."'"[25]

Both the plea bargain proffered to my brother and the terms of the clemency request required that he deny his own reality as a thinking, speaking subject and accept the objective identity that the State would impose on him. This cruel irony was untenable to me. If my brother had lied that he was guilty as charged, then parole board officials might have thought of him more favorably. Though he had sworn in court to tell the truth, the same court required him to lie. In exchange for my brother's corroboration of the falsehoods perpetrated, the prosecutor would have reduced his charges and recommended a sentence of twenty years. My brother found this *bargain* repugnant. He was not willing to surrender his sense of self for this historical, court-sanctioned construction of him.

✗ ✗ ✗

My brother's hope and ours were unrealistic. The board was not there to retry his case but to grant or deny his request for clemency—and only as the request related to the verdicts against him. The conviction of kidnapper and rapist was the only "truth" the board could or would entertain. If my brother had "copped a plea" at the outset of this Maafic experience, he might have been released by now. But he would have been branded a rapist.

He would have had to live life labeled as a sex offender and forever endure the restrictions and stigma associated with that conviction. If he were to see the light of day beyond prison walls, he would have had to identify as a kidnapper and rapist and wear the badge of shame that—like all badges or markers burned into or tattooed on the skin, coded in body mutilations or printed on armbands or sewn onto the fabric of one's clothing, emblazoned in yellow stars or scarlet letters—is intended to separate, isolate, humiliate, and imprison a person, no matter where that person may be or however the person is trying to live a sovereign life.

When the funeral attendants closed the lid that blocked my mother's face from view, the finality of her physical existence as my mother set in. When the members of the board closed the case of my brother's appeal—even before they voiced their denial of his request—I got that these people who represent the relentless overreach of the policing powers of the State never intended for me to see my brother again in life as a "free" person.

When the board moved on to another case, I was still stuck in my silo contemplating what life without the possibility of parole meant. It's not a sentence; it's a predestination that precludes "an expectable future."

## NOTES

1. Mark D. Plaisance and Francis Rougeau, "Original Appeal Brief of Appellant Bobby Plant," Louisiana First Circuit Court of Appeal, January 24, 2001, 1.

2. Plaisance and Rougeau, "Original Appeal Brief of Appellant Bobby Plant," title page.

3. Radley Balko, "7th Circuit Pokes a Hole in Prosecutorial Immunity," *The Washington Post*, January 30, 2014, https://www.washingtonpost.com/news/opinions/wp/2014/01/30/7th-circuit-pokes-a-hole-in-prosecutorial-immunity/.

4. Equal Justice Initiative, "Research Finds Evidence of Racial Bias in Plea Deals," October 26, 2017, https://eji.org/news/research-finds-racial-disparities-in-plea-deals/.

5. "Prosecutors can engage in either horizontal overcharging by filing charges for distinct crimes resulting from similar offensive conduct, or vertical overcharging by charging harsh variations of the same crime when the evidence only supports lesser variations." H. Mitchell Caldwell, "Coercive

Plea Bargaining: The Unrecognized Scourge of the Justice System," *Catholic University Law Review* 61, no. 1 (Fall 2011): 85, https: https://scholarship.law .edu/cgi/viewcontent.cgi?article=1003&context=lawreview.

6. Berdejó, "Criminalizing Race," 1191. While Berdejó's study shows that outcomes for Black and white defendants are similar in severe felony cases, the outcomes are nevertheless inherently disparate given the racial disparities evident in the data related to initial charges, convictions, and sentencing.

7. Plaisance and Rougeau, "Original Appeal Brief," 2, 4.

8. Plaisance and Rougeau, "Original Appeal Brief," 9, 10.

9. Plaisance and Rougeau, "Original Appeal Brief," 14, 15.

10. Berdejó, "Criminalizing Race," 1190.

11. Berdejó, "Criminalizing Race," 1195–96.

12. Plaisance and Rougeau, "Original Appeal Brief," 5.

13. Berdejó, "Criminalizing Race," 1189, 1196, 1198, 1238.

14. Berdejó, "Criminalizing Race," 1192–93.

15. Bobby D. Plant, letter to author, June 15, 2022.

16. Bobby D. Plant, letter to author, circa 1999.

17. Berdejó, "Criminalizing Race," 1192.

18. Michelle Alexander, *The New Jim Crow: Mass Incarceration in the Age of Colorblindness* (New York: The New Press, 2012), 139.

19. Reuben Jonathan Miller, "The Afterlife of Mass Incarceration," interview by Terri Gross, *Fresh Air*, NPR, March 24, 2021, https://www.npr.org/2021 /03/24/980778161/the-afterlife-of-mass-incarceration.

20. "Research Resources," Innocence Project, accessed 6/22/2023, http:// innocenceproject.org/research-resources/; and "DNA Exonerations in the United States (1989–2020)," Innocence Project, accessed 6/22/2023, https:// innocenceproject.org/dna-exonerations-in-the-united-states/.

21. United States Supreme Court et al., *The Dred Scott Decision: Opinion of Chief Justice Taney* (New York: Van Evrie, Horton & Co., 1860), https://www.loc.gov /item/17001543/.

22. Gilda Graff, "The Name of the Game Is Shame: The Effects of Slavery and Its Aftermath," *The Journal of Psychohistory* 39, no. 2 (2011): 136.

23. Dona Marimba Richards, *Let the Circle Be Unbroken: The Implications of African Spirituality in the Diaspora* (1980; Lawrenceville, New Jersey: Red Sea Press, 1992), 12.

24. Reuben Jonathan Miller, *Halfway Home: Race, Punishment, and the Afterlife of Mass Incarceration* (New York: Little, Brown and Company, 2021), 9; and Miller, "The Afterlife of Mass Incarceration."

25. Graff, "The Name of the Game Is Shame," 135, 140.

# CHAPTER 4

# "AIN'T THAT PECULIAR"

## "Slave Plantations," Angola Prison, and Perpetuity, Part I

MY BROTHER TOLD ME THAT he did not want to be buried at Angola. So on one visit home, I called the funeral home that my dad had recommended. Not all establishments provide services for imprisoned persons. But as it turned out, the one my dad recommended did write policies and handle services for incarcerated family members, so I set up an appointment. My dad wrote a check to cover the first two premium payments, and I made the monthly payments that would have the policy paid in full over the next five years. I don't recall why, but $5,000 was the maximum policy amount the company allowed for incarcerated individuals.

Later, my dad would secure a plot for my brother in the same cemetery where my dad now rests, in Baton Rouge. And upon my dad's death in 2018, the family had Bobby's headstone put in place, with his name, birth date, and those dashes that poets and philosophers write about. And in case my dashes were to be chiseled into dates before my brother's, I would acquire an extra life insurance policy with Bobby as my beneficiary.

My brother is in his early sixties, and his health is relatively very good. He is counted among America's growing number of "aging prisoners behind bars."[1] Given the state of Louisiana's history of excessive sentencing, its predilection for life sentences without the possibility of parole, the national "tough-on-crime" politics of the 1980s, the "truth-in-sentencing" politics of the 1990s, and mandatory sentencing, Angola, like other penal institutions across the country, has a largely aging population.[2]

"In 2020, 61,417 people who are at least 55 years old were serving life sentences. . . . In fact, the number of people in prison today who are age 55 or older has tripled since 2000." 2000 is the year in which my brother was sentenced to life. Nearly 6,000 prisoners in Louisiana are "lifers,"[3] 36 percent of whom are fifty-five years of age and older.[4] And 4,400 of those "lifers" are imprisoned at Angola, 97 percent of whom will die in prison.[5] Burial in the prison's Point Lookout cemeteries has been, almost inevitably, the period that dots the end of a life sentence in Angola, where "life" literally means "unto death."

Situated north of the prison and east of Lake Killarney, Point Lookout II was opened in 1996 after a mass grave—containing the remains of those disinterred by the flood of 1927—was discovered in the first Point Lookout cemetery. While 332 graves in Point Lookout I were marked, the grave of the unknown number of disinterred remains unmarked.[6] Initially, the grave markers of incarcerated persons "carried no names, just numbers"—those "inmate" identification numbers issued by prison authorities. Now the names of the deceased are included on grave markers along with the identification numbers.[7] I know, by heart, the number issued to my brother. This number has to be on all letters and communications, and you have to state it upon request at the front-office desk when you come for a visit.

Incarcerated persons who serve lengthy sentences often fall

out of touch with family and friends. For many convicted persons, a lengthy distance from home attends the lengthy sentence to which they have been condemned. Angola is over fifty miles, forty-five minutes or so—because of the low speed limits in small towns along the way—and even longer if fog has set in, and about a quarter tank of gas from Baton Rouge. Many families across the state don't have the resources to cross the Angola divide. Distance sometimes fosters disconnection. And so, when an incarcerated person dies, oftentimes, no one claims his remains.

These unclaimed individuals are interred in Angola's cemeteries. In other cases, families don't have the means to cover the cost of burying a loved one. And there are those who, having spent so much of their life within the gates of Angola, choose to remain. One in two imprisoned men who die in Angola is buried on prison grounds. As the lay journalist and prison historian Douglas Dennis puts it, "Even your bones don't get a second chance to get out."[8]

## ANGOLA PLANTATION TO
## ANGOLA PENITENTIARY

America is distinguished as the world's "incarceration capital." Per capita, Louisiana has the highest number of people serving no-parole sentences.[9] And Angola, the largest maximum-security prison in America, is also the largest penal complex in the world.[10] Comparable in size to New York's Manhattan Island, Angola prison spans eighteen thousand acres. This antebellum property is encircled by the Mississippi River on the north, west, and south sides and the northern tract of Tunica Hills on the east side, "an area of snakes, trees and wild animals."[11]

What became the expansive grounds of the Angola penitentiary was originally a tract of land formed from several Spanish land grants made in the late eighteenth and early nineteenth centuries. Between 1827 and 1834, Francis Routh acquired most of the property, subdividing it into three cotton plantations: Bellevue, Lake Killarney, and Lochlomand. Routh formed a partnership with planter and trafficker Isaac Franklin, who had waxed rich from his dealings in the "domestic slave trade." Franklin and his associates "were considered the leading long-distance slave traffickers in the country and credited with supplying some two thirds of all slaves transported to the Deep South." When Francis Routh faced financial ruin in 1837, Franklin assumed all of the property.[12]

In the 1840s, Isaac Franklin augmented the property with a fourth plantation—Angola. Loango Plantation was created from the lower section of the Angola tract, and Panola Plantation was subdivided from the upper part of the Bellevue tract. Franklin had married Adelicia Hayes of Tennessee in 1839, and their family resided mainly on the Angola Plantation. Fourteen two-room "slave cabins" were built in proximity to the two-story "big house." Franklin died in 1846, and Adelicia married Alabama lawyer Joseph A. S. Acklen in 1849. A prenuptial agreement, however, left the inheritance of all property and assets in Adelicia's hands.

Joseph Acklen had nevertheless succeeded in tripling his wife's fortune. Additional properties were acquired, including the 640-acre Monrovia Plantation, east of the Bellevue and north of the Lochlomand plantations.[13] By 1860, on the eve of the country's Civil War, the Acklens boasted two million in real estate and a million in personal assets. With a yield of 3,149 bales of cotton in the previous year, the Acklens were the third-largest cotton producers in the state of Louisiana. "Some 659 slaves worked 4,000 acres." Quarters for the enslaved had increased from fourteen to forty-four cabins, and 128 of the 659 enslaved laborers lived on the Angola Plantation proper.[14]

By late nineteenth century, all seven contiguous plantations would be referred to by the single name of "Angola."[15] This vast empire, however, fell into decline with the advent of war. Both Union and Confederate officials made demands upon the Acklens. Joseph Acklen would write in August of 1863 "that all was in ruins and the fields wasting, that the Confederates had taken all his mules and horses, and that he had been subjected to all the 'kinds of lies and slanders that malice could invent.'"[16] Acklen died shortly afterward in September of 1863. Adelicia would marry William Cheatham in 1867.

But as with Acklen, the marriage to Cheatham had entailed a prenuptial agreement. So Adelicia remained in control of her Louisiana holdings. Nevertheless, crop failures over the ensuing years and heavy taxes compelled Adelicia and her son William Acklen to sell the plantation estate in 1880. In 1885, Adelicia separated from Cheatham. She died in 1887 at age seventy, "having outlived two of her three husbands and six of her 10 children." For more than thirty years, the Angola property, the wealth it generated, and the people utilized to generate that wealth who were themselves considered "property," belonged to this "petite, sharp-witted" Adelicia Hayes, one of the wealthiest women in antebellum America.[17]

⚐ ⚐ ⚐

As the replacement of the "slave quarters" on the Angola Plantation with tenant housing signaled the transition from the antebellum to postbellum eras in America, so the sale of the plantation property to partners Louis Trager and Samuel Lawrence James heralded Angola's transition from "slave plantation" to penitentiary. James was a civil engineer, levee contractor, and a former major in the Confederate Army. The state of Louisiana officially granted James a five-year lease in 1870[18] to manage The Walls, Louisiana's first state penitentiary, which opened in 1835 in Baton Rouge, Louisiana.[19]

The State gave James's firm the right of use of "all Louisiana convicts"[20] and authority "to lease out convicts to work on private plantations and public works projects." With this turn of events, the Angola estate was poised to become one of the primary sites where the politics of the criminal-exception loophole of the Thirteenth Amendment would merge with Southern planters' greed for excessive profit, power, and prestige. Once the State extended the original five-year lease to twenty-one years, Angola mutated "from one of Louisiana's major antebellum plantations to its sole maximum security penitentiary."[21]

Upon acquiring the 10,015-acre plantation estate, Samuel James moved his family into "the Angola big house" and moved his sharecroppers and the State's incarcerated persons into "the existing buildings on the properties."[22] Trager and James dissolved their partnership in 1882, leaving James with the Angola, Loango, Bellevue, and Lake Killarney plantations, a partition of eight thousand acres. Angola became known as the "James prison camp,"[23] and Samuel James became known as the "notorious" prison lessee who "maintained the most cynical, profit-oriented, and brutal prison regime in Louisiana history."[24]

An avaricious businessman and a formidable political tactician, James was considered "untouchable." Absolute power corrupts absolutely, and Samuel James wielded absolute control over the lives of those leased to him by the State. James had initially set up a number of factories within The Walls wherein imprisoned persons produced textiles as well as shoes, bricks, and barrels. A local journal article proclaimed that production at the prison was on such a scale that it "would stimulate Louisiana's economy by increasing demand for cotton, wool, lumber, and other raw materials."[25] But James found that subleasing "convicts" to planters and levee- and railroad-construction work camps was exceedingly more lucrative.

As prison labor replaced free, white, "unshackled" labor and fatalities of imprisoned persons mounted, public outcry grew.[26] But James had made a deal with Louisiana state officials at the outset of his twenty-one-year lease: "he would pay [the State] $5,000 the first year, $6,000 the second, and so on up to $25,000 for the twenty-first year"—and James would pocket the profits.[27] Simply put, the convict-leasing system sprang "primarily from the idea that the possession of a convict's person is an opportunity for the State to make money," regardless of the means.[28]

James's methods entailed employing imprisoned persons with private individuals or corporations that awarded him the greatest profits. He cared nothing about the barbaric treatment that imprisoned persons suffered. They were brutally beaten, worked barefoot in cold weather, were forced to work though ill from malaria and other diseases, and slept in wet and muddy clothes.[29] Thusly, between 1870 and 1901, Samuel James, with the later assistance of his son, Samuel Lawrence James, Jr., also known as Law James, built an Angola prison empire and turned a profit for the State. Meanwhile, "approximately 3,000 prisoners died under the James lease" and on the watch of Louisiana state officials.[30]

In addition to utilizing "convict labor" as house servants and field hands for himself, family, and friends, Samuel James collected "rent" from several hundred Negro families who worked as sharecroppers at Angola. A percentage or share of their crops paid the rent on the land they worked and the shacks they occupied. Crop shares paid the debt accrued from groceries, supplies, and sundries bought on credit at James's plantation stores, and crop shares paid for the mules that croppers bought "on time" from James.[31]

When the State negotiated a ten-year lease with the senior James in 1890, the clamor of concerned citizens against the continuing brutal treatment suffered by convicted persons on his plantation, in the prison, and at labor camps was raised anew. Regular reports by the Louisiana State Penitentiary Board of Control, beginning in the 1890s, documented and disclosed the squalid condition of prison cells and camp sites and the continuing, staggering death rates of those imprisoned. In 1893, James would be editorialized in the Baton Rouge *Daily Advocate* as one who "has grown fat and insolent upon the gold he has coined out of the groans and tears and blood of his helpless victims."[32]

Law James managed the Angola properties in the late 1880s and inherited the estate after his father's death in 1894. Law James's oversight of the lease he inherited was no less appalling. "One brutal year, 1896, saw 216 of 1,001 inmates perish."[33] Such details were discussed in the state legislature and in the press, reigniting public debates over the brutality of the convict-leasing system, its merits, and its relationship to the unrest among free laborers. The State would finally, in 1898, adopt a constitutional ban declaring that "no convict sentenced to the State penitentiary shall ever be leased, or hired to any person, or persons, or corporation, private or public, or quasi-public, or board, save as herein authorized." In 1900, the State would buy Angola from Law James.[34]

In 1922, the State also acquired the Panola, Monrovia, and Lochlomand plantations held by William and Claude Acklen, as well as the land east of Angola extending to Tunica Hills. These purchases increased the Angola prison estate from eight thousand to eighteen thousand acres.[35] Although Louisiana had officially outlawed the convict-leasing system, state officials continued to exploit the Thirteenth Amendment's "Punishment Clause" as articulated in Article III, Section 3 of its own state constitution: "There shall be neither slavery nor involuntary servitude in this State, otherwise than for the punishment of crime, whereof the party shall have been duly convicted."[36]

Rather than lease convicted persons to middlemen like Samuel James, who would then sublease them to planters and industrial companies, Louisiana officials elected to resume management of imprisoned persons. In 1916, officials opted to construct a penitentiary at Angola, centralizing the population of imprisoned persons that had been strewn across the landscape of Louisiana's prisoner work camp sites. The State would then, in its own turn, exploit the labor of the incarcerated men in the cultivation of livestock and the farming of cash and subsistence crops on Angola's own plantations. By the mid-1920s, those incarcerated in the penitentiary at Angola tended over 3,000 head of cattle; 387 mules; 200 horses; 20,000 fowl. "Of the 17,800 acres under cultivation, 6,000 were in pasture and 8,000 planted in sugar."[37]

And by the twenty-first century, on any given workday, "groups of inmates carrying hoes, shovels and sling blades head to fields where they grow four million pounds of produce, ranging from corn to wheat, each year."[38]

## "LIFE" *IS* A BADGE OF SLAVERY

From cotton to sugar, from corn to cowpeas, wheat, and soybeans, the crops at Angola have rotated, but the hands that have planted and picked its fields—from the antebellum era into the twenty-first century—have consistently been Black and bound. Any number of historians, activists, lawyers, politicians, and journalists have described the Louisiana State Penitentiary at Angola as a modern-day slave plantation. "From a Slave House to a Prison Cell: The History of Angola Plantation," "American Slavery, Reinvented," and "How the 13th Amendment Kept Slavery Alive: Perspectives from the Prison Where Slavery Never Ended" are typical article titles that seek to capture the incongruity of slavery in a modern society that aspires to be free and democratic.[39]

"Before the Civil War, Angola was a plantation," states Jeffrey Goldberg in the documentary film *Angola for Life*. "Today there's a reasonable chance that some of the men working this farm are descendants of the slaves who once picked cotton here. Once a prison doctor clears an inmate for work, that prisoner's got a job whether he likes it or not."[40] And that "prisoner" will comply or be punished. As my brother Bobby explains it, "Your first job when you arrive at Angola, if you are a abled body you will work the fields."[41] "We are given a choice, work or get locked up in a cell. So we are force to comply."[42] He goes on:

*For the first year I was here I didn't get any money from the state for my job. I worked in the fields doing whatever the task was for that day. Now in those 11 months in the field I never got paid. I think that process is still the same way. Everyone work the fields when they come into the prison for free.*[43]

Typically, newly incarcerated persons in Angola are required to work only ninety days in the fields, my brother elaborates. After that, a person can submit an application to the classification office for a job change. However, those new to the system often learn how the system works through trial and error:

*The reason I work 11 months in the fields was because I didn't know the process. So once I found out the process, I was moved from the field to a new job . . . as a yard orderly. . . . As a yard orderly you only have one detail and that is to take care of the area of the yard [around a particular camp]. You may only need to cut grass and trim around the building but only the part that you are assigned to. . . . I work the fields from mid 2000 to June of 2001. I worked as a yard orderly from 2001 to mid 2002.*[44]

My brother's description of his first year in prison can be compared with what historians have described as the "breaking in" or "seasoning" period experienced by "salt water" Africans—those who survived the Middle Passage to find that they would be forced to work cane fields in the Caribbean and South and Central America or tobacco, cotton, or rice fields in the US for the rest of their lives. My brother had survived two years at East

Baton Rouge Parish Prison—his Middle Passage. Then, in 2000, when he was sentenced to "life at hard labor," he would be forced to work the fields of Angola.

In the state of Louisiana, conviction of a felony carries a penalty of death or imprisonment "'at hard labor,' which means incarceration in state prison."[45] Though the International Covenant on Civil and Political Rights—a covenant ratified by the United States and interpreted by the United Nations—allows for the sentencing of imprisoned persons to "hard labor," "it does not allow for that labor to be exacted under exploitative circumstances that violate basic tenets of human dignity."[46]

Despite US federal and international prohibitions, the officials of the Louisiana State Penitentiary at Angola are guilty of extracting the labor of those imprisoned under "gratuitously harsh conditions" while subjecting imprisoned persons to "a daily dose of humiliation." Those who work the fields—for upwards of "three years without pay" or for pennies per hour—are subjected to extreme heat and cold. They collapse from dehydration or exhaustion, or they are exposed to freezing temperatures, "sometimes without proper clothing."[47]

Louisiana was one of three case-study states in a 2022 American Civil Liberties Union and University of Chicago Law School Global Human Rights Clinic report that examined prison labor nationwide. In addition to the purely "punitive exploitation" of imprisoned laborers, Angola prison officials violated basic codes of decency outlined by the American Correctional Association— "the voice of the U.S. corrections profession since 1870." In a 2016 resolution, the Association agreed that "decent work, pay, and working conditions" for imprisoned workers was imperative, and it called "for the repeal of the 13th Amendment clause that excludes incarcerated people from its protection against slavery and involuntary servitude."[48]

Investigators found that the incidents and badges of slavery were prevalent in Angola's administration of hard labor. "Field laborers work with limited access to water, minimal rest, and no restroom facilities, under the supervision of armed correctional officers on horseback."[49] Investigations, which also included on-site field research and interviews of current and former imprisoned laborers, documented the persistence of systemic racism. The daily dose of humiliations experienced by the disproportionately African American population in Angola is laced with racial harassment, taunts, and belittlement. The psychological and emotional toll such treatment takes is evident in the palpable despair expressed during the interview of this anonymous incarcerated person:

> Now we are really slaves all over again. We work for free, hard labor, must work or you will be beaten. . . . Most of the deputies from warden on down are real racist and will let you know can't nothing we can do. One of the deputies told me the reason they named this Angola because that's where slaves escaped from the motherland, and that will never happen again because it's legal now. So we lost.[50]

⚔ ⚔ ⚔

Even as some incarcerated persons may speak of the benefits they experience from the work that they do, the punishment factor of prison labor is entailed both in the circumscribed choices in the kind of work done and, particularly, in the fact that the work is compulsory. No one can "quit" his sentence of hard labor, and refusing to work comes at a cost. "Working the fields [consists] of many different tasks," my brother told me.

> One day you might be picking vegetables next day you might be throwing hay the next day we may be painting a building. Sometime we would have to clean out canals and ditches that has many snakes in them. Now according to the season we may pick pecans. Summer time we may cut tall grass with swing blades or use hoes to cut or chop grass from under the fence line.[51]

The initial years of working in the fields of Angola prison can be compared with the initial years of working in colonial plantation fields as an enslaved worker. The seasoning period, a time of acclimation and adjustment, was not only intended to accustom enslaved Africans to constant work, it was also intended to break their spirit—that is, to diminish their humanity and force them to submit to a nonhuman existence of "slave," brute, chattel, cattle, object. In like manner, the experiences of condemned African Americans and other Americans sentenced to imprisonment at hard labor in Angola were intended to turn imprisoned persons into "convicts." My brother tells me that this is too often the case.

> Prison has messed up so many men and women mentally and the big thing is they don't know it. Some say they are not, but after 15 years and more, yes, you have been [affected]. The every day things that you hear and see is in you, want it or not. Sometimes you might say the words you heard or do what you saw and you know that's not you. It don't take

*much to make somebody mad around here because every-body is already mad for being here.*[52]

At the outset of Reconstruction, the ruling class of the South sought to regain its economic stability and dominance by expanding and exploiting the convict-leasing system of the antebellum period. Doing so was a conscious choice. As Nathan Cardon pointed out in his history of the convict-leasing system, "A return to leasing convicts was not an inevitable outcome of the postwar years' racial and labor tensions."[53] It was not inevitable, but it was desirable. Rather than pay an honest wage to "free and honest" workers, Southern planters and businesspersons conspired with politicians and the courts in the criminalization of the newly freed Black labor force and poor whites and reinstituted slavery by another name: convict leasing.

Those cunning enough to manipulate the system to their profit found it even more lucrative than the Peculiar Institution of the antebellum period. No buildings to maintain, no staff, penitentiaries in the South "had become large rolling cages that followed railroad building or ramshackle stockades deep in the forests, swamps, and mining fields." "Throughout the South, states were leasing to powerful politicians, Northern corporations, mining companies, and planters, and they imposed little or no restrictions on what type of work businesses could force prisoners to do or how many hours they could work them."[54]

Corrupted by greed marinated in resentment, and with no incentive to be otherwise, lessees and other neo-"masters" who engaged in sharecropping, debt bondage, and other forms of re-enslavement were cruel, merciless, and sadistic in their treatment of free Black citizens. As one Southerner reported: "Before the war, we owned the negroes. If a man had a good negro, he could afford to take care of him: if he was sick get a doctor. He might even put gold plugs in his teeth. But these convicts: we don't own 'em. One dies, get another."[55]

This kind of categorical disregard for Black life and suffering characterized European attitudes and behavior at the outset of their deracination and enslavement of Africans. Until the desire for greater profit prompted those engaged in trafficking enterprises to take some regard for the life and health of their "human cargo," morbidity and death rates seemed inconsequential. Through the crisis of being extracted from their homeland, tightly packed on transatlantic voyages, and the bewilderment at being brutally subjugated to perpetual, forced labor on an unrecognizable island or continent, enslaved Africans suffered mortality rates upwards of 50 percent at certain points during the phenomenon of the Maafa.

In his history of Portuguese and Brazilian trafficking in context of merchant capitalism, Joseph Miller draws this portrait of death in relation to trafficking enterprises out of the Angola of Central Africa:

Of 100 seized in Africa, 75 would have reached the marketplaces in the interior; 85 percent of them, or about 64 of the original 100, would have arrived at the coast; after losses of 11 percent in the barracoons, 57 or so would have boarded the ships; of those 57, 51 would have stepped onto Brazilian soil, and 48 or 49 would have lived to behold their first master in the New World. The full "seasoning" period of 3–4 years would leave only 28 or 30 of the original 100 alive and working. A total "wastage" factor of about two-thirds may thus be estimated for the late-eighteenth-century Angolan trade, higher earlier in the trade, probably a bit lower by the 1820s.[56]

&#x2612; &#x2612; &#x2612;

The brutal treatment of Black people and the "wastage" of human life as described by Miller was evident also in the convict-leasing system that was foundational to the origins of the Louisiana State Penitentiary at Angola. And this convict-leasing system—baptized in the antidemocratic spirit of the criminal-exception loophole that preserved "slavery and involuntary servitude" as punishment for crimes—has much in common with the *asiento* system of sixteenth-century Europe.

*Asientos* were monopoly contracts that the Spanish Crown awarded to individuals, corporations, or nation-states, granting them the exclusive right and authority to supply captured Africans to Spanish and Portuguese colonies in the Americas. Like convict leases, *asientos* went to bidders who could pay the most for the exclusive license to traffic in Africans and who could also demonstrate their capacity to fulfill the contract.

Like lessees of convict leases, *asientistas*—recipients of *asientos*—paid a fee to the government for the prized licenses.[57] Like convict leases, the *asientos* were awarded for a fixed period of time. The leases awarded to Samuel Lawrence James, for example, were for five, twenty-one, and ten-year periods, respectively. *Asientos* also had varying contractual periods and, like convict leases, could be awarded for up to thirty years.

Where the holder of *asientos* would employ traffickers to acquire the "human cargo" that would then be auctioned off in the colonies, the holders of convict leases were supplied their cargo of "convicts" by the State—via the courts that maintained a steady stream of the "duly convicted" *criminals* that the states were authorized to treat as "slaves." The systemic criminalization of newly freed Black citizens was prevalent throughout the South. One lessee, Georgia legislator James Monroe Smith (quoted in Oshinsky 1997), jocosely told county officials, "You had better send me some more n[——]s or I will come down and take the courthouse away from you."[58]

America's convict-leasing system preceded the Civil War and Reconstruction era. During the antebellum years, most incarcerated persons and victims of the convict-leasing system were white.[59] In postbellum America, "seven out of ten prisoners were now black." By 1890, there were around twenty-seven thousand "convicts" laboring on plantations, in groves, and in railroad, levee, sawmill, turpentine, or mining camps.[60] And the infamous Black Codes and the court systems that implemented them guaranteed that thousands of Black men and boys, primarily—along with Black women and girls—were sent to these labor camps.

After paying a fee for the lease and related charges, lessees like Samuel James, in a manner similar to so-called slave merchants, then basically auctioned convicted persons to the highest bidder among the individuals, corporations, and industrial companies that coveted the sublease of a "cheap," low-maintenance labor force that had no apparent protection and that could not go on strike.[61] Indeed, the Louisiana legislature itself was said to function as "an auction mart" when senators debated bills to determine not only which lessee would be granted the State's convict-leasing contract but also how much a lessee would have to pay the State annually.[62]

The lot of those caught in the criminal-exception loophole was actually worse than that of enslaved persons of the antebellum era. Though public officials were aware of the brutality suffered by the prisoners and aware of other lessee violations, no interventions were made, as officials preferred to avoid having the so-called convicts "thrown upon the state." Moreover, many public officials were waxing rich from this neo-slavery.[63]

Isolated in work camps, at the mercy of unscrupulous overseers and guards, the imprisoned laborers could be made to produce "thirty percent more work than free laborers." Worked from "dawn-to-dusk" on "starvation rations" and severely beaten and tortured, they were forced to do the dangerous work that free laborers refused to do and were driven at a pace that free laborers wouldn't tolerate. Shackled together more often than not, chains clattering about their joints, this imprisoned labor force built railroad lines through canal swamps, tropical marshes, and palmetto jungles.[64]

Weakened by constant work, want of food, and insufficient amounts of clean water, convicted persons who were leased suffered "consumption and other incurable disease." They generally lived no longer than six years and died horrible deaths.[65] The death rate of convicted persons who were leased in the Louisiana convict system was 20 percent during its worst year, in 1882.[66] Across the South, those enthralled within the convict-leasing system were literally worked to death, with annual mortality rates ranging from 16 percent to 25 percent, and upwards of 40 percent for those in Alabama mining camps and 45 percent in some railroad camps in South Carolina.[67]

The idea among racialized whites—individually and collectively—that building private and public wealth out of the life, suffering, and death of Black people was their birthright is a very old idea. Even as the ruling "elites" and public officials in early America saw Black people as *essential* to American "development," industrialization, and economic prosperity, they *would not* as easily recognize the *essential* humanity and personhood of Black people, nor later, their citizenship. Having learned from an 1868 report that the majority of those they imprisoned were now Black men who had been arrested mainly for larceny, some concerned Louisiana prison officials "wondered if the legislature could 'inquire into the reason why so many are sent to this institution for the term of three, four, and six months, upon trivial charges? Does there not lurk, beneath, the low, mean motive of depriving them of the right of citizenship?'"[68]

By depriving African Americans of their right of citizenship, the state was also depriving them of their human rights of personal and collective sovereignty. Louisiana public officials knowingly permitted their Black citizens to be reduced to "slaves," even as some, in 1883, objected that the employment of "convicts" beyond prison walls brought "this species of slave labor in competition with honest industry to the great pecuniary profit of the lessee." Officials were knowledgeable, as well, that the lessees wielded "absolute power over the prisoners" and treated them with "vicious" cruelty.[69]

Though the federal government abolished "slavery and involuntary servitude" in 1865, it allowed a "species" of slavery to continue through the criminal-punishment loophole. Similarly, though the state government of Louisiana abolished convict leasing in 1901, it allowed a species of that system to continue through their profit-oriented and racialized "criminal justice" system. For, although the State ended the practice of leasing imprisoned persons to private individuals, the State itself would continue the leasing of imprisoned laborers through contracts with external corporations. Seen as an integral aspect of enforc-ing the convictions of "criminals" sentenced to "hard labor," the practice would be justified by state officials as a matter of seeing justice served.

As the historian Mark Carleton pointed out, "when the [Samuel James] lease did at last expire, the profit motive, by which it had hypnotized a generation of Louisiana lawmakers, survived as a dominant principle in the state's philosophy of prison manage-ment."[70] Rehabilitation was not the objective. Profit was.[71]

The convict-leasing system, like debt peonage and sharecrop-ping, functioned to undermine Black citizenship and sovereignty and preserve the hierarchies of race and class "in a world of eman-cipation," increased mobility, and an evolving industrial moder-nity.[73] In Louisiana, the leasing system—in addition to advancing industrial capitalism while stifling labor organization—served as a means of subordinating the state's Black citizenry, disempow-ering Black voters, and maintaining "elitist" white domination. As the "exclusive use of African American convicts on the state's chain gangs reassured the white public of their supposed supe-riority," so the demographics of the state's prison population and its disparate sentencing practices made it clear that African American men were targeted by the judicial system and that the judicial system was the state's mechanism of racial control.[73]

## NOTES

1. Lea Skene, "Louisiana's Life Without Parole Sentencing the Nation's Highest—and Some Say That Should Change," *The Advocate*, December 7, 2019, https://www.theadvocate.com/baton_rouge/news/article_f6309822-17ac-11ea-8750-f7d212aa28f8.html.

2. Marc Mauer and Ashley Nellis, *The Meaning of Life: The Case for Abolishing Life Sentences* (New York: The New Press, 2018), 25, 162; and Gary Fields, "As

Inmates Age, a Prison Carpenter Builds More Coffins," *The Wall Street Journal*, May 18, 2005, https://www.wsj.com/articles/SB111637661650736440.

3. Nellis, "The Facts of Life," 19.

4. Roby Chavez, "Aging Louisiana Prisoners Were Promised a Chance at Parole After 10 Years. Some Are Finally Free," PBS, November 26, 2021, https://www.pbs.org/newshour/nation/aging-louisiana-prisoners-were-promised-a-chance-at-parole-after-10-years-some-are-finally-free.

5. Fields, "As Inmates Age, a Prison Carpenter Builds More Coffins."

6. Fields, "As Inmates Age, a Prison Carpenter Builds More Coffins"; and "The Unique Burial Practices at the Louisiana State Penitentiary," Historic Houston, http://historichouston1836.com/the-unique-burial-practices-at-the-louisiana-state-penitentiary/.

7. "Death Behind Bars (Part I)," *Witness*, Al Jazeera English, posted August 23, 2007, YouTube video, https://www.youtube.com/watch?v=RtU3iFZNtzw.

8. Fields, "As Inmates Age, a Prison Carpenter Builds More Coffins."

9. Chavez, "Aging Louisiana Prisoners Were Promised a Chance at Parole After 10 Years."

10. W. T. Whitney, Jr., "Louisiana's Angola: Proving Ground for Racialized Capitalism," *People's World*, June 25, 2018, https://www.peoplesworld.org/article/louisianas-angola-proving-ground-for-racialized-capitalism/.

11. Fields, "As Inmates Age, a Prison Carpenter Builds More Coffins."

12. Joanne Ryan and Stephanie L. Perrault, "Angola: Plantation to Penitentiary," US Army Corps of Engineers, New Orleans District, 2007, 1, https://www.crt.state.la.us/Assets/OCD/archaeology/discoverarchaeology/virtual-books/PDFs/Angola_Pop.pdf.

13. Ryan and Perrault, "Angola: Plantation to Penitentiary," 2, 5.

14. Ryan and Perrault, "Angola: Plantation to Penitentiary," 5.

15. Ryan and Perrault, "Angola: Plantation to Penitentiary," 1, 5, 8.

16. Ryan and Perrault, "Angola: Plantation to Penitentiary," 5.

17. Ryan and Perrault, "Angola: Plantation to Penitentiary," 2, 31.

18. Ryan and Perrault, "Angola: Plantation to Penitentiary," 7. The five-year lease was originally issued to the John Huger and Charles Jones company. Samuel James immediately bought them out. James had established James, Buckner, and Company in 1869. And in 1870, the state legislature approved of the buyout and negotiated a twenty-one-year contract with James. (Nathan Cardon, "'Less Than Mayhem': Louisiana's Convict Lease, 1865–1901," *Louisiana History: The Journal of the Louisiana Historical Association* 58, no. 4 [2017], 417–41, 425, https://www.jstor.org/stable/26290931.)

19. Marianne Fisher-Giorlando, "The Walls," *64 Parishes*, https://64parishes.org/the-walls.

20. Shane Bauer, *American Prison: A Reporter's Undercover Journey into the Business of Punishment* (New York: Penguin Press, 2018), 121.

21. Ryan and Perrault, "Angola: Plantation to Penitentiary," 7–8, 30.

22. Ryan and Perrault, "Angola: Plantation to Penitentiary," 8. Samuel James and Louis Trager would dissolve their partnership in 1882. James retained the Angola, Bellevue, and Loango plantations, and later, the Lake Killarney

plantation. Trager returned the Panola, Lochlomand, and Monrovia property to William and Claude Acklen in 1893 in a rescission. (Ryan and Perrault, "Angola: Plantation to Penitentiary," 12.)

23. "History of the State Penitentiary," Angola Museum at the Louisiana State Penitentiary, https://www.angolamuseum.org/history-of-angola.

24. Ryan and Perrault, "Angola: Plantation to Penitentiary," 8, 31.

25. Bauer, *American Prison*, 121–22.
    In 1871, James imported one hundred fifty Chinese workers to augment his labor pool: "Brought by steamer from Alabama, they were likely the first Chinese to settle in Baton Rouge." (Bauer, *American Prison*, 121–22.)

26. "History of the State Penitentiary"; and Cardon, "'Less Than Mayhem,'" 417–41.

27. Bauer, *American Prison*, 121.

28. Bauer, *American Prison*, 123.

29. Bauer, *American Prison*, 129; and Cardon, "'Less Than Mayhem,'" 417, 436.

30. Ryan and Perrault, "Angola: Plantation to Penitentiary," 8.

31. Ryan and Perrault, "Angola: Plantation to Penitentiary," 10.

32. Cardon, "'Less Than Mayhem,'" 437.

33. Cardon, "'Less Than Mayhem,'" 436.

34. *Constitution of the State of Louisiana: Adopted in Convention at the City of New Orleans, May 12, 1898* (New Orleans: H. J. Hearsey, Convention Printer, 1898), https://babel.hathitrust.org/cgi/pt?id=hvd.hl47v7; and "Louisiana's Constitutions," The Law Library of Louisiana, https://lasc.libguides.com/c.php?g=967774&p=6992518.

35. Ryan and Perrault, "Angola: Plantation to Penitentiary," 12.

36. "Louisiana's Constitutions," The Law Library of Louisiana, https://lasc.libguides.com/c.php?g=967774&p=6992518.

37. Ryan and Perrault, "Angola: Plantation to Penitentiary," 12.

38. Fields, "As Inmates Age, a Prison Carpenter Builds More Coffins."

39. Krissah Thompson, "From a Slave House to a Prison Cell: The History of Angola Plantation," *The Washington Post*, September 21, 2016, https://www.washingtonpost.com/entertainment/museums/from-a-slave-house-to-a-prison-cell-the-history-of-angola-plantation/2016/09/21/7712eeac-63ee-11e6-96c0-37533479f3f5_story.html; Whitney Benns, "American Slavery, Reinvented," *The Atlantic*, September 21, 2015, https://www.theatlantic.com/business/archive/2015/09/prison-labor-in-america/406177/; and Daniele Selby, "How the 13th Amendment Kept Slavery Alive: Perspectives from the Prison Where Slavery Never Ended," Innocence Project, September 17, 2021, https://innocenceproject.org/news/how-the-13th-amendment-kept-slavery-alive-perspectives-from-the-prison-where-slavery-never-ended/.

40. *Angola for Life: Rehabilitation and Reform Inside the Louisiana Penitentiary*, written by Jeffrey Goldberg, Sam Price-Waldman, and Kasia Cieplak-Mayr von Baldegg, posted September 9, 2015, on *The Atlantic*, https://www.theatlantic.com/video/index/404305/angola-prison-documentary/.

41. Bobby D. Plant, letter to author, May 14, 2022.

42. Bobby D. Plant, letter to author, May 14, 2022.

43. Bobby D. Plant, letter to author, May 14, 2022.

44. Bobby D. Plant, letter to author, May 14, 2022.

45. E. A. Gjelten, "Louisiana Felony Crimes and Sentences," NOLO, last modified May 16, 2023, https://www.criminaldefenselawyer.com/resources/criminal -defense/state-felony-laws/louisiana-felony-class.htm.

46. ACLU and The University of Chicago Law School Global Human Rights Clinic, *Captive Labor: Exploitation of Incarcerated Workers*, June 15, 2022, https:// www.aclu.org/sites/default/files/field_document/2022-06-15-captivelabor researchreport.pdf, 82.

47. ACLU and The University of Chicago Law School Global Human Rights Clinic, *Captive Labor*, 6, 55, 64, 66.

48. ACLU and The University of Chicago Law School Global Human Rights Clinic, *Captive Labor*, 6, 19.

49. ACLU and The University of Chicago Law School Global Human Rights Clinic, *Captive Labor*, 34.

50. ACLU and The University of Chicago Law School Global Human Rights Clinic, *Captive Labor*, 66–67.

51. Bobby D. Plant, letter to author, May 2022.

52. Bobby D. Plant, letter to author, May 16, 2022.

53. Cardon, "'Less Than Mayhem,'" 424.

54. Bauer, *American Prison*, 122, 125.

55. Bauer, *American Prison*, 122, 130.

56. Joseph C. Miller, *Way of Death: Merchant Capitalism and the Angolan Slave Trade, 1730–1830* (Madison, Wisconsin: The University of Wisconsin Press, 1996), 440–41.

57. In an exceptional case in 1868, the state of Mississippi contracted to pay plantocrat Edmund Richardson $18,000 per year to maintain its prisoners. "Richardson got to keep all of the profits he derived from the labor of these convicts." Richardson's contract established the convict-leasing system in Mississippi. (David M. Oshinsky, *"Worse Than Slavery": Parchman Farm and the Ordeal of Jim Crow Justice* [New York: Free Press, 1997], 35.)

58. Oshinsky, *"Worse Than Slavery,"* 67.

59. Bauer, *American Prison*, 120. Notably among the mostly Black convicts were Irish immigrants. See, for example, Fisher-Giorlando, "The Walls."

60. Bauer, *American Prison*, 120, 123.

61. Bauer, *American Prison*, 122, 125.

62. Mark T. Carleton, "The Politics of the Convict Lease System in Louisiana: 1868–1901," *Louisiana History: The Journal of the Louisiana Historical Association* 8, no. 1 (1967): 20, https://www.jstor.org/stable/4230931.

63. Carleton, "The Politics of the Convict Lease System in Louisiana," 13.

64. Bauer, *American Prison*, 124–25.

65. Even when compared with enslaved laborers on the infamous Louisiana sugar plantations of the early to mid-nineteenth century, those laboring within the convict-leasing system fared relatively worse. Like the enslaved laborers in Jamaican cane fields, leased "convicts" in the cane fields of Louisiana could drop dead from overwork and abuse "after seven years of labor" (Khalil Gibran

Muhammad, "Sugar," in *The 1619 Project: A New Origin Story*, eds. Nikole Hannah-Jones et al. [New York: One World, 2021], 71–87). According to an 1850 census, the average age of enslaved persons in the US South was twenty-one (Stampp, *The Peculiar Institution*, 318). Recent research indicates that life expectancy of enslaved persons was differentiated by material conditions, medical care, type of labor performed, sex, and locale, among other factors. The average twenty-one-year life span of enslaved persons in the Deep South was considerably longer than "free" Black persons laboring as "convicts" in postbellum America could hope for. And beyond the Deep South, the life expectancy of the enslaved sometimes extended beyond that of whites. In certain counties in Virginia, for example, "'more slaves than whites died of old age' between 1853 and 1860," and in 1850, "there were more centenarians among Blacks than Whites.") ("Health History: Health and Longevity Since the Mid-19th Century," Stanford Medicine Ethnogeriatrics, https://geriatrics .stanford.edu/ethnomed/african_american/fund/health_history/longevity.html.)

66. Christina Pruett Hermann, "Specters of Freedom: Forced Labor, Social Struggle, and the Louisiana State Penitentiary System, 1835–1935" (PhD diss., Michigan State University, 2015), 252.

67. Bauer, *American Prison*, 130.

68. Cardon, "'Less Than Mayhem,'" 421.

69. Carleton, "The Politics of the Convict Lease System in Louisiana," 5–25, 8, 16, 21.

70. Carleton, "The Politics of the Convict Lease System in Louisiana," 25.

71. Some apologists for the convict-leasing system claim that states were overburdened by the cost of maintaining large numbers of prisoners in the aftermath of the Civil War. However, Louisiana was the first state to utilize the convict-leasing system, beginning in 1844. And as Mark Carleton states in "The Politics of the Convict Lease System in Louisiana," "at no time between 1874 and 1901, not even during the depressed 1890's, did Louisiana's annual expenditures exceed her revenues" (7).

72. Cardon, "'Less Than Mayhem,'" 419–20.

73. Cardon, "'Less Than Mayhem,'" 420, 423, 441.

# CHAPTER 5

## "AIN'T THAT PECULIAR"

### "Slave Plantations," Angola Prison, and Perpetuity, Part II

THE EXCESSES ASSOCIATED WITH THE convict-leasing system in Louisiana and other Southern states persist in the current demographics and disparities within America's prison-industrial complex. "One of every seven people in prison in the United States—a total of more than two hundred thousand people—is currently serving a life prison term."[1] In Louisiana, 4,700 defendants have been sentenced to life without a chance for freedom, a number that exceeds the life sentences handed down in the states of Texas, Arkansas, Mississippi, Alabama, and Tennessee combined.[2] Just as the majority of Louisiana's "convict" laborers were Black, 75 percent of those sentenced to life without parole within Louisiana's penitentiaries are Black. One in three persons sentenced to life or other types of "virtual" life sentences in Louisiana will be worked until he dies behind bars.[3]

A life sentence can mean life imprisonment with the possibility of parole, life imprisonment without the possibility of parole, or the "virtual life" sentence. This type of life sentence entails sentencing a person to fifty or more years or sentencing a person to consecutive terms of twenty-five or more years.[4] Whether or not a person is sentenced to life at a Louisiana State Penitentiary, with or without the possibility of parole, "at hard labor" is an inextricable component of a life sentence. And even when a life sentence carries the possibility of parole, at Angola, this possibility has seldom parlayed into release. And oftentimes, those who agreed to a plea deal in order to escape a threatened life-without-parole sentence or death sentence find that the deal has been reneged on.[5] Moreover, even those at Angola who were not sentenced to "life" in any form ultimately were doomed to "life." The very environment at Angola, as my brother depicts it, remains a desperate one.

"Along with the death penalty," observes researchers Mauer and Nellis, "the most distinctive aspect of the American punishment system" is its "broad use of life imprisonment." And this severe and excessive punishment—which is imposed on nonviolent "offenders" as well as those charged with violent offenses—is disproportionately imposed on people of color. "Two thirds of people serving life sentences are people of color, including nearly half (48 percent) who are African American, a total of one hundred thousand people. As a result, one of every five African Americans in prison is serving a life sentence."[6]

In the same way that American colonial officials systematically codified into law the debasement, and then the perpetual enslavement, of Black people, so lawmakers of antebellum and postbellum America instituted a body of laws to maintain the racial, class, and economic hierarchies that undergird American society to this day. The 1664 Maryland law that formally established the doctrine of *"Durante Vita"* enslavement of Black people, which was the bedrock of America's Peculiar Institution of slavery, was recodified as the life imprisonment sentence that is the bedrock of penal institutions like the Louisiana State Penitentiary at Angola and others across the nation.

The two distinctions that made America's institution of slavery peculiar are the same attributes that distinguish America's institution of mass incarceration: race-based and perpetual subjugation or punishment for the duration of one's life. Colonial law progressively changed the status of Black people from servants to chattel to slaves *for life*. Winthrop Jordan makes the very important point that the involuntary servitude to which many white persons were subjected was wholly different from the conditions of *slavery* that were imposed on Black people:

> In considering this development, it is important to remember that the status of slave was at first distinguished from servitude more by duration than by onerousness; the key term in many early descriptions of the Negro's condition was perpetual. Negroes served "for ever" and so would their children. Englishmen did not do so. Servitude, no matter how long, brutal, and involuntary, was not the same thing as perpetual slavery. . . . Hereditary lifetime service was restricted to Indians and Africans.[7]

This doctrine of *"Durante Vita"* was not peculiar to the American South, nor was it unique in American colonial and post-bellum jurisprudence. This notion of the *perpetual* service and enslavement of Africans and other Indigenous peoples is rooted in what is called the "papal bulls" (officially sealed decrees) of certain popes of the Catholic Church, going back to the fifteenth century. Issued by Pope Nicholas V in 1455, the papal bull *Romanus Pontifex* granted King Alfonso of Portugal these rights, in accord with the politics of the "Doctrine of Discovery":

to invade, search out, capture, vanquish, and subdue all
Saracens [Moors or Muslims] and pagans whatsoever, and
other enemies of Christ wheresoever placed, and the kingdoms, dukedoms, principalities, dominions, possessions,
and all movable and immovable goods whatsoever held and
possessed by them and to reduce their persons to perpetual slavery, and to apply and appropriate to himself and
his successors the kingdoms, dukedoms, counties, principalities, dominions, possessions, and goods, and [the right] to
convert them [those things] to his and their use and profit.[8]

It is with this authority that Portuguese and Spanish monarchs
issued *asientos*, or monopoly licenses. This 1455 decree was a follow up to the 1452 papal bull *Dum Diversas* that established the
"Doctrine of Discovery," which was intended to regulate the com-
peting claims of Christian European monarchies over the lands of
non-Christian, non-European Indigenous peoples. In the decree
of 1455, Pope Nicholas reiterated the authority that he granted to
King Alfonso and indicated that the declarations granted were to
be adhered to *"Dum Diversas"* ("until different"), that is, until
the Catholic Church declared otherwise—or, in plain English,
"for ever."[9] The core tenets of these decrees are still referenced in
US law and continue to infuse interpretation of the law with the
attitudes of white supremacy and white nationalism.[10]

From the Vatican and the imperialist courts of Europe and
England to the federal, state, and municipal courts of the United
States of America, the practice of reducing Black people to "perpetual slavery" for the "use and profit" of the white power structure has been a constant in global economic history. And yet
the racialized, elitist, and excessive fiats, declarations, customs,

statutes, and court decisions that infringe on the innate freedoms and personal and collective dignity and sovereignty of others originate in politically constructed absolutist doctrines of "divine right." But actually, these sweeping fiats come from a place of confusion about *human* identity.

"Man," writes the philosopher Albert Camus, "is the only creature who won't be what he is"—and that is a being with limits.[11] The humanity of any one human reflects all humankind, and thus the innate freedom of any human being must have limits that respect the freedom that is the inalienable right of all others. To be boundless, to be without limits, is unnatural, it is absurd, and it is evidence of an exaggerated sense of self. Thought and action that disrespect limits in the reckless pursuit of greed and glory generate an absurd reality wherein tyranny, terror, and falsehood reign.[12]

⚹ ⚹ ⚹

In his preface to *The Peculiar Institution: Slavery in the Ante-Bellum South*, the historian Kenneth M. Stampp wrote that "southern slavery" was "America's most profound and vexatious social problem." Apologetic historians have constructed and advanced the absurd story that the Black Belt of the South, with its subtropical climate, "created a demand for labor" and thus "black labor" was *necessary* for America's development and economic prosperity. Far from such chronic excusatory claims, Stampp finds at the cornerstone of America's Peculiar Institution a frantic "race for wealth" and a lust for "absolute power and authority."[13]

What was absurd and peculiar about Southerners who practiced and defended "chattel slavery" was their exaggerated sense of self as an aristocratic "master class" and the delusion that their "superior" position in America's sociopolitical and economic hierarchy was natural, providential, and therefore idyllic. The title of Stampp's work, *The Peculiar Institution*, alludes to the arguments of this elitist group in justifying and protecting "southern slavery." Chief among this group was South Carolina's John C. Calhoun, who celebrated the "peculiarities" of the American South and popularized the phrase "Peculiar Institution."

"The truth can no longer be disguised," wrote Calhoun (quoted in Guelzo 2012), "that the peculiar domestick institution of the Southern states" was being subverted by Northern abolitionists and the federal government.[14] With states' rights and the doctrine of nullification as his backdrop, Calhoun portrayed the tyrannical ruling class of the South's slavocracy as an aristocratic and benevolent oligarchy and euphemistically described the enslaved Black men, women, and children whom they reduced to chattel as their fitted, well-adapted, and happy "peculiar labor."[15]

As the offspring of the planter class were taught that building their wealth at the expense of Black life was their birthright, so the offspring of Black people were to be "properly raised" to understand "that it is their duty, to regard [their masters] with benevolence, to administer to their wants, and to protect them from injury."[16] Where white children were to inherit the earth, as it were, Black children faced a bankrupt future and permanent dispossession. So in addition to the chains and the chain gangs, the overseers and corrupt public officials and the patrollers and the prisons, the indoctrination and enslavement of Black children were the essential means through which the white power structure sought to realize the doctrine of *durante vita* and keep Black people in hereditary perpetual slavery. *"Negroes served 'for ever' and so would their children."*

The bankrupted birthright and the doctrine of perpetual slavery to which African American babies were subjected was encoded in the policies of the Louisiana State Penitentiary. In 1848, the Louisiana legislature passed "An Act Providing for the disposal of such slaves as are or may be born in the Penitentiary, the issue of convicts." The act provided that "the issue of any slave confined in the Penitentiary for life, born during said confinement, shall inure to the said State, and become property thereof."[17]

Between 1835 and 1865, 179 African American women were incarcerated in the Louisiana State Penitentiary.[18] White women "came and went" through the prison's "solid iron doors" that had barely a "twelve-inch opening."[19] But government officials and prison wardens established the pattern that "once incarcerated, black women were there to stay."[20] During this period, thirty-three of these women were enslaved, and twenty-six of that number were imprisoned for life. Three hundred dollars compensated the "owners" of enslaved women who were sentenced to life. The state of Louisiana then claimed the "convict" women and any babies they might birth as state "property." In essence, state public officials became the new "masters." Prison wardens, other civil servants working within or in association with the prison, and convict lessees became their new "overseers."

Once a baby lived to reach ten years of age, the clerk at the penitentiary notified the sheriff. Officials then placed an advertisement for the upcoming auction of prison children in the state newspaper. After thirty days, the children were "auctioned on the steps of the county courthouse in Baton Rouge" and were sold for "cash on delivery."[21] In a journal article about other auctions of children he had witnessed, a Dr. John Theophilus

Kramer wrote, "I shall never forget those looks of deep sorrow, which I perceived in the faces of all those poor children upon the auction stand. I know that they participated in the distress of their mothers; I believe that they were conscious of their horrible fate in that awful hour—to be sold for money to the highest bidder."[22]

The proceeds from the sale of auctioned Black children were to be paid "to the State Treasurer" for the funding of free schools for white children.[23] Sheriff's records list the names of the babies born in prison. These records include the names of most of the mothers. The names of the men who fathered the babies were not recorded. Among the men who bought the auctioned children were prison board members and officials and convict lessees who also happened to own plantations.

Researchers speculate that prison officials and employees who worked in proximity with the imprisoned women "could have fathered the children they purchased."[24] In her article "Gazing upon the Invisible: Women and Children at the Old Baton Rouge Penitentiary," Connie H. Nobles relates that the area containing women prisoners was "encircled by a fence" that separated them from the male prisoners. Given the "public/private landscape of domination," Nobles asked: "Where did the rape of (black) women considered property take place. . . . Where were these slave babies born?"[25]

The imprisonment of enslaved women was not common in the antebellum South, and Louisiana was the only "slave state" that passed legislation mandating that children of Black, enslaved women be auctioned. Fifteen babies were born imprisoned and enslaved. Between 1849 and 1861, eleven were auctioned off. After the Union Army won the Battle of Baton Rouge, the four remaining children, ages one to ten, were evacuated from the prison.[26]

It was a peculiarity of the Louisiana justice system that its antebellum "convicts of color" were "twice condemned": Enslaved for life. Imprisoned for life.[27] Where gender intersected with race and class, Black women enslaved for life were thrice condemned, as they were vulnerable to sexual violence, rape-related pregnancies, and the auctioning of their children. The peculiarities of the Louisiana State Penitentiary generated absurd realities for Black people. And those peculiarities reflected the corruption and greed of a penal system controlled by politicians who were motivated by the pursuit of profit.[28]

The pelican is fabled to feed her children with her own blood. The Pelican State thus appears to have reversed the custom, and fed herself with the blood of her own children.[29]

⌖ ⌖ ⌖

About a hundred miles south of Angola prison, on the west bank of the Mississippi, in St. John the Baptist Parish, is the Whitney Plantation Museum. It is the only plantation museum that honors the lives of the enslaved people whose labor enriched plantation owners, their families, and the regional economy. Prominent in the interpretive history of the Black people who labored there are the *Children of Whitney*.[30] Life-size clay sculptures of Black girls and boys sit on the porch of "slave cabins" or stand, backs against the cabin's sun-bleached cypress walls. They occupy the pews of the "Anti-Yoke" Baptist Church or sit cross-legged in the Amen Corner, their faces poised in the direction of the pulpit.[31]

They appear in the historic buildings and about the grounds of the 1,800-acre plantation. The figure of a girl, Hannah Kelley, stands sentinel at the foot of a four-post bed in the "big house," waiting.

The Whitney Plantation Museum is described as "a site of memory and consciousness." The 350 names engraved on the granite slabs of the Wall of Honor at the museum pay homage to the life and legacy of persons who built and worked the Whitney Plantation.[32] The Field of Angels memorial is dedicated to the 2,200 children who died, enslaved, in the St. John the Baptist Parish from 1823 to 1863. A memorial hall displays the names of 107,000 *documented* persons who were enslaved in Louisiana from 1719 to 1820.[33] And the 1811 Slave Revolt Memorial commemorates the revolt of between two hundred and five hundred African and African American insurgents in the St. Charles, St. James, and St. John the Baptist parishes, the largest revolt of enslaved people in American history.[34]

⚔ ⚔ ⚔

The spirit of the children at the Whitney Plantation, as evoked by their sculpted images, underscores the cruelty of the doctrine of perpetual, intergenerational enslavement. Kenneth Stampp argued that the magnitude of the impact of "southern slavery" on the whole country compelled close study. He described this impact, in Maafic terms, as "disastrous."[35] Sixty-eight years after the publication of *The Peculiar Institution*, the human response to the disaster of slavery is ongoing, for as much as African Americans are dedicated to honoring and celebrating the cycle of life, antidemocratic public officials and private individuals seek to perpetuate the cycle of Black impoverishment, imprisonment, and intergenerational enthrallment in local, state, and federal criminal legal systems.

A collateral consequence of the preservation of "slavery and involuntary servitude" as punishment for crime is that millions of American children have a parent in the prison system. Over 5 million children have had a parent locked up at some point in the child's life, and "on any given day," 2.7 million children have a parent in jail or prison. Long-term, harsh sentencing "creates a lasting barrier between parents and children."[36]

When my brother Bobby was sentenced to life, his relationship with his children was affected. Where he has had direct communication with the first son and, until recently, mostly indirect communication with the second, he has had no communication with his daughter for over twenty years. This daughter is also my niece, whom I've seen, in person, only twice when she was a child and not once since my brother's incarceration, as the charge and conviction of rape has precluded familial communications. I could walk past her in the Mall of Louisiana and not know it.

Like the ten-year-olds who were taken from their mothers and auctioned off beyond prison walls, modern American children, separated from their parents and families by prison walls and court-mandated restrictions, also feel "deep sorrow" and suffer psychological distress. I witnessed this distress in my niece. It pained me that she had been so summarily cut off from her father and from us over twenty years ago. That little Zoom window wherein we all gathered for the Louisiana state parole board meeting could not contain the anguish, pain, and grief that I observed. It was apparent to me that, as my nephew spoke of his improved relationship with his father, my niece was only present to a relationship full of her father's absence.

A parent's incarceration in today's America also contributes to or exacerbates the economic hardship a child experiences. It is both ironic and unconscionable that an incarcerated parent can be sentenced to life at hard labor and precious little of that labor will benefit his or her child. Yet this economic deprivation is the fate of 13 percent of African American children. Poverty affects a child's ability to do well in school, contributes to antisocial behavior, and puts that child at risk later on for academic suspension, expulsion, delinquent behavior, juvenile detention, and punitive education policies that push Black children out of school and into "the system."[37]

The zero-tolerance and exclusionary policies enacted by many schools across the nation contribute to the school-to-prison pipeline (that typically reflects the experiences of Black male students) and the "school-to-confinement pathways" (that reflect the experiences of Black female students). Reports like those published in the *School Psychology Review* indicate that zero-tolerance federal and state mandates are often interpreted by school authorities to extend beyond incidents involving firearms and drugs to include "nonviolent infractions" to which authorities apply "predetermined consequences, most often severe and punitive in nature, that are intended to be applied regardless of the gravity of behavior, mitigating circumstances, or situational context."[38]

Zero-tolerance school policies are applied disparately to African American students, who are suspended at higher rates compared with white students for similar misbehavior and are twice as likely to be expelled.[39] Zero-tolerance school policies that disproportionately affect African American students and other students of color eerily parallel mandatory and extreme sentencing policies that are applied disparately to African American adult "offenders" for violent as well as nonviolent offenses. As generations of enslaved *and* imprisoned Black men and women were "twice condemned," so generations of Black students in twenty-first-century American schools face "double jeopardy."[40]

The belief that operators of public and private prisons use the reading scores of third graders to plan for additional prison beds or for the building of a new prison has been largely debunked. Though this belief has been adjudged an "urban myth," some see in it the truth of a hard reality. Researchers have learned that the reading levels of third-grade students is an important indicator of student performance in successive grades. They explain that reading skills are taught in first through third grades, "the time when students shift from learning to read and begin reading to learn."[41] When reading skills are compromised, so is the child's future. In third grade, students are typically eight or nine years old, a critical age for children, academically and socially speaking. If no interventions are made, a student who is not reading at grade level is likely to struggle, stumble, and fall victim to "the system."

The prospects of academically "at-risk" African American children and teenagers are peculiarly comparable to the prospects of African American children of the antebellum era. Kenneth Stampp's description of the "education" of enslaved youth invites a comparison:

> The master, not the parents, decided at what age slave children should be put to work in the fields. Until they were five or six years old children were "useless articles on a plantation." Then many received "their first lessons in the elementary part of their education" through serving as "water-toters"

or going into the fields alongside their mothers. Between the ages of ten and twelve the children became fractional hands, with a regular routine of field labor. By the time they were eighteen they had reached the age when they could be classified as "prime field-hands."[42]

Stampp was insistent that America's Peculiar Institution "deserves close study if only because its impact upon the whole country was so disastrous." What Kenneth Stampp wrote in 1956 is still true in 2024. He held that his work had "a peculiar urgency, because American Negroes still await the full fruition of their emancipation—still strive to break what remains of the caste barriers first imposed upon them in slavery days."[43]

## NOTES

1. Marc Mauer and Ashley Nellis, *The Meaning of Life: The Case for Abolishing Life Sentences* (New York: The New Press, 2018), 25, 162; and Gary Fields, "As Inmates Age, a Prison Carpenter Builds More Coffins," *The Wall Street Journal*, May 18, 2005, https://www.wsj.com/articles/SB111637661650736440.

2. Lea Skene, "Louisiana's Life Without Parole Sentencing the Nation's Highest—and Some Say That Should Change," *The Advocate*, December 7, 2019, https://www.theadvocate.com/baton_rouge/news/article_f6309822-17ac-11ea-8750-f7d212aa28f8.html.

3. Ashley Nellis, "Still Life: America's Increasing Use of Life and Long-Term Sentences," The Sentencing Project, May 3, 2017, 7, https://www.sentencingproject.org/publications/still-life-americas-increasing-use-life-long-term-sentences/.

4. Mauer and Nellis, *The Meaning of Life*, 9–10.

5. See, for example, Roby Chavez, "Aging Louisiana Prisoners Were Promised a Chance at Parole After 10 Years. Some Are Finally Free," PBS, November 26, 2021, https://www.pbs.org/newshour/nation/aging-louisiana-prisoners-were-a-at-parole-free.

6. Mauer and Nellis, *The Meaning of Life*, 14–16.

7. Winthrop D. Jordan, *The White Man's Burden: Historical Origins of Racism in the United States* (New York: Oxford University Press, 1974), 45.

8. Tonya Gonnella Frichner, "Preliminary Study of the Impact on Indigenous Peoples of the International Legal Construct Known as the Doctrine of Discovery," United Nations Economic and Social Council, Permanent Forum on

Indigenous Issues, Ninth Session (February 4, 2010), 8, https://www.un.org/esa/socdev/unpfii/documents/E.C.19.2010.13%20EN.pdf.

The first set of bracketed words are the author's. The latter bracketed words or phrases are original to the quoted text.

9. Jordan, *The White Man's Burden*, 35.

10. Frichner, "Preliminary Study of the Impact on Indigenous Peoples," 16–17.

11. Albert Camus, *The Rebel: An Essay on Man in Revolt*, rev. ed. (New York: Alfred A. Knopf, 1956; New York: Vintage International, 1991), 11.

12. Camus, *The Rebel*, 13, 283.

13. Stampp, *The Peculiar Institution: Slavery in the Ante-Bellum South* (New York: Vintage Books, 1956), vii, 4, 18, 82, 422.

14. Allen C. Guelzo, *Fateful Lightning: A New History of the Civil War and Reconstruction* (New York: Oxford University Press, 2012), 52.

15. John C. Calhoun, *Union and Liberty: The Political Philosophy of John C. Calhoun*, ed. Ross M. Lence (1811; Indianapolis: Liberty Fund, 1992), 322.

16. Stampp, *The Peculiar Institution*, 421–22.

17. Brett Josef Derbes, "'Secret Horrors': Enslaved Women and Children in the Louisiana State Penitentiary, 1833–1862," *The Journal of African American History* 98, no. 2 (2013): 277–90, https://doi.org/10.5323/jafriamerhist.98.2.0277.

18. Derbes, "'Secret Horrors,'" 281. State prisoners were originally confined "in a colonial-era Spanish jail in New Orleans." In 1832, the Act to Establish the Louisiana Penitentiary was passed. Between 1833 and 1835, "convicts" from the New Orleans parish jail constructed Louisiana's first state penitentiary in Baton Rouge, called "The Walls." The Louisiana State Penitentiary is also distinguished as "the first penal institution established in the Trans-Mississippi region" (Derbes, "'Secret Horrors,'" 279–80).

19. Connie H. Nobles, "Gazing upon the Invisible: Women and Children at the Old Baton Rouge Penitentiary," *American Antiquity* 65, no. 1 (2000): 5–14, https://www.jstor.org/stable/2694805; and Derbes, "'Secret Horrors,'" 280.

20. Nobles, "Gazing upon the Invisible," 10.

21. Derbes, "'Secret Horrors,'" 277, 280; and Bauer, *American Prison*, 96.

22. Derbes, "'Secret Horrors,'" 288.

23. Shane Bauer, *American Prison: A Reporter's Undercover Journey into the Business of Punishment*, New York, Penguin, 2018, 96.

24. Derbes, "'Secret Horrors,'" 285–86.

25. Nobles, "Gazing upon the Invisible," 7.

26. Derbes, "'Secret Horrors,'" 278, 286–88.

27. Jeff Forret, "Before Angola: Enslaved Prisoners in the Louisiana State Penitentiary," *Louisiana History: The Journal of the Louisiana Historical Association* 54, no. 2 (2013): 133–171, https://www.jstor.org/stable/24396520.

28. Derbes, "'Secret Horrors,'" 278.

29. Derbes, "'Secret Horrors,'" 288. The brown pelican is the state bird of Louisiana.

30. The *Children of Whitney* is a series of clay sculptures that represent the children and teenagers who were enslaved on the Whitney Plantation. The narratives associated with each rendering were taken from Works Progress Administration interviews of the formerly enslaved adults who were children at the time of

emancipation. See "The Children of the Whitney," Whitney Plantation, https://www.whitneyplantation.org/history/the-big-house-and-the-outbuildings/the-children-of-the-whitney/.

31. Renamed Antioch Baptist Church in 1890, Anti-Yoke Baptist Church was established in 1870. "This name spoke freedom—not tied or bound to anyone." ("The Antioch Baptist Church," Whitney Plantation, https://www.whitney plantation.org/history/the-big-house-and-the-outbuildings/the-antioch-baptist -church/.)

32. Ibrahima Seck, *Bouki Fait Gombo: A History of the Slave Community of Habitation Haydel (Whitney Plantation), Louisiana, 1750–1860* (New Orleans: University of New Orleans Press, 2014), 157–58.

33. Seck, *Bouki Fait Gombo*, 163–65; and "Whitney Plantation History," Whitney Plantation, https://www.whitneyplantation.org/history/. Dr. Allées Gwendolyn Midlo Hall began gathering data for the Afro-Louisiana History and Genealogy, 1719 to 1820 Database in 1984, documenting 107,000 lives of enslaved Africans and African Americans. "They estimate, for every one she's able to verify and document, there are two to three people, this state, this time period, alone, they will never verify or document." (Whitney Museum docent lecture, May 8, 2019. Transcription by the author.)

34. Seck, *Bouki Fait Gombo*, 111–15; "Resistance," Whitney Plantation, https://www.whitneyplantation.org/history/slavery-in-louisiana/resistance/; and Daniel Rasmussen, *American Uprising: The Untold Story of America's Largest Slave Revolt* (New York: HarperCollins Publishers, 2011), 1.

35. Stampp, *Peculiar Institution*, vii.

36. Nazgol Ghandnoosh, Emma Stammen, and Kevin Muhitch, "Parents in Prison," The Sentencing Project, November 17, 2021, 1–2, https://www.sentencingproject .org/publications/parents-in-prison/.

37. Ghandnoosh, Stammen, and Muhitch, "Parents in Prison," 1.

38. Francis L. Huang and Dewey G. Cornell, "Teacher Support for Zero Tolerance Is Associated with Higher Suspension Rates and Lower Feelings of Safety," *School Psychology Review* 50, nos. 2–3 (2021): 388–405, https://doi.org/10.1080 /2372966X.2020.1832865; Monique W. Morris, *Pushout: The Criminalization of Black Girls in Schools*, New York: New Press, 2016, 12.

39. Huang and Cornell, "Teacher Support for Zero Tolerance," 390.

40. "Double jeopardy" describes the influence of impoverished conditions on the reading skills of young students. See Donald J. Hernandez, "Double Jeopardy: How Third-Grade Reading Skills and Poverty Influence High School Graduation," The Annie E. Casey Foundation, April 2011, 3, https://www.fcd -us.org/assets/2016/04/DoubleJeopardyReport.pdf.

41. Hernandez, "Double Jeopardy," 4.

42. Stampp, *Peculiar Institution*, 57–58.

43. Stampp, *Peculiar Institution*, vii.

# CHAPTER 6

# AMERICAN PLANTATION LULLABIES[1]

The court system have been playing with people's lives for a long time because they have the power. Most DA's want convictions so that they might go higher in their career. These people have no regards to anyone but themselves. I was thinking about when Jesus went before Governor Pilate and Pilate told him, "I have power to crucify you and have power to release you."

The courts have been playing this [role] a long time. They even let a robber go to keep a innocent man, which was Jesus. The courts will [wheel and deal] with your life. But Jesus said "He that delivered me unto thee hath the Greater sin." There are so many men here that the courts have taken their lives and some are dead and gone. Some of the [Innocent] men here now has one eye, some have scars in their face, neck, body from trying to survive, some have mental issues. All because the courts has the power, they really dont care if you are Innocent or guilty its all about their conviction career.

They are not concern about justice for a real victim. In reality its all about them. In my case I know the judge know that I am Innocent of this charge but the judge can't go against her DA because a house divided cannot stand.

*But like Jesus said, "He that delivered me unto Angola hath the Greater sin." Their day is coming.*[2]

WHAT MY BROTHER WAS GETTING at here was the problem of a rigged court system and the unfettered corrupt prosecutorial power at its center. In the American criminal justice system, prosecutors exercise virtually absolute power. They determine what constitutes a crime, which crimes are deemed a priority, which violators of the crime will be targeted for prosecution, which charges will be brought and prosecuted, and they set the terms of punishment for those "duly convicted" of the crime or crimes with which they have been charged.

"Duly convicted" implies that a sentence of "hard labor" (i.e., slavery or involuntary servitude) was obtained in accordance with "due process of law" procedures, as the Criminal Punishment Clause requires. It suggests that a defendant was accorded "the equal protection of the laws." The "duly convicted" stipulation of the Thirteenth Amendment, like the due process and equal protection provisions of the Fourteenth Amendment, was intended to protect newly emancipated Black citizens both from the unjustified deprivation of "life, liberty, or property" *and* from the "badges and incidents of slavery."

The Due Process Clause in the Fifth Amendment, which applies to federal government—like that in the Fourteenth, which applies to the states—entitles every citizen to fair treatment during any legal proceeding that would deprive that person of life, liberty, or property. But how is fairness assured, how is equal protection provided, and how is justice served when district attorneys and prosecutors—the very guardians of the justice system—can, with near impunity, manipulate the system to accord with their personal interests and career ambitions?

During the plea-deal process of my brother's case, the district attorney asked my brother's public defender what charge he and my brother would settle for. "On the table" was a charge of "simple rape" (twenty-five years imprisonment at hard labor) and several "lesser" charges, including second-degree battery (five years imprisonment at hard labor). The district attorney scoffed at the idea of settling for the second-degree battery charge.

In reaction to this idea, my brother writes that "the D. A. said something like I guess you would because it don't carry any time. So the D. A. said we are going with the [Aggravated] Rape"—the charge which carried a sentence of life imprisonment at hard labor.[3] What the district attorney wanted was clear to my brother. "Say you are guilty and take the 25 years. Or we will make you guilty and give you life in prison. That's the bottom line," my brother wrote. "Going through the court system I found out the hard way that they don't play fair."[4]

How is a defendant provided equal protection of the laws when the laws favor the State and its representatives? Louisiana is one of twenty-three states that require a grand jury indictment in certain serious felonies, and "the prosecution controls almost every aspect of the proceeding."[5] "The jurors, ordinary citizens, are schooled in the law, presented evidence, and instructed about the case or issue before them by the prosecutor acting alone."[6] The defendant's right to equal protection is further nullified by the legal convention that "grand-jury proceedings are secret"[7] and only the prosecutor is allowed to present evidence or address issues "behind the closed doors of the jury."[8]

Historically, the grand jury was meant to protect the sovereign rights of "the people" from the overreach of State power, as "exercised through a local prosecutor."[9] Its purpose was to keep the government from unduly taking a person to trial without sufficient probable cause that the person committed a crime. However, even former grand jurors have complained that "most grand jurors are only too obliged to act as a rubber stamp for the prosecution rather than as an investigative body."[10] As a rule, "judge, defendant, defense attorney, the press, [and] the public" are absent from grand jury proceedings.[11] And although in some states a defendant may request permission to provide testimony, "neither the defendant nor the attorney for the defendant has a right to be present."[12]

My brother only learned incidentally that he was indicted by the Louisiana grand jury. "They indicted me on what they call a secret-indictment," he wrote.

*I never knew that I was indicted until one of the guys in jail read it in a newspaper, the next day. I went to court the day before the guy read it to me. It said I was indicted for the rape and kidnapping of [his fiancée]. . . . Now here is the thing I dont understand, they brought me to court that day but I was rescheduled. I never saw anybody. So the next day the guy in jail showed me the paper where it said I was indicted at court. I was indicted without evidence that a rape took place.[13]*

On pain of the penalty for perjury, defendants and witnesses alike are instructed to tell nothing but the truth. Yet prosecutors have the legal authority to construct fabrications and are empowered by the government to tell lies by omission. "That is to say, even if the prosecution is aware of a witness or physical evidence that may tend to show that the defendant did not commit the crimes in question, the prosecution is not required to and typically will not present this evidence to the grand jury."[14]

How is justice served when justice takes a back seat to winning a conviction for the State? "There was no evidence," my brother writes, "no clothes, no underwear no [samples] of DNA because there was nothing found . . . to compare it to. They never asked me for blood work or anything."[15] In my brother's case, the evidentiary facts of the case were immaterial. At one point during his pre-trial incarceration, my brother met with another public defender who had been assigned to him, as his appointed lawyer was unavailable and my brother's court dates had been rescheduled several times. My brother was told that his appointed lawyer was in rehab. "While [the court-appointed public defender, 'a Black man'] is in REHAB the court assigned me a white man, temporary. My next court date came and this is what happen":

*OK when everyone is brought over from the jailhouse, we are placed in what they call a holding tank. Now when the P. D. come for his people only he will call your name and [you] line up on the hallway. Now he calls about 4 guys out first and he tell them what going to happen when we or they get in court. So when he came to me he did not say a word. He had a big book in his hand. It was a law book that headed like a dictionary with the words at the top of the pages. He said nothing to me. But open that book and pointed at the word at the top of that page, and the word was RAILROAD.*

"I looked it up in the Dictionary, and this is what he was trying to tell me: To convict a person in a hasty manner by means of FALSE charges or insufficient evidence. So now the next time I come to court, [the lawyer appointed originally] is back from

REHAB. It is now TRIAL TIME. For two days of trial, he didn't do nothing but only act as if he was defending me, only for a show. . . . They gave me a drug addict for a representative," my brother confided. "I never told this to anyone because no one offer to help me."[16]

At the beginning of the jury trial, my brother recalled that the prosecutor "said to the jury, I have to tell you, the state has no [evidence] or proof."[17]

⌘ ⌘ ⌘

In his reflections on the trial and death sentence of Jesus, my brother wrestled with the idea that the innocence of a person is neither here nor there when a prosecutor is intent on finding a person in custody guilty of *something*, even if she has to utilize some loophole, some ambiguity in the law, in order to advance and prosecute a case and argue for conviction. Accordingly, even as my brother spoke about the "secret-indictment" and the warning that he was being railroaded, Jesus was himself arrested "under cloak of darkness,"[18] was interrogated, and was sent "bound unto Caiaphas the high priest."[19] Caiaphas, who assumes the role of prosecutor, casts about for witnesses whose testimony would support criminal charges—beyond the level of an infraction or misdemeanor—in violation of provincial law. Inflammatory speech and charges of disturbing the peace in Judaea were "hardly grounds for prosecution" under Roman law, and neither "crime" warranted the death penalty.[20]

Construing a statement Jesus reiterated about "sitting on the right hand of power" to be a capital crime punishable by death, Caiaphas indicts Jesus, then dispatches him, "bound," to "the judgment hall" before Pilate.[21] Though the stories interpreting the motivations and circumstances surrounding Jesus's death may be varied and controversial, the events of his arrest and prosecution are consistent through scriptural texts and historical narratives.

What also remains consistent over time and across generations is the question of the role of race and class in the formulation of the American legal process and the use of the court system to leverage political power in maintaining America's social and economic status quo. In John 11:50, Caiaphas proclaims "that it is expedient for us, that one man should die for the people, and that the whole nation perish not."[22] Scholars theorize that Caiaphas's "hasty" indictment of Jesus had to do with containing Jesus's growing popularity and preventing further demonstrations, like the incident with the money changers, which were upsetting the socioeconomic status quo and which might provoke the unwanted presence of Roman forces.[23]

As with the notion that "one man should die for the people," has it not also been reasoned expedient to allow one American demographic to suffer rather than to engage in the long and difficult work to end slavery once and for all? What remains consistent, also, is the question of the systemic biases and prejudices inherent in the justice system and the reality of a brutal and "bent" court system that delivers a jaundiced justice.

Consider, for instance, the controversial case of the Exonerated Five, whose 1989 conviction for the beating and rape of a woman jogger in New York's Central Park was overturned in 2002. One of the defense lawyers in the case had stated early on that the prosecutor's case against the teenagers was thin, as there was "no blood on their clothing, the semen doesn't match, the DNA test come back negative. There's nothing that links these boys to the crime."[24]

Prosecutors maintained otherwise. Writing in *The Wall Street*

*Journal*, Linda Fairstein, who "was one of the supervisors who oversaw the team that prosecuted the teenagers," concurred with the decision that "the rape charges against the five be vacated," given that the actual perpetrator had confessed and DNA tests substantiated the confession. "I agreed with that decision, and still do," she wrote in her opinion piece. However, Fairstein objected, "other charges, for crimes against other victims, should not have been vacated." She maintained that evidence supported the convictions for "first-degree assault, robbery, riot and other charges."[25]

A string of "other charges," i.e. "stacking," virtually guarantees that a suspect will be charged with *something*, whether she is guilty of that particular *something* or not. No matter how flimsy the evidence, prosecutors don't necessarily choose to take a case to trial because the evidence is solid, irrefutable, and provides proof "beyond a shadow of a doubt." They also will try a case because they believe that they can win it; they believe that they can tell the more compelling story. And, based on my own *voir-dire* experiences as a potential juror, they can even override the whole concern with the shadow of a doubt by undermining the critical and intellectual importance of doubt itself. Countless cases have been won not only with insufficient evidence but also with contradictory evidence. This fact of legal life in America is the basis of organizations like the Innocence Project.

A sixth teenager who was arrested in connection with the Central Park case avoided the rape charge and trial because he acquiesced to a plea deal. The "deal" the prosecutors offered was that he would not be charged with rape if he pleaded guilty to the lesser charge "that he and several others" had assaulted and robbed a male jogger. A July 2022 review of the case found that the accused, who was fifteen years old at the time, had "pleaded guilty involuntarily 'in the face of false statements' and under 'immense external pressure.'"[26]

His conviction, like the Exonerated Five, had been overturned. Prosecutors said that "statements implicating [the teenager] in the violence that night also were unreliable," as witnesses had recanted their stories.[27] The sixth teenager had served more than three years behind bars. The Exonerated Five had endured six to thirteen years in prison. All had had their convictions vacated, and the Exonerated Five had won a $41 million settlement that charged "malicious prosecution, racial discrimination, and emotional distress."[28] Yet the damage had been done. Families were separated, parents lost jobs, one parent suffered a stroke, family members were evicted from their homes or were forced to relocate.

All six of the exonerated men, African American and Latino, who ranged in age from fourteen to sixteen when arrested and convicted, were still struggling with the trauma of incarceration. As one among them put it thirty years later, "Even our conversations is different. It's not normal. Our conversations'll be about prison, about how we had to survive in prison."[29] Prosecutors and other agents of the criminal-punishment system seem oblivious to the sufferings of those they deliver into the prison-industrial complex. "These people have no regards to anyone but themselves," my brother says matter-of-factly, as he also bears witness to the physical abuse and mental distress to which incarcerated persons are subjected. He concludes that "it's all about their conviction career."[30]

One wonders whether this point of view pertains to prosecutor Fairstein, who praised the investigation conducted against the arrested teenagers as "brilliant." And even when the same criminal-punishment system declared that the youths had been "wrongfully convicted," Fairstein betrayed "no regrets."[31] Rather, she argued that some of the convictions should have been upheld and added, as if in a whimper, that they were not "totally innocent."[32]

And, of course, she may have been totally right that they were not totally innocent. But who is? There are so many acts of commission and omission that have been codified into law as *crimes* that we all engage in criminal behavior on a regular basis. From talking loudly or playing music above a certain decibel level past a certain time, jaywalking, making a "rolling stop," and littering, to ignoring the lead content in drinking water, manipulation of municipal zoning laws to create "slums" and "food deserts," circumventing campaign finance laws with "dark money," and targeting civilians during military campaigns, all constitute outlaw behavior.

American citizens commit an incalculable number of legal violations every single day and several times in any given day. "Only a tiny fraction of those violations, however, are ever targeted for punishment."[33] So none of us is without civic sin, yet only some of us are targeted, criminalized, and cast into the hell of the criminal-punishment system. The choices made by those who run America's punishment bureaucracy determine which laws are enforced and in which precincts, who will be punished for "alleged" crimes, and what methods will be used in the procedure identified and advertised as "law enforcement."[34]

The outcome of the policing policies of the American criminal bureaucracy is the criminalization of American citizens. It has been well established that the activity of those elected, appointed, and employed to enforce the "rule of law" have disproportionately trained their sights on Black people, other people of color, and low-income whites. It has been well established that officials and bureaucratic agents of federal, state, city, and county government have used their positions to bring the weight of policing and the police force to bear on individuals of color and low-income communities.

Far from being fair and just in their application of "the rule of law," these officials and agents of the State indiscriminately break the law in surveilling, searching, arresting, charging, and caging millions of Americans. Constitutionally guaranteed and protected rights are broken a million times a day. In fact, the rule of law imposed on African Americans looks quite like the 1740 slave codes of South Carolina. And the policies, practices, and tactics of enforcers of the law in contemporary American society, as applied to African Americans, closely resemble those of colonial officials and the "slave patrols" they deputized to extend their power and control over Black populations, both the enslaved and the nominally free. (See Appendix.)

Elitist officials and bureaucratic agents of the State victimize those individuals and communities that have relatively little social and political capital and also, ironically, little economic capital. I say "ironically" because the wealth extracted from the criminalization of vulnerable populations has built the mass incarceration empire and has contributed to the public coffers and to the salaries of prosecutors, judges, public defenders, bailiffs, clerks of court, guards, police departments, wardens, parole officers, and the personnel of allied corporate entities.

Every night in our country, 2.2 million adult and juvenile American citizens are locked up in detention centers, jails, and prisons. More than half a million of those confined are legally innocent, as they have been convicted of nothing. Their bodies are caged nonetheless, as they cannot pay the bail a judge has set—if, indeed, a judge has permitted bail to be set. Even though "eighty and ninety percent of the people charged with crimes are so poor that they cannot afford a lawyer,"[35] their meager incomes collectively fund municipal, state, federal, and corporate budgets. They sustain an injustice empire that cages and crushes them and their families and communities.

The greed that galvanizes America's peculiar criminal-punishment empire also bends the arc of justice in the nation's courts. Greed incentivizes their inclination to ignore the "rule of law" when it comes to pretrial release of those in custody. The jailing of an indigent African American defendant in New Orleans, Louisiana, is a case in point. In his observations of the proceedings of this case, Alec Karakatsanis explains the economic imperatives at work in both the transfer of Black and brown bodies into the system of "mass human caging" and the extraction of wealth from Black and brown communities:

> After all, in Louisiana, it's not surprising that the judge would require as many people as possible to pay for their release from jail: the public defender who represented the man, the prosecutor who argued against the man, the sheriff who shackled the man, and the judge who ruled on the man's case all take a percentage cut of the money if the man pays for his release. If the man's family could pay the $2,600 that a for-profit bail company requires for a $20,000 bond, then these local officials would get $600 of that payment. (The for-profit company would keep $2,000.)[36]

"Every year in New Orleans alone," reports Karakatsanis, this bail money amounts to about a quarter million *each* "for the budgets of the public defender, district attorney, and sheriff, and about $1 million for the budget of the court controlled by the local judges."[37] If convicted, the bail amount is forfeited, and fees are incurred. Take the case of rap artist Meek Mill (Robert Rihmeek Williams) for example, who was finally a freedman after twelve years of entanglement with the criminal-punishment system. He spent most of his early adult life in and out of courtrooms, jails, and prison in relation to a 2007 arrest at age nineteen on assault, gun, and drug charges. And he spent around $30 million on legal defense fees in his efforts to exist in freedom.[38]

The initial misdemeanor "illegal carry" firearms charge "typically warrants a fine and house arrest," but in 2009, Judge Genece Brinkley sentenced Meek Mill to eleven to twenty-three months in the county prison.[39] On probation for nearly ten years, the artist was accused of violating several among the "forty-five thousand federal and state laws [that] regulate the lives of the accused." These rules dictate the conditions to which individuals on parole or probation are subject to adhere.[40] In 2017, the same judge sentenced Mill to two to four years in state prison for a host of probation violations, including "popping wheelies" on a dirt bike without wearing a helmet.[41]

Citing "excessive supervision," instances of police "corruption," and "unfair processes" in the criminal court system as factors in Meek Mill's release from prison, Philadelphia District Attorney Larry Krasner announced that in the criminal case against Meek Mill, there would be no further penalty, incarceration, or probationary or parole supervision.[42] A successful recording artist and businessman, Meek Mill has used his platform to speak for those silenced behind and beyond prison bars. In his song "Mandela Freestyle" (2021), Mill tells his story about incarceration and the deceptions of a freedom wrapped in the barbed wires of technicalities and restrictions.

Once a guilty plea deal was negotiated, the Philadelphia District Attorney's office "nolle prossed (dropped) all remaining charges."[43] This action means that a district attorney's office is no longer willing (*nolle*) to pursue or follow (*pros*, from *prōse-quī*) the criminal case against Meek Mill any further. Such a legal declaration, theoretically, is an admission that prosecutors cannot prove their case, that evidence contradicts prosecutors' claims or the evidence is flawed, or that the district attorney believes an accused person is innocent.

Or, twelve years and $30 million later, the choice to *nolle prosequi* in the case against Meek Mill may have had something to do with the fact that "the FBI has had undercover agents in courtrooms monitoring Brinkley's handling of Meek Mill's case since April 2016" and that in 2018, the police officers involved in the case were being "investigated by federal authorities for several alleged acts of corruption."[44]

In his statement to the press, the DA said he knew "two things to be true": that Meek Mill was unfairly treated and that he was guilty—of *something*. According to the plea deal, Mill was "guilty of illegally possessing a firearm on the day he was arrested, a fact that he has established by his own testimony and public statements for years."[45] As with the Exonerated Five, Mill vowed to contest the charge. The point here is that even when the criminal-punishment system is revealed to be a destructive force in the lives of so many human beings, those who work in and profit from the injustices and the corruption inherent in the criminal-punishment bureaucracy continue to cloak the system in neutrality and infallibility. Because, after all—over the span of twelve years, wherein Mill was subjected to court-imposed incidents and badges of slavery—his freedom to travel was blocked, his communications were monitored, his ability to work to secure his profession was compromised.

The point here, too, is that in executing the *nolle prosequi*, Lady "Justice" is neither blind nor "race-neutral." The process of criminalization devastates the lives of individuals and their families and even whole communities. Which was the case of Michael Brown, his family, and his Ferguson, Missouri, community.

## NOLLE PROSEQUI

In November of 2014, the St. Louis County prosecutor announced that the St. Louis County grand jury declined to indict white police officer Darren Wilson for the fatal shooting of African American Michael Brown, Jr., having found that "no probable cause exists."[46] The US Department of Justice (DOJ) made a similar announcement, stating that the evidence gathered from their investigation "does not support the conclusion that Wilson's uses of deadly force were 'objectively unreasonable' under the Supreme Court's definition," and therefore there would be no indictment and the case would be "closed without prosecution."[47]

Although the Justice Department "declined" to indict Wilson, his case led to a thorough investigation of the Ferguson Police Department and Municipal Court. While the DOJ's March 2015 report stops short of advancing a cause-and-effect interpretation of the killing of Michael Brown, the evidence gathered revealed a "deep divide" between city officials and the African American residents of the Ferguson community.[48] Officer Wilson's killing of the unarmed eighteen-year-old recent high school graduate became a flash point that highlighted the harmfulness of social

injustice, economic marginalization, and political disempowerment and their fatal consequences.

Ferguson, Missouri, had been a "sundown" town—a place
where Black people could enter as the labor pool for whites, but
Black people couldn't live there and shouldn't be caught there
after dark. By 2014, African Americans made up 67 percent
of Ferguson's population. Nevertheless, the town's majority-
Black population was subjected to the oppressive authority of its
minority-white and racialized leadership. At the time of the DOJ
investigation, city officials—mayor, city council, city manager, finance director, municipal court judge, clerk of court, prosecutor,
and police chief—were all white. Of Ferguson's fifty-four police
officers, four were African American.[49]

Though no longer by definition a sundown town, the postbellum
twilight glow still lingered in Ferguson. The treatment of African
Americans by the town's white minority leadership mimicked "the
badges, incidents, and relics of slavery" that Black Americans were
subjected to after the Civil War.[50] The US Supreme Court's ruling
in the Civil Rights Cases of 1883 had overturned the 1875 Civil
Rights Act, leaving African American citizens vulnerable to incidents that could reduce them to *de facto reenslavement or legal
subjugation.*"[51] And the court's 1896 ruling in *Plessy v. Ferguson*
codified into law the ideology of a purported white supremacy and
the doctrine of "separate but equal."

The arguments in *Plessy v. Ferguson* issued from Judge John
Howard Ferguson's ruling in *The State of Louisiana v. Homer
Adolph Plessy*. Judge Ferguson upheld the Louisiana Railway
Accommodations Act (or the Separate Car Act) of 1890. That act
required that "all railway companies carrying passengers in their
coaches in this State shall provide equal, but separate, accom-

modations for the white and colored races."[52] The US Supreme Court's *Plessy v. Ferguson* ruling legitimized Louisiana's Black Codes while implicating the entire nation in the statutory assault on Black citizenship.

Even as the federal government would eventually move to restore and protect the civil rights of African Americans, the leadership in "former" sundown towns, as in other municipalities across the nation, found new ways to impose old prejudices and practices and thus maintain the status quo. Though the municipal codes in Ferguson, Missouri, were no longer identified or identifiable as black codes, the city's "race-neutral" laws were enforced more aggressively when infractions of codes involved Black residents.

DOJ investigators found that, rather than attending to their lawful responsibility of public safety, Ferguson's police department had been focused on generating revenue through practices that violated "the First, Fourth, and Fourteenth Amendments of the United States Constitution, and federal statutory law." The focus on money, investigators wrote, had "contributed to a pattern of unconstitutional policing" and had bent the municipal court toward the will of greed.[53]

The evidence in the DOJ investigation showed beyond a reasonable doubt that Ferguson's revenue-enhancing scheme intentionally targeted the African American community.[54] City officials, in collusion with the police chief and the municipal judge, had modified their criminal justice system to institute their own version of "debt slavery." The system was contrived to manipulate costs, terms, and dates of payment of tickets issued and fees charged, such that the circumstances would force an accumulation of debt from which the debtor would be virtually unable to extricate herself or himself.[55]

In Ferguson, minor infractions like failure to remove leaf debris, dog creating nuisance, parking violation, expired license plate, or no proof of insurance could result in crippling debt. Such infractions were among a host of noncriminal offenses for which a person "must appear" in court before the fine could be paid. When a person missed a court date or did not pay a fine on time, the court routinely issued a warrant for a person's arrest and incarceration. A person's inability to pay the fine incurred from a "failure to appear" charge typically resulted in more charges, more fines, more fees, which could lead to a suspended driver's license, incarceration, loss of employment, and loss of housing.[56]

The fact of citing a single individual with multiple offenses all at once, in and of itself, generated a financial challenge for those in Ferguson who were already "living in or near poverty."[57] The focus on monies due, rather than due process, compromised the ability of Ferguson's police department to provide equal protection for all its residents. Ferguson's "must appear" requirements for minor violations, together with its punitive "failure to appear" charge was a legal maneuver designed to shield "judges against the attack that the court is operating as a debtor's prison"— which it did.[58] The Ferguson court operated as such and utilized its police force "in large part as a collection agency," carrying out a "staggering" number of municipal arrest warrants—which had nothing to do with public safety but were issued "exclusively" to intimidate residents and to coerce payment.[59]

Between 2010 and 2014, "the City of Ferguson issued approximately 90,000 citations and summonses." From 2012 to 2014, "African Americans [accounted] for 85% of vehicle stops, 90% of citations, and 93% of arrests." They were almost exclusively targeted for certain "offenses": "from 2011 to 2013, African Americans accounted for 95% of Manner of Walking in Roadway charges, and 94% of all Failure to Comply charges." Documented cases of use of force involved African Americans 90 percent of the time, and in every incident of a canine bite where race data was available, "the person bitten was African American."[60] The arrest of a person for whom a warrant had been issued was a "highly discretionary" matter. Ferguson city officials justified the disproportionate number of African Americans trapped in their criminal justice system with the retort that African Americans were "disproportionately irresponsible."[61]

## "THE PRICE OF THE TICKET," OR HOW DO YOU SPELL WHITE PRIVILEGE?

Ferguson city officials consistently budgeted for ever-increasing amounts of monies from "enforcement of code provisions" and exceeded the targeted amount.[62] So by fiscal year 2015, with a general-fund projected budget of $13.26 million (as compared with a 2010 budget of $11.07 million), the $3.09 million to be collected from fines and fees had more than doubled the 2010 extraction of $1.38 million. The fiscal burden of $3.09 million was imposed on Ferguson's economically marginalized citizen-residents.

To the same extent that disparate "law enforcement" actions criminalized, punished, and disadvantaged the Black community in Ferguson, disparate "law enforcement" actions advanced the white community, pardoned their "mistakes," and situated whites above the "rule of law." In 2007, an African American woman resident was issued two tickets for a parking violation for which she was fined $151, plus fees. In financial straits and periodically unhoused, this woman missed court dates, and her attempts to make partial payments were initially rejected as the court demanded "payment in full." New fines and new fees mounted. She was arrested twice and was incarcerated for six days. In 2014, she was allowed to make partial payments. After having submitted $550, she still had an outstanding balance of $541. The price of her $151 ticket was $1,091.[63]

After playing basketball at a public park, an African American man sat in his parked car to cool down. With no probable cause, a police officer accused him of being a pedophile, patted him down, charged him with eight violations of the city's municipal code, and arrested him, "reportedly at gunpoint." Because of the charges against him, he lost the job he had held for several years as a contractor with the federal government.[64] There was no indication in the 2015 report that any conviction ensued, and yet there was also no indication that this individual was reinstated in his job. The price of his ticket was his livelihood, plus fines and fees.

The price of the $200 ticket for the friend of a relative of a white court clerk was the time it took the friend to email the court clerk and request intervention. "Your ticket of $200 has magically disappeared!" the clerk responded. A few months later, this same friend emailed the clerk regarding two more tickets: "Can you work your magic again?" The court clerk had one ticket dismissed and was waiting to hear back about the second. The price of the ticket for the wife of a man who had a friend who was also friends with a white court clerk was simply a matter of giving the ticket to her husband to take care of. When the friend faxed a copy of the ticket to the white court clerk, the clerk replied, "It's gone baby!"[65]

Where white court clerks in Ferguson were working white magic, white prosecuting attorneys were dispensing godly blessings. For the relative of a white police patrol supervisor in the

Ferguson Police Department, the price of a speeding ticket in a neighboring town was simply the act of the relative giving the ticket to the white Ferguson patrol supervisor. In an email with the subject heading "Oops," the police patrol supervisor requested the Ferguson prosecuting attorney's assistance with the ticket: "[h]aving it dismissed would be a blessing." The prosecuting attorney of the neighboring town granted the divine favor and informed the Ferguson attorney that he would "nolle pros the ticket."[66]

Similarly, the white mayor of Ferguson petitioned the city prosecutor on behalf of an associate who was ticketed for a parking violation. The mayor acknowledged that the associate "shouldn't have left his car unattended there" but pleaded that "it was an honest mistake . . . I would hate for him to have to pay for this." Apparently the prosecuting attorney hated it, too, for he instructed the court clerk, "to 'NP' [nolle prosequi, or not prosecute] this parking ticket."[67]

⌧ ⌧ ⌧

The other side of "white privilege" is Black disadvantage. As the socioeconomic politics in Ferguson illustrate, the benefits accrued to white Ferguson residents that stem from the "matrix of white privilege" are correlative with the disadvantages, deprivations, and dispossessions suffered by Ferguson's Black residents. Ferguson, Missouri, is one of many such towns and a microcosm of national politics.

The concept of "privilege" is considered a positive one. It implies that a person or group has some exceptional and typically desirable and enviable right, advantage, or honor. But these attributes of "privilege" are really generic and universal and can apply to all American citizens. What is typically understood as *white* privilege is a kind of privilege that (whether associated with race, class, caste, gender, sex, sexuality, etc.) is no privilege at all but is, as the professor and activist Peggy McIntosh describes it, an "unearned advantage" that gives the so-called privileged person "a license to be ignorant, oblivious, arrogant, and destructive."[68]

A spurious white privilege gives white Americans "an invisible weightless knapsack" of specialized provisions that enables them to escape penalties for minor infractions of the law, like traffic tickets, or even misdemeanors and felonies. It protects them from dangers and allows them to slip past loopholes in the law that are rigged to ensnare disadvantaged others. These provisions endow white Americans with "unearned power" that is "conferred systematically" by virtue of their white identity and status. Where some white Americans are consciously aware of the advantages associated with *"skin-color privilege,"* others, who take their advantages for granted, remain unconscious of how the myth of white privilege operates in their day-to-day life.[69]

In her analysis of the provisions of "white privilege," McIntosh examines a number of "special circumstances and conditions" in her personal and professional life which she recognizes as "unearned" but which she had been made to feel were hers, not because of any exceptional treatment, but hers "by birth, by citizenship, and by virtue of being a conscientious law-abiding 'normal' person of good will." It was her due. What reflection and research had her realize was that she was "'meant' to remain oblivious" about the unearned assets that she could "count on cashing in each day."[70]

"Privilege," though a seemingly ordinary word, is a legal term that pertains to laws that affect private individuals ("privi-," from *"privus,"* meaning "private" and "leg-," from *"lex,"* meaning "law"). As the Fourteenth Amendment declares, "No state shall make or enforce any law which shall abridge the privileges or immunities of citizens of the United States."[71] The systematic practice of "white privilege" in Ferguson was illegal both in its granting of unearned advantage to white residents and in abridging the privileges and immunities of its Black residents.

This system of privilege based on skin color seems unimportant to some, but as McIntosh has pointed out, this is mainly because in our society, privilege is generally extolled as something positive, "a favored state, whether earned, or conferred by birth or luck."[72] However, privilege systems engender disparities, inequities, and imbalances that result in deprivations and disadvantages for others. To a not-insignificant extent, the poverty suffered by African American residents in the Ferguson community, for example, was directly related to the policy and practice of "white privilege." These politics inflected by race and class and caste are instructive when we consider that in 2021, 11 percent of Americans, some 37.9 million people, were living in poverty. African Americans experienced the highest rate of poverty in the country. At a poverty rate of 22.6 percent, nearly 11 million African Americans were living in impoverished conditions.[73]

Like a high-interest, platinum credit card that is advertised as a promise to high-ticket material acquisition, privilege, and adventure, the "white privilege" bill comes due. Not only do disadvantaged groups suffer the consequences of this purchase, white-skinned people do so as well. The negative effects of "white privilege," like its seeming positive effects, are hidden in the matrices of mutually reinforcing privilege systems and are obscured with discourses about entitlement, meritocracy, superiority, and natural selection.

The sociopolitical blight of privilege systems arrests individual human development and thus obstructs societal progress. It undermines equality and democracy in America as it enables those who are favored to systematically overpower disfranchised others. The system arbitrarily *"confers dominance,* gives permission to control, because of one's race or sex." Unearned advantage and power "does not confer moral strength."[74] As it allows a person to avoid responsibility and escape accountability, it does not build character. As it encourages and nourishes arrogance, intolerance, and insensitivity, it has the effect of diminishing a person's humanity.

The assets and the alleged benefits associated with the system called white privilege are intentionally cloaked in invisibility. As practical dimensions of this system are not to be discerned, its consequences are not intended to be felt. As McIntosh informs us:

Obliviousness about white advantage, like obliviousness about male advantage, is kept strongly inculturated in the United States so as to maintain the myth of meritocracy, the myth that democratic choice is equally available to all. Keeping most people unaware that freedom of confident action is there for just a small number of people props up those in power, and serves to keep power in the hands of the same groups that have most of it already.[75]

James Baldwin observes the fact that like those of us whose ancestors traversed the Middle Passage of the "triangular slave trade," white immigrants from Europe experienced a unique but comparable Middle Passage. Though the currents that drove us to America were sourced by different powers, we were all washed upon these shores by the very same waves. Baldwin counseled

European Americans to reexamine their history, to recall whence they came, and to tell the truth about it. However, Baldwin states,

> This is precisely what the generality of white Americans cannot afford to do. They do not know how to do it—: as I must suppose. They come through Ellis Island, where *Giorgio* becomes *Joe*, *Pappavasiliu* becomes *Palmer*, *Evangelos* becomes *Evans*, *Goldsmith* becomes *Smith* or *Gold*, and *Avakian* becomes *King*. So, with a painless change of name, and in the twinkling of an eye, one becomes a white American.[76]

Despite ostracism and abuse, those Europeans considered inferior "became white" and began to rise in the world, whereas Black people began to sink and became pariahs to those granted skin-color privilege. The jettisoning of name, history, and culture, however, would neither quell the storm of the Middle Passage, nor would the skin color alone substitute a discarded identity. "The price the white American paid for his ticket," writes Baldwin, "was to become white—: and, in the main, nothing more than that, or, as he was to insist, nothing less."[77] In any case, in a democratic republic that is committed to the kind of equal justice that promotes the more perfect union, there are limits that prohibit the abridging of the privileges and immunities of fellow and sister citizens. It is for us all to realize that supremacy based on skin pigmentation is a political fiction, manipulated at the will of the politician, and that the only thing that is supreme is Love.

## NOTES

1. This chapter title recognizes Me'Shell NdegéOcello's album *Plantation Lullabies*, Maverick Records, 1993.
2. Bobby D. Plant, letter to author, May 12, 2022.

3. Bobby D. Plant, letter to author, June 15, 2021.

4. Bobby D. Plant, letter to author, April 26, 2021.

5. Greg Hurley, "The Modern Grand Jury," National Center for State Courts, January 2015, 1, http://ncsc.contentdm.oclc.org/cdm/ref/collection/juries/id/281.

6. Gordon Griller, "The Modern Grand Jury (Part II)," National Center for State Courts, February 2015, 1, http://ncsc.contentdm.oclc.org/cdm/ref/collection/juries/id/282.

7. Hurley, "The Modern Grand Jury," 2.

8. Griller, "The Modern Grand Jury (Part II)," 1.

9. Hurley, "The Modern Grand Jury," 1.

10. Griller, "The Modern Grand Jury (Part II)," 2.

11. Griller, "The Modern Grand Jury (Part II)," 1–2.

12. Hurley, "The Modern Grand Jury," 1.

13. Bobby D. Plant, letter to author, May 19, 2022.

14. Hurley, "The Modern Grand Jury," 1.

15. Bobby D. Plant, letter to author, April 26, 2021.

16. Bobby D. Plant, letter to author, June 11, 2021.

17. Bobby D. Plant, letter to author, June 8, 2021.

18. Jean-Pierre Isbouts, "Meet the High Priest Behind Jesus's Rushed and Rigged Trial," National Geographic, April 19, 2019, https://www.nationalgeographic.com/culture/article/why-caiaphas-broke-jewish-law-indict-jesus.

19. John 18:24 (KJV).

20. Isbouts, "Meet the High Priest Behind Jesus's Rushed and Rigged Trial."

21. Mark 14:62 (KJV); and John 18:28 (KJV).

22. John 11:50 (KJV).

23. Isbouts, "Meet the High Priest Behind Jesus's Rushed and Rigged Trial."

24. "The Central Park Five: A Cautionary Tale of Injustice," interview by Maurice DuBois, CBS Sunday Morning, posted May 12, 2019, YouTube video, https://www.youtube.com/watch?v=1hf-bLR668g. Transcription by the author.

25. Linda Fairstein, "Netflix's False Story of the Central Park Five," The Wall Street Journal, June 10, 2019, https://www.wsj.com/articles/netflixs-false-story-of-the-central-park-five-11560207823.

26. Associated Press, "A 6th Teenager Charged in the 1989 Central Park Jogger Case Is Exonerated," NPR, July 26, 2022, https://www.npr.org/2022/07/26/1113614422/a-6th-teenager-charged-in-the-1989-central-park-jogger-case-is-exonerated.

27. Associated Press, "A 6th Teenager Charged in the 1989 Central Park Jogger Case Is Exonerated."

28. Alfred Joyner, "How Much Was the Central Park Five Settlement? 'When They See Us' Victims Sued New York City for $41M," Newsweek, June 19, 2019, https://www.newsweek.com/central-park-five-settlement-when-they-see-us-41m-1444765.

29. "The Central Park Five." Transcription by the author.

30. Bobby D. Plant, letter to author, May 12, 2022.

31. Jeffrey Toobin, "A Prosecutor Speaks Up," *The New Yorker*, November 24, 2002, https://www.newyorker.com/magazine/2002/12/02/a-prosecutor-speaks-up.

32. Fairstein, "Netflix's False Story of the Central Park Five."

33. Alec Karakatsanis, *Usual Cruelty: The Complicity of Lawyers in the Criminal Injustice System* (New York: The New Press, 2019), 38.

34. Karakatsanis, *Usual Cruelty*, 38–39. Karakatsanis discusses "the rule of law" and "law enforcement" as central features of the American criminal system. His discussion of how they are used to deceive and manipulate the masses informs my use of the phrases.

35. Karakatsanis, *Usual Cruelty*, 5, 14.

36. Karakatsanis, *Usual Cruelty*, 5.

37. Karakatsanis, *Usual Cruelty*, 5.

38. Kory Grow, "Meek Mill's Legal Troubles: A History," *Rolling Stone*, March 14, 2018, https://www.rollingstone.com/music/music-news/meek-mills-legal-troubles-a-history-117981/.

39. Grow, "Meek Mill's Legal Troubles"; and "TIMELINE: Meek Mill's Legal Troubles Date Back to 2007," CBS Philadelphia, April 25, 2018: https://philadelphia.cbslocal.com/2018/04/25/meek-mill-timeline/.

40. Reuben Jonathan Miller, *Halfway Home: Race, Punishment, and the Afterlife of Mass Incarceration* (New York: Little, Brown and Company, 2020), 9.

41. Grow, "Meek Mill's Legal Troubles."

42. Larry Krasner, "District Attorney Krasner Statement on Plea Agreement Resolving Commonwealth v. Robert Williams (Meek Mill)," Philadelphia District Attorney's Office, August 27, 2019, https://medium.com/philadelphia-justice/district-attorney-krasner-statement-on-plea-agreement-resolving-commonwealth-v-da3839aa7851.

43. Bobby Allyn (@BobbyAllyn), "It's now official: The 12-year-old case against Meek Mill is finally over," Twitter, August 27, 2019, 9:59 a.m., https://twitter.com/BobbyAllyn/status/1166349424899100672.

44. Grow, "Meek Mill's Legal Troubles."

45. Krasner, "District Attorney Krasner Statement on Plea Agreement."

46. Julie Bosman et al., "Amid Conflicting Accounts, Trusting Darren Wilson," *The New York Times*, November 25, 2014, https://www.nytimes.com/2014/11/26/us/ferguson-grand-jury-weighed-mass-of-evidence-much-of-it-conflicting.html; and Eyder Peralta and Bill Chappell, "Ferguson Jury: No Charges for Officer in Michael Brown's Death," NPR, November 24, 2014, https://www.npr.org/sections/thetwo-way/2014/11/24/366370100/grand-jury-reaches-decision-in-michael-brown-case.
    Wilson was cleared of criminal wrongdoing by the state of Missouri and the Justice Department, but in 2017, the city of Ferguson awarded Mr. Brown's parents, Ms. Lezley McSpadden and Mr. Michael Brown, Sr., $1.5 million to settle a wrongful-death civil suit against Officer Wilson, the Ferguson police chief, and the city of Ferguson. Where the DOJ's report only implied a connection between Ferguson's racially discriminatory police and municipal policies and the fatal shooting of Michael Brown, Jr., the civil lawsuit filed on behalf of Mr. Brown's parents claimed that "the city fostered a culture of pervasive hostility toward African-Americans that eventually led to the

18-year-old's death last August." (Koran Addo, "Michael Brown's Family Files Wrongful-Death Lawsuit," *St. Louis Post-Dispatch*, April 24, 2015, https://www.stltoday.com/news/local/crime-and-courts/article_c2c9fd8a-9664-5653-80f0-c38a507ca23e.html.)

47. "Department of Justice Report Regarding the Criminal Investigation into the Shooting Death of Michael Brown by Ferguson, Missouri Police Officer Darren Wilson," United States Department of Justice, March 4, 2015, 5, https://www.justice.gov/sites/default/files/opa/press-releases/attachments/2015/03/04/doj_report_on_shooting_of_michael_brown_1.pdf.

48. "Investigation of the Ferguson Police Department," United States Department of Justice, Civil Rights Division, March 4, 2015, 80, https://www.justice.gov/sites/default/files/opa/press-releases/attachments/2015/03/04/ferguson_police_department_report.pdf.

    Officer Darren Wilson served two years in the police department in Jennings, Missouri, and four years in the police department in nearby Ferguson. The city of Jennings was predominantly Black, and the police department was predominantly white. The Jennings City Council fired every police officer as tensions between Black residents and white officers rendered the police department dysfunctional.

    See Natalie DiBlasio, "What We Know About Ferguson Officer Darren Wilson," *USA Today*, August 19, 2014, https://www.usatoday.com/story/news/nation/2014/08/19/darren-wilson-ferguson/14280623/; and Carol D. Leonnig, Kimberly Kindy, and Joel Achenbach, "Darren Wilson's First Job Was on a Troubled Police Force Disbanded by Authorities," *The Washington Post*, August 23, 2014, https://www.washingtonpost.com/national/darren-wilsons-first-job-was-on-a-troubled-police-force-disbanded-by-authorities/2014/08/23/1ac796f0-2a45-11e4-8593-da634b334390_story.html.

49. "Department of Justice Report Regarding the Criminal Investigation into the Shooting Death of Michael Brown," 6–7.

50. Jennifer Mason McAward, "Defining the Badges and Incidents of Slavery," *Journal of Constitutional Law* 14, no. 3 (2012): 563, https://scholarship.law.upenn.edu/cgi/viewcontent.cgi?article=1046&context=jcl.

51. McAward, "Defining the Badges and Incidents of Slavery," 561.

52. "Supreme Court of the United States. Plessy v. Ferguson. May 18, 1896," *The Virginia Law Register* 2, no. 5 (September 1896): 327–47, https://doi.org/10.2307/1099065.

53. "Investigation of the Ferguson Police Department," 1–2.

54. "Investigation of the Ferguson Police Department," 76.

55. "Investigation of the Ferguson Police Department," 1–2.

56. "Investigation of the Ferguson Police Department," 4, 46.

57. "Investigation of the Ferguson Police Department," 62.

58. "Investigation of the Ferguson Police Department," 42–43, 56. The report noted: "While the City Council repealed the Failure to Appear ordinance in September 2014, many people continue to owe fines and fees stemming from that charge. And the court continues to issue arrest warrants in every case where that charge previously would have been applied." ("Investigation of the Ferguson Police Department," 43.)

59. "Investigation of the Ferguson Police Department," 55–56.

60. "Investigation of the Ferguson Police Department," 4–5, 62.

61. "Investigation of the Ferguson Police Department," 74.

62. "Investigation of the Ferguson Police Department," 9.

63. "Investigation of the Ferguson Police Department," 42.

64. "Investigation of the Ferguson Police Department," 3.

65. "Investigation of the Ferguson Police Department," 75.

66. "Investigation of the Ferguson Police Department," 75.

67. "Investigation of the Ferguson Police Department," 75.

68. Peggy McIntosh, "White Privilege and Male Privilege: A Personal Account of Coming to See Correspondences Through Work in Women's Studies," in *Critical White Studies: Looking Behind the Mirror*, eds. Richard Delgado and Jean Stefancic (Philadelphia: Temple University Press, 1997), 291–299, 295.

69. McIntosh, "White Privilege and Male Privilege," 291, 293, 296.

70. McIntosh, "White Privilege and Male Privilege," 291, 293.

71. Fourteenth Amendment: "Article XIV, Section1, The Constitution," from *The Debate on the Constitution, Part One*, ed. Bernard Bailyn (New York: Library of America, 1993), 985–86.

72. McIntosh, "White Privilege and Male Privilege," 296.

73. "Figure 3. Distribution of Total Population and Poverty by Race Using the Official Poverty Measure: 2021," United States Census Bureau, https://www.census.gov/content/dam/Census/library/visualizations/2022/demo/p60-277/figure3.pdf.

74. McIntosh, "White Privilege and Male Privilege," 296.

75. McIntosh, "White Privilege and Male Privilege," 298.

76. James Baldwin, "The Price of the Ticket," in *James Baldwin: Collected Essays*, ed. Toni Morrison (New York, Library of America, 1998), 841.

77. Baldwin, "The Price of the Ticket," 842.

# CHAPTER 7

# AN ACCOUNTING

## WHAT PROFITETH A MAN, WOMAN, TRIBE, TOWN, OR NATION TO GAIN "THE WORLD"?

Cities like Ferguson, Missouri, are implicated in the arc of Black impoverishment that stretches back to colonial America. As the Ferguson finance director, city manager, police department, and clerk of court utilized the city's accounting system in their collaborations to maximize revenue by targeting and exploiting African American residents, so colonial plantation owners also used accounting practices as a tactic of Black oppression.

Colonial planters utilized the tools of accounting to record agricultural experiments and to document the improved quality and the yield increase of their crops. They also used that accounting data to inform and manage production processes, monitor and control enslaved laborers, generate inventories and reports of capital assets, and estimate profits. In *Accounting for Slavery: Masters and Management*, the historian Caitlin Rosenthal traces the development of these early accounting systems and managerial practices, from their West Indian slave plantation origins to their evolution in the contemporary American corporate economy.

The most calculating colonial planters, disparaged as "book farmers," writes Rosenthal, maintained records as sophisticated and comprehensive as their industrial counterparts.[1] Slave plantations became laboratories for the systemization and the standardization of accounting practices "because neat columns of numbers translated more easily to life on plantations than they did in many other early American enterprises." This was particularly true of cotton plantations, where large-scale, "elite planters" and their managers meticulously recorded the pounds of cotton picked on a "slave-by-slave basis" on a given day and throughout a season.[2]

As the life force of Black men, women, and children was extracted to fuel the "human machine" that kept the wheels of production turning, planters focused keenly on labor productivity. They experimented with factors of time and motion and allocation of their "units of labor" and analyzed the data collected to improve efficiency, accelerate production, and increase profits.[3] Some planters held out material incentives and cash bonuses as rewards to push performance. Others were more likely to drive performance with the lash of the bullwhip and other forms of violence and intimidation, favoring punishment, rather than the trickery of rewards, to force maximum work productivity.

Given their near-absolute power and control over virtually every aspect of the lives of their "human capital," plantation owners and their team of managers and overseers could analyze labor productivity with precision. Their emphasis on monitoring and measuring the performance of their enslaved workforce foreshadowed "the rise of scientific management" that would be associated with Northern factories and industries and, later, with multistory mega-warehouses.[4] And their innovations in accounting technologies and their practical applications greatly influenced the accounting and managerial practices that characterized the early capitalist systems, like textile factories and railroad companies, that emerged in the late nineteenth century. That influence would reverberate into the twenty-first century, in the late capitalist-oligarchic practices of corporate America.

This history, "the business history of plantation slavery," observes Rosenthal, has been effectively erased from standard texts that surveyed historical developments in American business and management, and its omission constitutes a "denial of slavery" in the development of modern American capitalism. Though some studies recognized the plantation overseer as the "first salaried manager" in America, they also dismissed the plantation and its operations as an archaic relic of America's antebellum past.[5]

An inclusion of plantation slavery in business and management history complicates the official narrative. That history allows us to see clearly how what has been heralded as *sophisticated* and *innovative* in the business practices of "book farmers" and early industrialists has always been compatible with the barbarity that belies "vastly unequal power and wealth."[6] Embracing that history allows us to begin to get to the roots of an economic system that has been used as a tool of oppression against people of color and the working poor, as well as the unwitting white, middle-class American.

Recognition and appreciation of this otherwise hidden and rejected history helps us to see how we all have become enthralled in the nightmare of relentless productivity—not unlike a cow who is forced to lactate her whole abbreviated life—in service to the powerful few, the ten-percenters, the neo–"master class." So that the wheels of plantation production would never stop spinning, the children of the enslaved were entrained at an early age to perpetuate the cycles of slave-plantation life. Plantation owners and their attorney-managers and overseers allocated groups of children to pulling grass or weeding with hoes sized for the hands of the youngest of children and made as small as "No. 0." Such tasks and processes prepared their youthful "property" for a lifetime of "constant work."[7]

Similarly, Americans, particularly marginalized Americans, have been expected to work constantly. The history of this push toward relentless productivity remains largely obscured. "We live in a global economy where the labor of production is often invisible," explains Caitlin Rosenthal:

> Distance and quantitative management facilitate this erasure, and assumptions about capitalism and freedom help conceal it. Neither "free" trade nor "free" markets have any necessary relationship with other kinds of human freedoms. Indeed, the history of plantation slavery shows that the opposite can be true.[8]

Among the assumptions that Rosenthal references is the assumption that the free enterprise system of capitalism, together with the spirit of innovation and the properly implemented hierarchies of accounting and management systems, would benefit the whole of American society: "higher profits for business, higher earnings for laborers, and lower prices for consumers."[9] However, this purportedly *free* enterprise system is part of an economic continuum that is rooted in the worldview and the practical reality of plantation slavery. And at the core of this economic worldview is the "master-slave" construct.

At our peril, we dismiss and excuse the violence of the planter class, enabled and empowered by the "rule of law," in the dehumanization and objectification of an enslaved workforce. At our peril, we overlook the business administration of slave-plantation estates and their use of accounting and management practices to extract the maximum amount of labor possible from brutalized, captive human beings in the name of relentless production and profit. At our peril, we forget that economic freedom in America, then and now, meant the freedom to enslave others—*in perpetuity*.

At the 1787 Constitutional Convention in Philadelphia, delegate General Charles Cotesworth Pinckney expressed his opinion "that while there remained one acre of swampland uncleared of South Carolina, I would raise my voice against restricting the importation of negroes." The nature of their climate and swampy terrain obliged them, he declared, "to cultivate our lands with negroes."[10] Though pro-slavery colonists like Pinckney would subject Africans to enslavement, they would resist *slavery* themselves. English colonists revolted against England precisely because they perceived trade restrictions and imposed taxation to be acts of tyranny that reduced them to the condition not of ill-used subjects but of *slaves*:

> *Those* who are *taxed* without their own consent expressed by themselves or their representatives . . . are *slaves*. *We are taxed* without our consent expressed by ourselves or our representatives. *We* are therefore—SLAVES.[11]

Revolutionary diplomat John Adams underscored this perspective, stating that the colonists were "the most abject sort of slaves, to the worst sort of masters!" Apparently, as a political term, expounds A. Leon Higginbotham, Jr., "slavery" "had two different meanings": "for whites it described any enactment that limited their economic freedom of action or reduced the value of their property when they had not previously elected representatives to vote on that impediment." Ironically, Higginbotham mused, in relation to Black persons, "those arbitrary acts of physically enslaving blacks, despite the absence of black consent, were not embraced within the slavery definition whites used in condemning the king's abuses."[12]

The irony and the perfidy of monied white men claiming freedom for themselves while claiming others as their "private property," counting that "property" among their accumulation of capital, and then, a little further along the line of the economic continuum, talking about free enterprise and free market forces, cannot be lost on us. Such men perceived the abolition of the transatlantic trafficking of Africans and the dismantling of America's Peculiar Institution not so much as a moral and philosophico-political issue, but rather, as a government-imposed market regulation that affected their economic bottom line.[13]

Thus, plantation owners, slave dealers, and other antidemocratic and supremacist whites resisted the worldview reflected in the larger American principles of universal freedom, personal sovereignty, and equal opportunity. They would later conspire to plunge the nation into civil war in order to maintain control of the "peculiar labor" that was the engine of their wealth and the basis of their claim to aristocratic, elitist privilege.

⚅ ⚅ ⚅

At the sundown of antebellum America and upon the horizon of a democratic republic, at the economic crossroads of plantation slavery and free enterprise capitalism, at the juncture of the Southern plantocracy and Northern modernity, at the pivotal moment of the possibility of Black freedom and the contradicting proviso of the criminal-punishment loophole, hung the economic noose about the neck of the newly free African American citizen.

Persistent in the development of the American conscience has been the presence of the malevolent "master-slave" construct. Just as England's prohibition of the "slave trade" in 1807 and abolition of slavery in the Caribbean colonies in 1833 contributed to a "second slavery,"[14] so America's abolition of slavery in 1865 did not end the practice but ushered in the "free market" innovation of the convict-leasing system, reproducing the "master-slave" dynamic of the plantation and re-establishing the South's social, economic, and political hierarchy.

As violent punishment was the primary tool for enforcing plantation law and for pushing Black people to attain steadily increasing targets of maximum productivity, so punishment became the foundational basis of American penal institutions, and the violence of maximum sentences "at hard labor," as authorized by the Criminal Punishment Clause, became justified as fit punishment for the masses of incarcerated African American citizens in the South and beyond. For a consequence of the criminal-exception clause was that the early American barbarism of "slavery" leached into the whole of the nation, compromising America's modernism and thwarting its evolution into a more perfect union.

The loophole again established the "due subjection" of the Black person.[15] Once again, Black life became "human capital." Once again, Black men, women, boys, and girls became the "cheap" labor supply that would generate for both agriculturalists and industrialists the products and profits that they obsessed after. The convict-leasing system did not end when state and federal government officials resumed direct control of imprisoned populations. The leasing system simply became a contracting system where imprisoned laborers were contracted out. As "slaves" became "convicts," "leases" became "contracts."

America's criminal-punishment system is rooted in the same sociocultural worldview that evolved the slave-plantation system. Thus the function of America's mass incarceration system simulates the function of the slave-plantation system, and the pyramidal hierarchy of the criminal-punishment bureaucracy mimics the administrative structure of the slave plantation. Where the plantation estate owner and his main attorney were perched at the top of the administrative pyramid that accounted for and ordered the operations of plantation production, state officials and their prosecuting attorneys top the administrative pyramid of the criminal-punishment system (see Figure 2). Like the plantation attorney whose responsibility was to maintain a reliable supply of "slave labor," prosecuting attorneys in the criminal-punishment system initiate "the transfer of thirteen million bodies each year from their homes and families and schools and communities into government boxes of concrete and metal."[16]

Like their colonial and antebellum counterparts, modern American attorneys and politicians bank on the commodification of Black freedom. Our freedom is something we have had to purchase—if we could. If one could scrape up enough money, like Venture Smith; acquire the financial support of civic or religious activists, as did Elizabeth Keckley; or win the lottery, as was the case with Denmark Vesey, one might be able to get one's self purchased and experience some semblance of personal sovereignty.

# HIERARCHICAL LAYERS OF THE CRIMINAL PUNISHMENT BUREAUCRACY

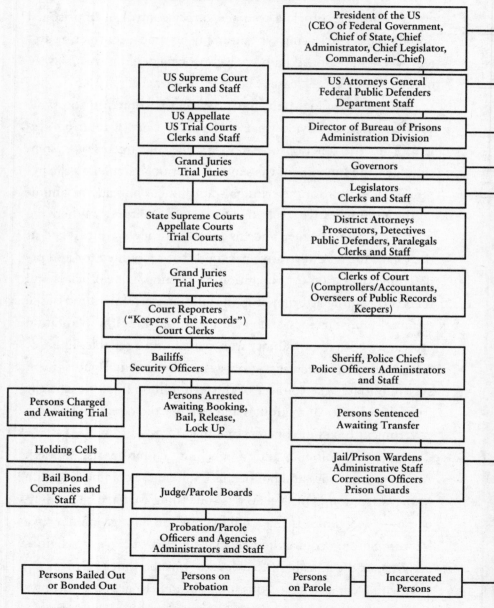

FIGURE 1. THE MULTI-LAYERED HIERARCHY OF THE CRIMINAL-PUNISHMENT BUREAUCRACY. AS WITHIN THE SLAVE PLANTATION ESTATE SYSTEM, ATTORNEYS, MANAGERS, PUBLIC OFFICIALS, AND CORPORATE HEADS OVERSEE THE FEDERAL AND STATE CRIMINAL

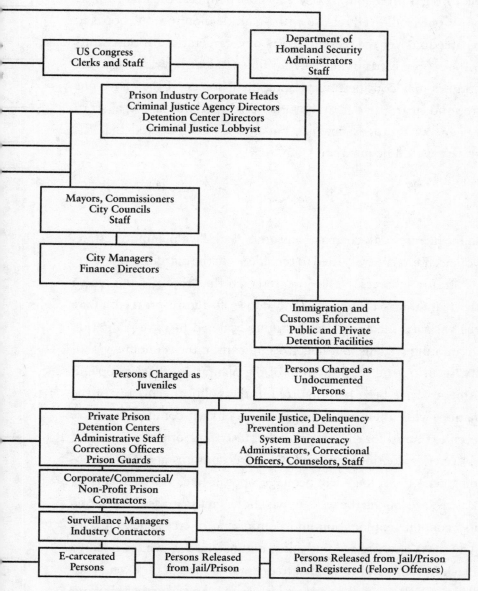

US Congress
Clerks and Staff

Department of
Homeland Security
Administrators
Staff

Prison Industry Corporate Heads
Criminal Justice Agency Directors
Detention Center Directors
Criminal Justice Lobbyist

Mayors, Commissioners
City Councils
Staff

City Managers
Finance Directors

Immigration and
Customs Enforcement
Public and Private
Detention Facilities

Persons Charged as
Juveniles

Persons Charged as
Undocumented
Persons

Private Prison
Detention Centers
Administrative Staff
Corrections Officers
Prison Guards

Juvenile Justice, Delinquency
Prevention and Detention
System Bureaucracy
Administrators, Correctional
Officers, Counselors, Staff

Corporate/Commercial/
Non-Profit Prison
Contractors

Surveillance Managers
Industry Contractors

E-carcerated
Persons

Persons Released
from Jail/Prison

Persons Released from Jail/Prison
and Registered (Felony Offenses)

INJUSTICE SYSTEM, AS THEIR ACCOUNTANTS, ADMINISTRATORS, CLERKS, AND RECORD KEEPERS
PROVIDE THE CONVENTIONAL AND DIGITAL TECHNOLOGY AND DATA THAT STRUCTURES,
UPHOLDS, REINFORCES, AND MAINTAINS THE CRIMINAL-PUNISHMENT BUREAUCRACY.

In "freedom," we struggle to remain free. Or, in the case of jailed or imprisoned loved ones like my brother Bobby, we struggle to regain freedom. If one can post bail, one breathes a little bit. If one is allowed release with an ankle monitor, one hopes to be able to cover the fees and costs of e-carceration. If one wants to be represented in court by an independent lawyer, desperate families may consider mortgaging their home—if they have one free and clear. My dad and brother discussed this last legal strategy in my brother's defense, but my brother believed that the system would be just.

☒  ☒  ☒

In the hierarchical schema of a prototypical slave-plantation estate, young children were "listed to the side"—in the margins, as it were, as "future laborers."[17] They represented the "stock" from which the plantation's economy would derive its future proceeds. Like the enslaved Black children marginally noted in slave-plantation accounting systems, but hugely significant in the economic viability, security, and profit margin of the plantation, Black people in America have been marginalized in the political economy of the nation, while the wealth and resources of their communities have been extracted for the benefit of "mainstream" others.

America continues to hold Black freedom hostage. Sharecropping, tenant farming, debt peonage, and the like, as well as convict leasing, are among the ways in which the "master class" reasserted its economic exploitation and domination of free Black citizens. This class of racialized and elitist and patriarchal whites resented Black freedom and continued to operate as though they were entitled to Black labor and productivity. In the same way that Haitians were forced to pay reparations to France in order to hold on to the independence that they fought for and won, so the Southern establishment demanded that Black people pay a premium for their freedom.

African Americans have historically paid a "color tax," as Martin Luther King, Jr., called it.[18] That tax includes the violent taking of Black lives and property, the exorbitant prices paid for the most basic necessities of daily life, the exclusion from state and federal financial programs and federally secured suburban housing opportunities, and the "weathering" consequent to enduring second-class citizenship.[19] Consider, for instance, these incidents, badges, and relics:

- Dispossession of millions of acres of African American farmland[20]
- Government-sanctioned residential segregation[21]
- Inadequate or infrequent provision of basic city or county services
- Denial of veteran benefits
- Root shock: deracination of African American families and communities through urban renewal and re-development programs[22]
- Redlining
- Food deserts
- Inadequate access to healthcare; implicit bias in assessment, treatment, and pain management
- Enthrallment in the American injustice system

The shackle around the ankle of the African in Angola, Dahomey, Gorée, became the ball and chain around the ankle of the "duly convicted," and the ball and chain became the GPS monitoring device around the ankle of persons on parole, persons on probation, persons convicted of nothing. The electronic monitoring device permits those unable to post bail to be released from jail to await their trial at home. Sometimes equipped with a two-way microphone, it allows law enforcement to track those under house arrest.

Known also as an "ankle bracelet," the device is considered a reform measure. In reality, the electronic chain is not an alternative to the incarceration of persons—who are presumed innocent, "It's an alternative *form* of incarceration," says the professor of law Kate Weisburd.[23] Also considered an *innovation* within the criminal-punishment industry, this electronic surveillance device is another means of generating profit for the industry and its criminal-punishment bureaucracy.

Pretrial defendants are required to pay private companies a daily, weekly, or monthly user fee, installation and removal fees, fees for violating rules associated with the use of the device, and fees for late payments. Defendants must also maintain landline or cell-phone services. The costs associated with the "bracelet" are charges in addition to other court costs. And the accumulation of costs incurred for this innovation often exceeds the original bail amount imposed. Bureaucrats who institute "'offender funded' payment plans" callously ignore that the same economic conditions that made it impossible for defendants and their families to make bail in the first place would also prevent them from keeping up with an e-surveillance payment plan, driving families into debt and the defendant back to jail.[24] Driving criminalized Black citizens and their families into debt replicates the ruse of erstwhile plantocrats who, in reestablishing their social and economic control over freed Black folk, substituted the power of ownership of Black bodies for "the power of debt."[25]

The technological devices designed to enslave, imprison, detain, constrict, and control us have gone through many innovations and upgrades. Law enforcement agents have been weaponized, militarized, computerized, and armed with robots programmed to deliver payloads of C-4 explosives.[26] These "advancements" are used to continually and disproportionately keep Black people in the crosshairs. And yet, as with the minority-white inhabitants of eighteenth-century South Carolina, an anxious insecurity is the nation's abiding feeling because we refuse to look at the roots of our fear. Moreover, we continue to accept the problematic "law-and-order" discourse of run-of-the-mill politicians who are *against* criminal justice reform or *for* reforms that maintain the status quo and who avoid the deeper dive into a politics that supports societal transformation.

We care a great deal about how to physically subdue, subjugate, and destroy a human being. We've been indoctrinated to care a great deal about punishment and making people "pay." But we don't care enough about freedom—unless our little eddy of it appears threatened. We don't care enough about equality and inclusion—not as long as we feel ourselves somehow privileged or beyond "the law." And those among us who perceive ourselves as the true and protected class of Americans entitled to constitutional privileges and immunities, glory in the orchestrated subjugation of Black people and other peoples of color. As "now, more than ever," this faction among us appears "to measure their safety in chains and corpses."[27]

And all of us Americans have either been kept unaware of or have ourselves willfully ignored the history of the madness that developed on British and American slave plantations and the transmutation of that madness into the American "free enterprise" system. Collapsing American history into a sound bite that spins a politicized and deliberate misreading of "critical race theory" (or "CRT") simply extends the willful ignorance. An enchanted version of our history makes us gullible and complacent and leaves us uninformed and ill-equipped to reckon with the complexity of our inheritance.

Ignoring how the "slave-plantation" system converted human beings into "human capital" and how the legal system converted American citizens into "criminals" who become "human capital" prevents us from understanding how that same system is the foundation and impulse of today's sociocultural and economic phenomena of the haves and the have-nots, "the rich and the rest,"[28] and the one- to ten-percenters who control 90 percent of the nation's wealth, in contrast to the ninety-percenters who were left to occupy Wall Street, briefly.

Ignoring the continuum from "slave-plantation" production to modern corporate, high-tech mass production and distribution prevents us from seeing how we've become cogs in the same colonial and antebellum wheels that rolled over the masses of people for the profit of a few, producing unsustainable imbalances in financial and social wealth. Labeling "slave-planation" production as "archaic" and "preindustrial" and erasing the influential business history of plantation estates prevents us from identifying America's "Peculiar Institution" as an American industry. It keeps us from discerning how today's business conglomerates and corporations operate on the same "master-slave" paradigm and generate the same catastrophic social and political consequences. Journalist Matthew Stewart articulates the comparison:

In the first half of the 19th century, the largest single industry in the United States, measured in terms of both market capital and employment, was the enslavement (and the breeding for enslavement) of human beings. Over the course of the period, the industry became concentrated to the point where fewer than 4,000 families (roughly 0.1 percent of the households in the nation) owned about a quarter of this "human capital," and another 390,000 (call it the 9.9 percent, give or take a few points) owned all of the rest.[29]

Allowing "elite," antidemocratic politicians who have been funded and empowered by "elite," monopolistic corporations to short-circuit our critical-reasoning capacity and deaden our human endowment of empathy and compassion effectively blinds us to how they bind us to an economic system that has no humanity.[30] In other words, we're all free to be locked up, to be under constant surveillance, and to have our life force extracted from us in the name of continuous production, perverse consumerism, and corporate profit.

❌ ❌ ❌

Slavery has always been the ball and chain that puts the lie to the myth of a "free market" enterprise system. It has always loomed over the lot of the "'free labor' market" and has been the competitive edge for enslavers and their posterity who have historically found ways to disparage and spurn the free-wage earner. The relationship between employer and employee, between management and labor, between administrative "bosses" and their rank-and-file "subordinates" has been fraught with the kind of challenges and conflicts characteristic of feudal lords and peasants, and "masters" and "slaves."

We have all been drugged, chained, and turned into property, as Walter Mosley enlightens us in *Workin' on the Chain Gang: Shaking Off the Dead Hand of History*. Hundreds of TV, cable, and internet-streamed shows and entertainment are the opium. "And money is the super-drug, the one fix that you can't leave cold turkey—because the withdrawal would be fatal. Money has also formed the bonds of our imprisonment. Our labor binds us to systems that can see us only as units of value or expense."[31]

And these systems are not interested in us—only in our life force, the kind of labor our life force can undertake, the products or services it can produce, and the profits it can generate. The person has little value beyond this extraction. We may or may not be shocked to know that in accounting for the appreciation and depreciation of their "human stock," planters and overseers recorded the value of elderly enslaved persons as $0.00. "In the language of twentieth century business these slaves had a negative net present value, meaning the market deemed them less than worthless."[32]

The incidents and badges associated with chattel slavery—with that peculiar form of slavery that objectifies a human being as capital, cattle, a brute, a thing, a machine, as property—are more and more associated with all divisions of labor in the American workforce. Wherein comparisons have long been made between the enslaved laborer and the wage earner, the same comparison is now frequently made with salaried workers who had assumed themselves beyond the indignities suffered by "blue-collar" workers. Only a wish to move up into the class of the ten-percenters or a fear of plunging into the despair of becoming one of the working poor keeps the middle-class American worker from looking at her and his kinship with the historically marginalized, subjugated, and exploited African American.[33]

While millions of African Americans have been criminalized

and populate actual cells in America's jails and prisons, corporate workers—and those employed in institutions that are organized on the corporate model—have been reduced to units of labor that populate the cubicles in the offices of America's corporate fiefdoms and empires. The digitized details of their identity populate spreadsheets that organize the data under headings that denote their names, titles, employee numbers, and assignments. And their "output" is quantified and accounted for in the cells formed by the neat rows and columns that capture their productivity and calculate their worth.

As plantation estate owners and criminal-punishment bureaucrats utilized accounting data and a multilayered administrative hierarchy to manage operations and control enslaved and imprisoned workers, respectively, so executives of modern and contemporary institutions, industries, and corporations utilize accounting systems and managerial practices to facilitate their operations and control their "free" workers. Surveilling and timing workers in order to increase production efficiency did not begin with Henry Ford's stalking his assembly line of employees with a stopwatch.[34] No less than railroad company managers, Ford's "scientific management" approach to productivity, like that of Frederick Winslow Taylor, the "Father of Scientific Management," was preceded by and influenced by the processes of "scientific agriculture" as practiced by "book-farming" planters.

Before the 1888 invention of the employee time clock, there was the plantation timekeeper and the daily work log. Before Pinkerton detective agents monitored company employees during work hours, spied on them after hours, reported on their discontentment, disrupted unions, or infiltrated the meetings to form unions, there were "slave patrols." The Pinkerton Agency, a collaboration between Allan Pinkerton and his attorney, Edward

Rucker, was formed in the 1850s. Not coincidentally, the agency was originally called the North-Western Police Agency.[35]

Controlling the "labor supply" has been as much of an obsession with many modern and contemporary American entrepreneurs as it had been with their enslaving predecessors. In extracting the maximum amount of labor in the least amount of time from the human beings they relied on to mass produce their products and services, late nineteenth-, twentieth-, and twenty-first-century industrial and corporate employers took a page out of the accounting and management ledger of "slave-plantation masters." In doing so, they also imposed on their employees the incidents and badges of slavery.

What was corporate downsizing but a stratagem—comparable with the plantation practice of pushing the enslaved toward continuous and ever-increasing maximum output—that was employed to force one employee to do the work of two or three? What are high-tech employee-monitoring-and-tracking systems but digitized "slave-plantation overseers"? As plantation owners and overseers cared nothing about separating enslaved family members, corporate managers care neither about the longer hours, weekends, and holidays employees spend working, nor the collateral consequences of family alienation.

News articles and reports inform us that the scientific tracking of employee productivity has been on the rise since the 1980s.[36] In actuality, the current wave of workplace monitoring is part of a continuum that flows from the overseeing of the enslaved plantation worker to the surveilling of the corporate employee. Whether working in the public or private sector, whether working on-site or remotely, whether classified as a white-, blue-, pink-, tan-, or gray-collared worker, the American worker, more and more, is subject to the treatment of those in America who wore the iron collar of slavery.

Espousing the centuries-old narrative about "efficiency" and "productivity," employers continue to obscure their addiction to profit and justify the objectification and dehumanization of the American workforce. Where wage-earning workers have endured constant and invasive scrutiny, salaried "white-collar" and "pink-collar" workers are now commonly subject to the same indignities. Employee-monitoring-and-tracking software counts computer keystrokes, takes screenshots, and documents websites visited and emails sent and received. The algorithms of AI software detect what you might be thinking or feeling.[37] Visible and hidden cameras are strategically installed in the workplace to capture your movements and police your activities.

Employees who have jobs that require them to travel beyond the main office or those who work from home are not any less unfree. Their laptops or cell phones—typically provided by "the company"—function like the electronic ankle bracelet of someone under house arrest. And like someone under house arrest or like the "fugitive slave," when an employee—whether in the main office, home office, or mobile office—is "reported" in the monitoring system as "derelict," "inactive," "idle," or "offline," that employee is subject to being reprimanded or punished. The employee's paycheck, bonus pay, or promotion is affected by how the surveilling system classifies tasks and accounts for an employee's time. The computer-configured "productivity score" can influence whether an employee remains employed or is fired.[38]

Is it coincidental that at the core of computer terminology is a hierarchical model of control or communication that has been named "master/slave"?[39] This "technosocial" language describes the unidirectional control of one hardware device over one or more other devices. This "master-slave" terminology was first used in 1904 to describe a certain kind of clock, a two-part sidereal clock.[40] Applied to other technical systems as well, the "master-slave" terminology became more common in the US during the 1960s, in relation to computers.[41] Computer scientists explained the Dartmouth time-sharing system that facilitated computer programming in such terms:

> First, all computing for users takes place in the slave computer, while the executive program (the "brains" of the system) resides in the master computer. It is thus impossible for an erroneous or runaway user program in the slave computer to "damage" the executive program and thereby bring the whole system to a halt.[42]

Some researchers describe the language used to articulate the relationship between the two devices as "inaccurate," given that the devices actually operated autonomously. And though they acknowledge the "technosocial metaphor" to be controversial, the researchers believe the use of such terminology has nothing to do with historical slavery and that "there was no conscious intention to echo pre-Civil War discourse on runaway slaves." Perhaps, it was concluded, the metaphor operated within the tech community "at a subconscious level."[43] However, recent discussion in the tech community has reopened the subject for debate.[44]

⚔ ⚔ ⚔

The ubiquitous monitoring and tracking of wage-earning employees and the exponential expansion of such practices among salaried employees is explained by managers and CEOs as a matter of efficiency, security, and accountability. However, employees have experienced electronic nano-management as problematic in how it perceives and measures productivity. The currency of informal conversation, for example, is essential to human interaction, networking, and relationship building. But such activities are seldom integrated into monitoring systems, or they are not accounted for, and are thusly understood to be counterproductive. Employees also experienced constant surveilling and tracking as personally invasive, a violation of their constitutional right to privacy, and a denial of their personal sovereignty.

In the age of the electronic overseer, even taking a coffee break or the inevitable bathroom break has caused employees concern and distress. Caffeine used to be touted as a "gift to capitalism" because it improved focus and concentration, which were seen as the "keys to the safety and success of the machine-based labor that powered the Industrial Revolution." Since the 1940s, coffee breaks have been part of the work environment, as employers had "institutionalized a drug for the express purpose of improving productivity and quality control."[45]

The coffee break was formerly perceived as just the thing to power an employee through the eight-hour workday. It also had the effect of regulating and elevating an employee's mood, as the respite allowed for the fact that human beings are gregarious creatures. They need to gather socially. They need to express.[46] But the gift to capitalism is a casualty in the march toward greater efficiency and higher profit margins. "It is the nature of capitalism to apply its value system to everything."[47] And in its present configuration, humanity has no value. In the configuration of this economic system that assigns everything a specific value—as is the case in computer software programming—

technology itself has increased in value in direct proportion to the depreciation of human labor.

It is noteworthy that productivity technology has garnered a great deal of interest from investors. Employee-tracking or "performance-management" software is "one of the fastest-growing categories" in workplace technologies.[48] In step with investments in workplace monitoring are investments in "the so-called community-corrections market" that provides e-carceration services and devices like ankle monitors and "represents one of the fastest-growing revenue sectors" of the jail-prison industry.[49]

If the consensus is that efficiency and profit are the main, if not the only, endgame of capitalist production, then the masses of Americans are working themselves out of a job and are being abused and insulted in the process. Tracking-and-monitoring systems are basically designed to effectively separate labor from the laborer, as a cook would separate the yellow yolk of an egg from the surrounding egg white. In other words, computer programs, surveillance monitors, algorithms, webcams, GPS trackers, pressure and heat sensors, et cetera, are consciously aggregated by program and systems designers to extract a human being's physical, intellectual, creative, and even spiritual capacities. Technological programs and processes are calculated to exploit the human being as "company property" and to take what a person has to offer a company while diminishing her personhood and undermining her professionalism.

In the case of employees within the healthcare industry, for example, the constant accounting for "accomplishments" and time spent with clients intervenes in a healthcare provider's ability to provide the quality and standard of care she is trained and inspired to render. The pressure of economizing time spent with clients is exacerbated by constantly increasing caseloads. As a veteran hospice-care provider informed me, anymore, the kind of expertise that comes with graduate-level education, additional certifications, and experience is valued less and less. The recent change in the management of the organization that employed her brought with it the kind of pervasive and intrusive employee monitoring that has resulted in employee dissatisfaction, burn-out, and a high turnover rate.

In addition to being on call most of the time and spending her own time entering client data into the system, she was then required to train a new employee, a recent graduate with a bachelor's degree. She was expected to download her wealth of knowl-edge and expertise into the apprentice, as it were. The throughline in this case in point is the continued effort of "management" to convert the human worker into "interchangeable chattel." Once the perceived essential aspects of a profession are reduced to dis-crete units of tasks, rubrics, or objectives to be completed in an allotted period of time, then the employee doesn't need to think, reason, or exercise discretion, just do what the system dictates. Only a certain level of proficiency is required, rendering the highly skilled, professional, and credentialed employee obsoles-cent, disposable, easy to discard, like all the electronic gadgets and devices that crest American landfills.

⁂

The lawful ramifications of corporate surveillance of employees are legion. Lawsuits have been filed as a consequence of negative productivity reports and the invasion of employee privacy.[50] But in the main, surveillance of workers is practically normative. As the journalist Zoë Corbyn puts it, "Bossware is coming for almost every worker."[51] And even though Americans have the right to privacy, period, and in spite of the fact that "the people" are a sovereign power that is equal with the power of the state and federal government, one wonders whether the enslavement of the American worker can be effectively fought in the courts.

As the attorney Alec Karakatsanis says in relation to the imprisonment of millions of American citizens, "dismantling the system of mass human caging is not a legal battle for lawyers. It is, fundamentally, a political one. It is about power."[52] And so we need to understand that we are being disempowered. We need to investigate the means by which our constitutionally granted power is being undermined and nullified. We need to interrogate the oppressiveness of our own situations and be open to seeing the realities of marginalized "others," open to listening to historical narratives that are our common heritage, open to expanding our knowledge and evolving our consciousness. We need to ask questions of ourselves and our government.

What have the courts and the legislatures done about economic injustices, such as employer wage theft, for instance? What has Congress done about the unlivable wages of millions of Americans who are "tipped" employees, that is, employees whose incomes depend on tips? Tipped employees, who are predominantly females and people of color, are part of an industry that continues the legacy of "slavery." This legacy takes us back to post–Civil War America, wherein emancipated Black citizens could get jobs in service industries as waitresses, bellhops, and Pullman porters and such. But employers did not pay them wages. Their pay was only the tips they received. The "slave's wage" in these industries is still the rule.[53] Why does the gender pay gap persist despite the 1963 Equal Pay Act? Why is it that corporations, tech companies chief among them, rake in record profits while so many of their employees barely make a living wage and are thus mired in "wage slavery," struggling from paycheck to paycheck?

✖ ✖ ✖

With few exceptions, the law has not kept pace with employee-surveillance technology, and many employers "have carte blanche" in how they surveil employees.[54] And when employees, unions, and advocates of fair labor practices seek workplace reforms and government regulations to protect workers' civil and human rights, business groups oppose their efforts and corporations set up offices in DC to constantly lobby Congress. Certainly, reforms and regulatory legislation should be sought. At the same time, one must consider the fact that the same hierarchy of attorneys, politicians, and judges that empowered slavocracies and that today maintain the criminal-punishment system have also empowered corporate America.

As corporate America has continually diminished the personhood of working Americans, ironically, the Supreme Court granted corporations personhood in their 2010 *Citizens United* decision. The ruling was a corporate coup. It gave corporations "the same speech rights as individuals and opened the door to billionaire-funded Super PACs and unlimited, undisclosed 'dark money.'"[55] This decision introduced monetized interpretations of First Amendment rights of free speech, overturned laws governing campaign financing, and "shifted the balance of power in candidate fundraising even more sharply toward the elite 'donor class' and away from ordinary citizens."[56] Given that money wins campaigns and the "elite 'donor class'" supplies the most money, it is a no-brainer just whose interests most elected officials will work to advance—especially if that official desires reelection.

For the same reasons that plantation owners resisted the abolition of slavery, the neo–"master class" of "elite" politicians and lawyers and judges resists supporting state and federal abolition amendments: money. Not simply for the acquisition of obscene amounts of money but for the acquisition of obscene amounts of money derived from disempowered, debased human beings over whom the neo–"master class" exercises tyrannical control. Collaborations among corrupt government officials, politicians, and corporate "elites" have undermined democratic processes and have engendered "an economic system that perverts our labor in order to create riches based on a sub-culture of poverty and crime."[57] To the extent that entrepreneurs are obsessed with excessive profit, elitist prestige, and oligarchic and tyrannical power, they remain fixated not so much on "cheap" labor but on cheapening the laborer.

Writing in the June 2018 issue of *The Atlantic*, Matthew Stewart dubbed the 9.9-percenters (as distinguished from "the so-called top 1 percent") as "the new American Aristocracy." Like the old administrative hierarchy of the slave-plantation estate, they are "the staff that runs the machine that funnels resources from the 90 percent to the 0.1 percent. We've been happy to take our cut of the spoils. We've looked on with smug disdain," Stewart states, "as our labors have brought forth a population prone to resentment and ripe for manipulation."[58] They, the "new aristocracy," are the elitist CEOs who extract marrow from employees to fatten the portfolios of stakeholders and shareholders. They are the officials of the criminal-punishment bureaucracy—the prosecutors, judges, and public defenders who also get their cut of bail money or proceeds from "ankle bracelets."

This "new" class of American "aristocrats," like their pro-slavery predecessors, are "accomplices in a process that is slowly strangling the economy, destabilizing American politics, and eroding democracy," as Stewart observes.[59] But I would change out the word "slowly" for "imperceptibly" or "insidiously," because it's not happening slowly. Only if you're not unhoused, criminalized, caught in "wage slavery," rendered a climate-change refugee, or are otherwise *dis*advantaged or *under*privileged can you say the country's sociopolitical and economic debacle is happening slowly. Ignorance is bliss only for those who don't *yet* feel the impact of their ignoring the adverse experiences of other Americans.

The contemporary class of elitists, like their forebears and predecessors, figured out how to game the system, then *mastered* the game. They buy up real estate in the same obsessive and greedy fashion as did colonial and antebellum plantocrats. They objectify the "productive classes" in ways similar to the objectification of enslaved persons. They will speculate the nation into a financial crisis and destabilize the housing market while consolidating their own wealth, enjoying the sail of golden parachutes, and remain indifferent to "passing privilege along at the expense of other people's children."[60] They flout antitrust laws in their pursuit of monopolistic control, find loopholes in labor and tax laws, devise systems of wealth preservation, and then construct economic moats around their exclusivity.

They, the "new aristocrats," laud themselves as diverse, as they are "(somewhat) more varied in skin tone and ethnicity." But their predecessors tolerated Black, Semitic, Slavic, and female enslavers, too—to the extent that these presumed inferior others aligned themselves with the status quo and remembered their place. Moreover, the lawyers who do their bidding fit the profile Karakatsanis associates with "American prosecutors": they are "mostly men, almost all white, and share a number of other similarities across religious, class, and educational backgrounds."[61] In a word, the "new aristocracy" is the same old "master class," motivated by greed and obsessed with control; they glory in the privilege obtained through systemic disparities and structured inequities.

Their attributes and orientation reflect the archetypal "master" in Albert Camus's philosophy of the absurd. They are tyrants who scorn the idea of equality and anoint themselves superior, ascribing to themselves total authority and thereby disempowering the perceived inferior other—"the slave." The basic fiction of such a worldview requires that tyrants deal in the currency of lies in order to uphold an exaggerated sense of self. Victims of their own lies, they feel themselves entitled, which has them believe that there are no limits that they need to respect. Of course, not recognizing limits, exceeding limits results in excess, imbalance, and injustice.

The excess that exudes from tyrannical power is often expressed in the humiliation of the "othered," in violence against the "othered." In their treatment of other human beings as something other than human and in their attempts to convert human beings into "slaves" or chattel or units of labor, these self-deluded "superhumans" or would-be "masters" commit horrendous acts of violence. But the impossibility of the "master-slave" order breeds a harrowing silence that yet speaks. And the oppression born of injustice inevitably compels pushback, resistance, rebellion. The rebel, the activist, the protestor, the whistleblower confronts the unnatural order of things. In rejecting servitude, terror, and falsehood, they align themselves with and embody the values of freedom, truth, dignity, respect, democracy, and personal and collective sovereignty.

❌ ❌ ❌

The Maafic experience of the enslavement of African peoples and the colonization and criminalization of African Americans is heinous. As overwhelming as this experience may be to contemplate in and of itself, it is but part and parcel "of a much larger malignancy." As the objectification and dehumanization of the entire American labor force demonstrates, economic exploitation and oppression is not "a Black thing." A consequence of the so-called "New World" Atlantic economy, *slavery*, or the process of turning people into cogs in the wheels of producing "goods and services," has its roots in Europe. "Mass oppression for mass production" in America reveals itself as "part of the Western psyche."[62]

Importantly, "slave-based" economic oppression is also reflective of the modus operandi of the Western patriarch. His obsession with controlling the processes of production in America is matched only by his obsession with controlling the reproduction of human life itself. It is the white, Western patriarch who would insinuate himself between the Black woman's womb and the issue of her womb. Patriarch and third US president Thomas Jefferson wrote in a 1792 letter to then president George Washington of his discovery of a phenomenon he conceived of as "silent profit." Jefferson, "a meticulous record keeper," had calculated that at Monticello "there was approximately a 4 per cent annual increase in the population of slaves." He accounted a credit of "four per cent annum, for their increase over and above keeping up their own numbers."[63]

Jefferson saw the birth of Black babies as an opportunity for white families to improve their fortunes, free themselves from debt, and establish economic security. Projecting an even greater yield in the investments in "human stock," Jefferson proffered his insights in subsequent letters to friends, "recommending that a family in financial distress lay out, 'every farthing . . . in land and negroes, which besides a present support bring a silent profit of from 5. to 10. per cent.'"[64]

Thomas Jefferson, a lawyer, was also a "book farmer." "He kept daily records of every receipt and expenditure that he made, no matter how small, for a period of over 60 years."[65] The science of accounting, along with the managerial services of Edmund Bacon, his primary overseer of sixteen years, enabled and facilitated control at Jefferson's Monticello plantation estate. *Control*—the *sanctum sanctorum* of America's Peculiar Institution—"has always been at the heart of modern accounting practice," writes Caitlin Rosenthal:

> The word "control" itself comes from an accounting document: the *contreroulle*, or counter-roll, a duplicate of a roll or other document, which was kept for purposes of cross-checking. At its origins, the word first meant "verification," but by the late sixteenth century it had come to encompass the direction, management, and surveillance that verification required.[66]

Slave-plantation accounting records had been omitted from American business history and the history of the development of business administration and management. "Slavery became a laboratory for the development of accounting," Rosenthal informs us, because more than in almost any other American industry or business enterprise, "the control drawn on paper matched the reality of the plantation more closely."[67]

Control is also a core attribute of the social institution of patriarchy. The once-hidden history of accounting, like the "silent profit" recorded in plantation account books, also speaks to the interconnecting and interlocking oppressions that have obscured the violent and controlling hand of patriarchy.

## NOTES

1. Caitlin Rosenthal, *Accounting for Slavery: Masters and Management* (Cambridge, Massachusetts: Harvard University Press, 2018), xii, 2.

2. Rosenthal, *Accounting for Slavery*, 86, 109.

3. Rosenthal, *Accounting for Slavery*, 115, 147.

4. Rosenthal, *Accounting for Slavery*, 86, 123.

5. Rosenthal, *Accounting for Slavery*, 6, 8.

6. Rosenthal, *Accounting for Slavery*, 7.

7. Rosenthal, *Accounting for Slavery*, 34.

8. Rosenthal, *Accounting for Slavery*, 8.

9. Rosenthal, *Accounting for Slavery*, 7.

10. A. Leon Higginbotham, Jr., *In the Matter of Color: Race and the American Legal Process: The Colonial Period*, (New York: Oxford, 1978), 151.

11. Higginbotham, *In the Matter of Color*, 375.

12. Higginbotham, *In the Matter of Color*, 375–76.

13. Rosenthal, *Accounting for Slavery*, xiv.

14. Those engaged in the institution of enslavement in the Caribbean migrated to places where slavery was still permitted and reinforced the institution in those places.

15. David J. McCord, ed., *The Statutes at Large of South Carolina, Volume Seventh, Containing the Acts Relating to Charleston, Courts, Slaves, and Rivers* (Columbia, South Carolina: A. S. Johnston, 1840), 397, https://www.carolana.com/SC/Legislators/Documents/The_Statutes_at_Large_of_South_Carolina_Volume_VII_David_J_McCord_1840.pdf.

16. Alec Karakatsanis, *Usual Cruelty: The Complicity of Lawyers in the Criminal Injustice System* (New York: The New Press, 2019), 146.

17. Rosenthal, *Accounting for Slavery*, 23.

18. Martin Luther King, Jr., "Address to Chicago Freedom Festival," March 12, 1966, https://www.crmvet.org/docs/6603_sclc_mlk_cfm.pdf.

19. In *Weathering: The Extraordinary Stress of Ordinary Life in an Unjust Society* (New York: Little Brown, 2023), public health researcher and professor Arline T. Geronimus delineates weathering as "a process that encompasses the physiological effects of living in marginalized communities that bear the brunt of racial ethnic, religious, and class discrimination" (10–11).

20. See, for example, Vann R. Newkirk II, "The Great Land Robbery: The Shameful Story of How 1 Million Black Families Have Been Ripped from Their Farms," *The Atlantic*, September 2019, i, 74–85.

    While African Americans were being evicted, unhoused, and squeezed into urban ghettos and assaulted in suburban towns, they were being evicted and swindled out of their property and driven off their land in rural America. In this article, the journalist Vann R. Newkirk II tells "the shameful story of how 1 million black families have been ripped from their farms." Two generations into the Reconstruction era, African Americans had begun to amass significant landholdings. Through the Southern Homestead Act of 1866, squatter's rights, collective enterprises, and the largesse of some sympathetic white American landowners willing to sell parcels of land to Black folk, African Americans began to put down roots and establish themselves—as citizens. In the late nineteenth and early twentieth centuries, African Americans held titles to millions of acres of farmland. In Mississippi alone in 1910, "there were 25,000 black farm operators" and Black-owned farmland "totaled 2.2 million acres . . . some 14 percent of all black-owned agricultural land in the country, and the most of any state." (Newkirk, "The Great Land Robbery," 78.)

    The wealth that African Americans had accrued by the 1920s would be "lost." Throughout the twentieth century in the Southern Delta, Black-owned land, like Black people themselves, would seemingly disappear. Some loss of land was due to the vagaries involved in a farming economy—weather, market fluctuations, mechanization, industrialization, and unwise or unfortunate business ventures. For African Americans specifically, however, racism was another variable that factored into the "losses" of land, capital, and investments.

21. See, for example, Richard Rothstein, *The Color of Law: A Forgotten History of How Our Government Segregated America* (New York: Liveright Publishing Corporation, 2017), which reveals how the federal government's racially discriminatory policies in the housing market, financial industries, the labor market, and the distribution of military benefits effectively segregated America and initiated, through its own offices and the offices of state and local government, the structural economic and social inequities and disparities prevalent in contemporary society.

    See also Richard Rothstein, "The Making of Ferguson: Public Policies at the Root of Its Troubles," Economic Policy Institute, October 15, 2014, https://files.epi.org/2014/making-of-ferguson-final.pdf.

22. See Mindy Thompson Fullilove, *Root Shock: How Tearing Up City Neighborhoods Hurts America, and What We Can Do About It*, second edition (New York: One World/Ballantine, 2004; New York: New Village Press, 2016).

23. Kate Weisburd et al., "Electronic Prisons: The Operation of Ankle Monitoring in the Criminal Legal System," The George Washington University Law School, September 27, 2021, https://papers.ssrn.com/sol3/papers.cfm?abstract_id=3930296.

24. Ava Kofman, "Digital Jail: How Electronic Monitoring Drives Defendants into Debt," *ProPublica*, July 3, 2019, https://www.propublica.org/article/digital-jail-how-electronic-monitoring-drives-defendants-into-debt.

25. Rosenthal, *Accounting for Slavery*, 179.

26. Sara Sidner and Mallory Simon, "How Robot, Explosives Took Out Dallas Sniper in Unprecedented Way," CNN, July 12, 2016, https://www.cnn.com/2016/07/12/us/dallas-police-robot-c4-explosives.

27. James Baldwin, "An Open Letter to My Sister, Miss Angela Davis," *The New York Review of Books*, January 7, 1971, https://www.nybooks.com/articles/1971/01/07/an-open-letter-to-my-sister-miss-angela-davis/.

28. Tavis Smiley and Cornel West, *The Rich and the Rest of Us: A Poverty Manifesto* (New York: Smiley Books, 2012).

29. Matthew Stewart, "The 9.9 Percent Is the New American Aristocracy," *The Atlantic*, June 2018, https://www.theatlantic.com/magazine/archive/2018/06/the-birth-of-a-new-american-aristocracy/559130/.

30. "Capitalism has no race or nationality. Capitalism has no humanity. All that exists in the capitalist bible is the margin of profit, the market share." (Walter Mosley, *Workin' on the Chain Gang: Shaking Off the Dead Hand of History* [New York: Ballantine, 2000], 12.)

31. Mosley, *Workin' on the Chain Gang*, 6.

32. Rosenthal, *Accounting for Slavery*, 141.

33. In analyses of the 2016 presidential election, for example, some pundits speculated that while the results reflected a "racially charged reaction to a black president and multicultural society, others have dismissed such claims, instead suggesting that the country's college educated are out of touch with noncollege educated and working class citizens." (Patton O. Garriott, "Race Trumps Class? Whiteness, Social Class and the 2016 Presidential Election," American Psychological Association, January 2017, https://www.apa.org/pi/ses/resources/indicator/2017/01/race-class.)

   Exit polls also indicated that election results reflected middle-class America's frustration with wage and salary stagnation and the fear of falling out of the "shrinking middle class" and becoming part of the economically marginalized "others." "Of the one in three Americans who earn less than $50,000 a year, a majority voted for Clinton. A majority of those who earn more backed Trump," and "54% of male college graduates voted for Trump, as did 45% of female college graduates." (Jon Henley, "White and Wealthy Voters Gave Victory to Donald Trump, Exit Polls Show," *The Guardian*, November 9, 2016, https://www.theguardian.com/us-news/2016/nov/09/white-voters-victory-donald-trump-exit-polls.)

34. Rosenthal, *Accounting for Slavery*, 5–6, 8; Ifeoma Ajunwa, Kate Crawford, and Jason Schultz, "Limitless Worker Surveillance," *California Law Review* 105, no. 3 (June 2017): 735–76, https://papers.ssrn.com/sol3/papers.cfm?abstract_id=2746211.

35. Ajunwa, Crawford, and Schultz, "Limitless Worker Surveillance," 738.

36. See, for example, Jodi Kantor and Arya Sundaram, "The Rise of the Worker Productivity Score," *The New York Times*, August 14, 2022, https://www.nytimes.com/interactive/2022/08/14/business/worker-productivity-tracking.html.

37. Zoë Corbyn, "'Bossware Is Coming for Almost Every Worker': The Software You Might Not Realize Is Watching You," *The Guardian*, April 27, 2022, https://www.theguardian.com/technology/2022/apr/27/remote-work-software -home-surveillance-computer-monitoring-pandemic.

38. Kantor and Sundaram, "The Rise of the Worker Productivity Score."

39. "Slave": "Designating a subsidiary device; *esp.* one which is controlled by, or which follows accurately the movements of, another device. Opp. master." *Shorter Oxford English Dictionary on Historical Principles*, fifth edition, volume 2, eds. William R. Trumble and Angus Stevenson (Oxford: Oxford University Press, 2002), 2, 868.

40. Sidereal clocks measure time relative to fixed stars versus measuring time relative to our sun.

41. Ron Eglash, "Broken Metaphor: The Master-Slave Analogy in Technical Literature," *Technology and Culture* 48, no. 2 (2007): 360–69, https://www.jstor .org/stable/40061475.

42. Eglash, "Broken Metaphor," 363.

43. Eglash, "Broken Metaphor," 364.

44. Tyler Charboneau, "How 'Master' and 'Slave' Terminology Is Being Reexamined in Electrical Engineering," All About Circuits, October 6, 2020, https://www .allaboutcircuits.com/news/how-master-slave-terminology-reexamined-in -electrical-engineering/.

45. Colleen Walsh, "How Caffeine Changed the World," *The Harvard Gazette*, August 20, 2020, https://news.harvard.edu/gazette/story/2020/08/author-michael -pollan-discusses-how-caffeine-changed-the-world/.

46. Jessica Hester, "A Brief History of the Coffee Break," *Bloomberg*, September 29, 2015, https://www.bloomberg.com/news/articles/2015-09-29/a-brief-history-of -the-office-coffee-break.

47. Mosley, *Workin' on the Chain Gang*, 11.

48. Kantor and Sundaram, "The Rise of the Worker Productivity Score."

49. Kofman, "Digital Jail."

50. Kantor and Sundaram, "The Rise of the Worker Productivity Score."
    Although workplace monitoring of employees is pervasive and laws have not kept pace with technological innovations that facilitate employee surveillance, some employees have filed grievances and lawsuits based on the constitutional protection of privacy rights. Articles like Will Yakowicz's "When Monitoring Your Employees Goes Horribly Wrong" (*Inc.*, July 6, 2015, https:// www.inc.com/will-yakowicz/drones-catch-employees-having-sex-and-other -employee-monitoring-gone-wrong.html) warn employers of the limits of their powers of surveillance. And Mark S. Spring and Dan M. Forman's "Invasion of Privacy Lawsuits Will Be on the Rise in California Where Employers Use Monitoring/Tracking Technology" (*California Labor & Employment Law Blog*, November 28, 2022, https://www.callaborlaw.com/entry/invasion-of -privacy-lawsuits-will-be-on-the-rise-in-california-where-employers-use -monitoring-tracking-technology) announces an increase in employee legal actions against workplace privacy violations.

51. Corbyn, "'Bossware Is Coming for Almost Every Worker.'"

52. Karakatsanis, *Usual Cruelty*, 10.

53. Taylor Mooney, "The Disturbing History of Tipping in the U.S.: 'It's Literally a Slave Wage,'" *CBS News*, March 30, 2020, https://www.cbsnews.com/news /tipping-jobs-history-slave-wage-cbsn-originals-documentary/. See also Elise Gould and David Cooper, "Seven Facts About Tipped Workers and the Tipped Minimum Wage," *Working Economics Blog*, Economic Policy Institute, May 31, 2018, https://www.epi.org/blog/seven-facts-about-tipped-workers-and-the-tipped -minimum-wage/; Libby Wann, "American Tipping Is Rooted in Slavery—and It Still Hurts Workers Today," Ford Foundation, February 18, 2016, https://www .fordfoundation.org/news-and-stories/stories/posts/american-tipping-is-rooted -in-slavery-and-it-still-hurts-workers-today/; and Laura Testino, "Fact Check: Tipping Began amid Slavery, Then Helped Keep Former Black Slaves' Wages Low," *USA Today*, December 16, 2020, https://www.usatoday.com/story/news /factcheck/2020/12/16/fact-check-tipping-kept-wages-low-formerly-enslaved -black-workers/3896620001/.

54. Kantor and Sundaram, "The Rise of the Worker Productivity Score."

55. "Buckley v. Valeo," Federal Election Commission, https://www.fec.gov/legal -resources/court-cases/buckley-v-valeo/; "Citizens United v. FEC," Federal Election Commission, https://www.fec.gov/legal-resources/court-cases /citizens-united-v-fec/; and Adam Lioz, "Stacked Deck: How the Racial Bias in Our Big Money Political System Undermines Our Democracy and Our Economy," Dēmos, July 23, 2015, 33, https://www.demos.org/sites/default/files /publications/StackedDeck2_1.pdf.

56. Lioz, "Stacked Deck," 9.

57. Mosley, *Workin' on the Chain Gang*, 3.

58. Stewart, "The 9.9 Percent Is the New American Aristocracy."

59. Stewart, "The 9.9 Percent Is the New American Aristocracy."

60. Stewart, "The 9.9 Percent Is the New American Aristocracy."

61. Karakatsanis, *Usual Cruelty*, 39.

62. Mosley, *Workin' on the Chain Gang*, 9–10.

63. Charles Richard Baker, "What Can Thomas Jefferson's Accounting Records Tell Us About Plantation Management, Slavery, and Enlightenment Philosophy in Colonial America?," *Accounting History* 24, no. 2 (2019): 236–252, https://doi .org/10.1177/1032373218772589.

64. Rosenthal, *Accounting for Slavery*, 130.

65. Baker, "What Can Thomas Jefferson's Accounting Records Tell Us?," 249.

66. Rosenthal, *Accounting for Slavery*, 3.

67. Rosenthal, *Accounting for Slavery*, 4.

# CHAPTER 8

# PATRIARCHY—
# THE SLAVERY WE SWIM IN

MY BROTHER IS NOT A completely innocent man, though not guilty of all the charges of which he was convicted in 2000. As he refused to plead guilty to the rape of his fiancée, my brother, without hesitation, pleaded guilty to battery. It wasn't the first time.

My brother had physically abused his fiancée before. He had described to me in a phone conversation the circumstances of a previous altercation wherein he realized she had been lying to him about money, about a car, et cetera. Feeling manipulated and made a fool of. His reaction was to "beat" her. During the parole board Zoom meeting, he expressed his regret. He talked about the anger management classes that he had taken. He shared his realization that what he had done was wrong, inexcusable. That he had no business putting his hands on her. But his fiancée was not the first woman he had abused.

His wife of four years shot him with a .22-caliber pistol. This incident followed "a fight" that my brother said happened after he learned his wife was having an affair. As the shooting was not fatal, her fear of him had not subsided. Thus, according to my brother's deductions, she had conspired to have him shot a second time. Factors in his deductions: A gun, a .45, kept under the seat of his car, that was missing—after he allowed his wife to use his car. A knock at the door that only he was home to answer. The bullet casings from the second shooting were fired from a .45-caliber handgun.

His body is still home to one of the three bullets fired during the second shooting. My brother wrote, "The doctor removed one bullet and left one in me because he said it won't [cause] no problem where it was." The third bullet wasn't recovered. No one was arrested for the attempted murder of my brother.[1]

My brother recognized that his wife had shot him in self-defense. But for the grace of God, as they say, the situation could have been even worse. But he said he had forgiven his wife for both shootings and told all of us that we should hold no hard feelings against her because he was at fault. "I'm 40 year older now," he wrote recently. "I was very [dumb] when it came to having a wife. I think if I was in her shoes, I [would] have done the same thing. I had pushed her to the limit. . . . I should have kept my hands to myself."[2]

## WHAT EVER HAPPENED TO "SISTER, I'M SORRY"?[3]

When our dad died, I called Angola prison to speak to the assistant warden, to ask that my brother be released to attend the funeral. I gave him the pertinent information. Permission was granted.

My dad was the main and constant support of my brother, from his arrest to his life of imprisonment at hard labor in Angola. "Daddy believed me, so he was on my side all the time," my brother wrote. "He went to every court date. He made sure [that the witness in my brother's defense against the rape and kidnapping charges] showed up for court, also."[4] My dad had visited my brother as regularly as the prison allowed—twice a month. He cared nothing about hurricanes and high water if he was intent on seeing my brother. Bobby would have to call him sometimes to dissuade him from coming to the prison due to weather or road conditions, as my brother was always concerned for our dad's safety.

At the repast, I observed my brother as he got up from the table where he sat next to me. Dressed in prison-institution orange, shackled, chains connecting wrist and ankle restraints. Taking carefully measured steps, he made his way to his former wife. They stood together, speaking quietly, intimately. My sister-in-law (for she remained part of our family despite their divorce) told me that he had approached her to apologize to her. She said that first, he asked her if he could speak with her.

She was feeling uneasy, but the room was full of people and their son was close by. So she told him yes, he could speak with her. He told her that he had resolved that if he ever had the chance to speak to her again in life, face-to-face, that he would apologize to her and tell her how sorry he was for abusing her and tearing their family apart. That she had been a good wife. That nothing she had done was her fault. He had told her these things, she said. Then he asked her if she would forgive him. My sister-in-law accepted my brother's apology. She felt that he had changed. For the first time since things went wrong between them, she did not feel fear in his presence. So she forgave him, too.

✄ ✄ ✄

In a letter my brother wrote since that time, he told me that he regretted his behavior, that violence was not the answer to the issues he experienced in his relationships. Although he knows better now, he had believed that he abused his fiancée *because* she had provoked him. That he had abused his wife not only *because* he believed she was unfaithful to him but also *because* his mindset was that he "owned" his wife. A big part of his problem, he wrote, was that he felt the women in his life were his possessions:

> *Well what made me think I own my wife, I thought by me paying the bills and being the only one working you had to do what I said. I was running it. I was young and wanted control of everything, even my wife. It was my way or the highway.*[5]

My brother had objectified his wife and his fiancée as his "property." And he used violent physical force to try to control them. And there were others. This kind of behavior is usually seen through the sociological lens of sexism and toxic masculinity. This kind of behavior is not unique to my brother. Although he would be the first to say that the prevalence of domestic abuse in our society does not excuse his behavior or absolve him of his responsibility to exercise self-restraint—or, as he put it, to keep his hands to himself—the use of violence to assert authority, dominance, and control is not *just* commonplace in intimate relationships; it is characteristic of a much larger social malignancy: patriarchy.

The sexism apparent in my brother's relationships is not separate from the racism and classism that factored into his life sentence at Angola prison. The racism that objectifies and enslaves and the sexism that objectifies and enslaves are part and parcel of a common oppressive ideology. In 2018, a woman was found inside the "dark prison" of a shipping container. She was shackled at the ankles and chained around the neck "like a dog," the chain around her neck connecting her to a wall of the steel container. She was tortured there and used as a "sex slave."[6] In 2016, a star athlete at a "prestigious school" was found guilty of three felony charges, including assault with the intent to rape an unconscious woman behind a dumpster. More concerned about the impact of prison on the life of the "Olympic hopeful" than on the impact statement of the now conscious and speaking woman, the judge handed down a lenient, six-month *jail* term that would likely be reduced to ninety days with good behavior.[7]

The instances of racism, sexism, classism, and elitism evident in the above examples are not separate, discrete forms of social injustice, but are aspects of the interconnected, interlocking oppressions that, perceived disparately, render patriarchy invisible. As white people historically have not been raced, men have not been gendered. Both *white* and *male* have been considered normative and standard in American society, and all other social demographics have been considered as deviations from the norm. As *the norm*, the white male doesn't stand out. His privilege is not remarkable. And to the extent that he is not "seen" and his privilege is unremarked, he moves "through the world with relatively little awareness of the causes or consequences of male privilege and white privilege and the social oppression they produce."[8]

In *The Gender Knot: Unraveling Our Patriarchal Legacy*, the sociologist Allan Johnson explains further, "If male gender is invisible, then patriarchy is invisible," and that invisibility allows those who benefit from patriarchy to avoid any responsibility for addressing the consequent oppression that is inevitable.[9]

Defining oppression as a problem only for the oppressed is as old as oppression itself. It does not protect or enhance the status of men, whites, or the "upper" classes to look critically at systems that privilege them over women, people of color, and the working and so-called lower classes. Instead, the path of least resistance is to be charitable or to focus on how oppressed groups can solve their problems or advance their standing as having "special interests." But advantaged, dominant groups are rarely portrayed as problematic or even as groups, much less as having special interests.[10]

"Patriarchy is *not* a way of saying 'men,'" Johnson clarifies, and it is not synonymous with maleness, individual men, or with manhood. Patriarchy is "a kind of society in which men *and* women participate."[11] Even as the oppression of women is a key aspect of patriarchy, patriarchy's main preoccupation concerns the domination, control, and fear of other men.

The social construct of Western patriarchy features a hierarchical social structure that "promotes male privilege," which is propagated via the core principles of male domination, male identification, male centeredness, and obsession with male control.[12] These core principles make up the roots of the patriarchal tree. "Perhaps more than anything else, what drives patriarchy as a system," writes Johnson, "what fuels competition, aggression, oppression, and violence—is a dynamic relationship between control and fear."[13] The control-fear spiral that is an integral aspect of the "master-slave" dynamic was ever-present throughout colonial and antebellum America and is prevalent within contemporary American society.

Patriarchy encourages men to seek security, status, and other rewards through control, to fear other men's ability to control and harm them, and to identify being in control as both their best defense against loss and humiliation and the surest route to what they need and desire. In this sense, although we usually think of patriarchy in terms of women and men, patriarchy is more about what goes on *among men*. The oppression of women is certainly an important part of patriarchy, but, paradoxically, oppression of women may not be the *point* of patriarchy.[14]

✕ ✕ ✕

An illustration of the point Johnson makes is clearly seen in the social policy advocated in the 1965 *Moynihan Report*. In this classic diatribe against the Black family, Senator Daniel Patrick Moynihan reprimanded Black men for not becoming men in the tradition of the Western patriarch. He berated them for not being in control of *their* women. Moynihan prophesied doom for Black society as a whole—lest Black men assume their rightful *patriarchal* authority in the Black household and implement the mandated white, patriarchal, middle-class model of family life. This censor, broadcasted on the national stage, had a lot to do with the "I Am a Man" placards present at Civil Rights demonstrations.

"Ours is a society which presumes male leadership," asserted Assistant Secretary of Labor Moynihan.[15] But leadership here seems to be confused with masculinity, authoritarianism, tyranny, autocracy, absolutism, dictatorship—*and* being part of the white, male-dominated "master class." In any case, in the absence of a male *head* of household—like Black houses, Black land, and Black communities—Black American society could also expect condemnation. And judgment for the entire disastrous calamity, Moynihan reckoned, fell on the head of the Black woman, whose fertility rates he measured in his figures and graphs, concluding that the Black woman was promiscuous and *her* "illegitimate" children a danger to (white) society.

Even when Moynihan acknowledged that the politics of race and class figured into the political economy of America, he never ushered in figures and graphs to account for the systemic exclusion of African Americans from economic opportunities and the ongoing wealth extraction that engendered and maintained cycles of poverty among working-class and poor, urban African Americans. He never marshalled stats to illustrate how wealthy whites become wealthier at the expense of Black folk and other marginalized groups that patriarchal white men maneuver into disadvantaged spaces.

In his report, it was the financial bottom line that preoccupied Moynihan. He expressed alarm over the deterioration of the integrity of the Black family structure, which he declared as "a case for national action," but in actuality, his report was the "hue and cry" that warned against an increase in "the number of welfare dependent children."[16] As the assistant secretary of labor, Daniel Moynihan emphasized a connection between employment and family stability, and unemployment and social pathology. And it was as a privileged, patriarchal white man that he would presume to admonish Black men about their employment status and their supposed impotence as the head of the Black household while at the same time dismissing or ignoring all the public policies and private practices that have exploited Black men's labor and undermined their paternity.

A foundational principle of patriarchy is control—over the self and over subjugated others. As a core value around which private and public life is to be ordered, control or the perceived lack of control figures into how white American patriarchs view, evaluate, and judge the society of othered cultures. In the spirit of the political "elites" of antebellum America, Moynihan set himself up as the "aristocratic" gatekeeper who regulates privilege and dispenses disadvantage in accordance with the values of the white patriarchs that he represents. He determined that Negroes as a group are all to be disadvantaged because of the employment record of working-class and poor, urban ("ghetto") Negroes.

In his article "Employment, Income, and the Ordeal of the Negro Family," a fall 1965 publication that echoes the earlier *Report*, Moynihan wrote, "From the very outset, the principal measure of progress toward equality will be that of employment. It is the primary source of individual or group identity. In America what you do is what you are: to do nothing is to be nothing; to do little is to be little. The equations are implacable and blunt, and ruthlessly public."[17]

Implacable and blunt though they may be, the equations are not purely mathematical. They are political constructs designed not only to interpret labor market analyses and interrelated sociological indices in ways that demean and pathologize African Americans but also to blame them for the economic oppression they experience while hiding the white, male, and privileged hand that controls labor market dynamics. To speak of "employment" in abstract terms, as though it were some autonomous, authoritative entity that has power and agency to put the entire Black population in peril of remaining ostracized denizens *in perpetuity* distracts from the raced and gendered controlling hand that leaves patriarchy invisible.

In a report that was controversial when he published it and that still remains part of contemporary political discourse, Daniel Patrick Moynihan iterated that three centuries of injustice were at the root of the problems that Negro families were facing. He implicated unemployed and underemployed Black men in the continuation of the problems. The issue of employment "is already, and will continue to be, the master problem," he declared.[18] Though likely a pun not intended, Moynihan couldn't have been more honest. Control of Black men's labor—which is to say how to employ or how to control Black men's bodies—has historically been a problem of the so-called "master" within America's Peculiar Institution.

How to extract his labor, bind him to a plantation or workshop, and balk his rebellion were among the preoccupations of enslavers and residents in those colonies whose economies were directly fueled by the labor of enslaved Black persons. Whether Black men worked or not, how, and in what capacity has always been a matter of concern for racialized and patriarchal white men. Thus, in *The Moynihan Report: The Negro Family—The Case for National Action*, Moynihan enthralls Black men in a controlling, master narrative that casts them as "incompetent," "irresponsible," "weak," and "sexually unrestrained."[19]

But, in a perverse kind of patriarchal fraternity, it was the Black woman whom Moynihan demonized and targeted as the antagonist, the taproot of the "tangle of pathology" that plagued the Black family.[20] It was not unfair, racialized, and white, patriarchal, elitist labor policies and practices that he focused on in relation to struggling Black families, but the Black woman, both in terms of her work and her womb.

✠ ✠ ✠

At the intersection of the interconnecting and interlocking oppressions that structure and reinforce the social construct of patriarchy, we'll find the legacy of the iconic Fannie Lou Hamer. Born in 1917, Hamer was the youngest of twenty children. Her parents, Lou Ella and James Lee Townsend, were sharecroppers. At six years of age, Fannie Lou joined them in the cotton fields. She married Perry "Pap" Hamer, also a sharecropper, in the 1940s, and they later adopted two girls who were in need of a home. Mrs. Hamer had experienced several miscarriages, but her possibility of having a child biologically was callously taken from her when she was sterilized without her knowledge.

This practice of sterilizing Black women was popularly referred to as the "Mississippi appendectomy," a procedure performed by white doctors on Black women in Mississippi so regularly that it had become as routine as performing an appendectomy. It was 1961. Mrs. Hamer was hospitalized for a minor surgery when doctors also performed the hysterectomy. Doctors who routinely sterilized Black women apparently used other methods as well. For, by her own estimates, Mrs. Hamer stated that "about six out of the 10 Negro women that go to the hospital are sterilized with the tubes tied."[21]

This biographical fact of Hamer's life and biological fact of Black women's lives reveal another layer of cruelty against which Fannie Lou Hamer fought in her struggles for a transformed agrarian South, a transformed America, and a sustainable world. Before her activism and employment with the Student Nonviolent Coordinating Committee (SNCC), Fannie Lou Hamer's life was that of a sharecropper and a timekeeper in Ruleville, Mississippi. She and thousands of African American sharecroppers and tenant farmers, and farm owners and landowners alike, were treated like brutes, as "tongueless, earless, eyeless conveniences" for the white and patriarchal establishment in the Deep South.[22]

Yet Fannie Lou Hamer and seventeen others heard freedom's call to expressive humanity and full citizenship: "Will you register to vote?" the SNCC organizers asked at a mass meeting in August of 1962. The inspired cadre boarded a bus to the county seat in Indianola, Mississippi, to register to vote. Before Fannie Lou Hamer returned to the plantation where she was a tenant, W. D. Marlow, the planter and "landlord," stood at the ready to officially deliver her the ultimatum to withdraw her voter registration application or be evicted. Hamer had a ready response: "I didn't try to register for you," she addressed Marlow unapologetically. "I tried to register for myself."[23]

The die had been cast. Forced to leave "that same night," Hamer never looked back.[24] She joined forces with SNCC in 1962, initiating her public political activism and new employment as a community organizer and a different kind of field-worker. Violent reprisals against Hamer, her family and friends, and the general Black and female population in the Delta were ongoing.

In June of 1963, a highway patrolman and chief of police arrested Hamer and her civil rights cohort at a bus station in Winona, Mississippi. Hamer and her associates had attended a voter education workshop in Charleston, South Carolina, and were returning home on a Continental Trailway bus. At the bus station in Winona, some of her group went in to use the restroom while others entered the restaurant. They were refused service, and the state highway patrolman ordered them to leave. In reaction to one activist's assertion that segregation of facilities at bus stops were against the law, the officer of the law declared, "Ain't no damn law."[25]

What ensued was sheer barbarity. Five of the civil rights workers were arrested and forced into patrol cars. A county deputy kicked Hamer before forcing her into the police car. At the county jail, she was beaten. At the August 1964 Democratic National Convention, as the Mississippi Freedom Democratic Party (MFDP) petitioned the Credentials Committee for seats on the convention floor, Fannie Lou Hamer would protest these civil rights violations and acts of terrorism.

But she and her integrated coalition of delegates from the MFDP would do more than protest violent voter suppression and question the credentials of the all-white, segregationist delegates representing the Democratic Party in Mississippi. As cofounder of the MFDP, Fannie Lou Hamer questioned all of Mississippi and she questioned America. That is, she insisted on a dialogue. By implication, she insisted on being recognized as an equal: African American, woman, poor, yet human and citizen and therefore equal.

Mrs. Hamer's unvarnished, plainspoken narration of being arrested must have pulled the members of the Credentials Committee into the Winona county jail cell with her. Perhaps they, too, were chilled by "the sounds of licks and horrible screams" that Hamer heard while she sat there in a holding cell, waiting. They, too, must have been listening in when the three white men questioned her. When the three white men learned her identity and where she was from, the highway patrolman—one among the three men—told her, "We are going to make you wish you was dead."[26] The licks and screams that Hamer had heard earlier were a portent of things to come.

Hamer recounted for the Credentials Committee how these men had her beaten unmercifully. The patrolman ordered a jailed African American man to "take the blackjack" and beat Mrs. Hamer. This man was ordered to instruct Hamer to lie facedown on a bunk, then beat her. Once the first man had beaten her until he was spent, the officer ordered a second jailed African American man to resume the beating. Unflinchingly, Hamer narrated this terror and her trauma:

> I was holding my hands behind me at that time on my left side, because I suffered from polio when I was six years old. . . .
>
> The second Negro began to beat and I began to work my feet, and the State Highway Patrolman ordered the first Negro who had beat me to sit on my feet—to keep me from working my feet. I began to scream and one white man got up and began to beat me in my head and tell me to hush.[27]

The beating inflicted on Fannie Lou Hamer resulted in permanent kidney damage, a permanent limp, and a blood clot that nearly blinded her left eye. But it didn't stop her ability to see. As Black men had gained the right to vote with the Fifteenth Amendment, Fannie Lou Hamer, her mother, Ella Lou Townsend, and others among the women in Ruleville and throughout the Rulevilles of America had gained the right to vote with the Nineteenth Amendment, in 1920. Yet in the absurd and distorted reality of white and patriarchal "supremacists," not only were the voices of the women in Hamer's family to be suppressed but their bodies were to be objectified, dominated, exploited, and violated.

As we look into the causes of these attacks, again we find that the violence to which the men of Mississippi subjected Mrs. Hamer was not perpetrated *because* she was Black, *because* she was a woman, or even *because* she was a Black woman. The behavior of these men actually had nothing to do with the dimensions of

Hamer's beingness but everything to do with their own world-view and psycho-emotional constitution. The behavior of these men had more to do with having absorbed the Western patriarchal notion of ownership, of "private property," and of control of that property.

During, as well as after, the Civil War, many among the planter class continued to perceive African Americans as property—property that had been *taken* from them by the State, but property nonetheless. They had solemnly sworn that in upholding the US Constitution, they would "abide by and faithfully support all laws and proclamations which have been made during the existing rebellion with reference to the emancipation of slaves. So help me God."[28]

In spite of having signed an oath as a condition of their pardons (the condition being that they don't own people) they still, so help them God, instituted Black Codes and structured economic systems—sharecropping, tenant farming, debt peonage, and convict leasing among them—in order to ensnare the bodies of "free" Black folk for the purposes and conveniences of the "elite" class and to again extort the Black labor upon which white, patriarchal elitism depended.

⚜ ⚜ ⚜

As the notion of private property had something to do with the attitude of Mississippi landlords and lawmen toward Fannie Lou Hamer, the plantocrat's notion of controlling "the means of production" had something to do with the decision of doctors to perform a hysterectomy on Mrs. Hamer without her consent. And perhaps both the notions of "private property" and the obsession with controlling "the means of production," ultimately, have something to do with how humans understand their relation to Earth, to the land—to Pachamama, Terra, Gaia. For the understanding of this archetypal relationship informs humanity's understanding of its relationship to womankind.

Does one's understanding hold the relation between human beings and the land to be sacred and connected? Or is one's understanding inspired by daemonic notions of possession and disconnection? Does one's creation stories teach oneness, wholeness, and sacredness, or do they teach fragmentation, separation, and fear? In his comparative examination of shamanic mythology and Judeo-Christian belief, the shaman Alberto Villoldo considers the biblical story of Adam and Eve and the Garden of Eden.

Accordingly, the first humans forfeited their paradisical home as a consequence of yielding to temptation and eating forbidden fruit from the tree of knowledge. Eve and Adam both ate of the fruit. They both were cast out of Eden as punishment. They both "fell from grace," but the blame fell on Eve (Adam's second wife?). Subordinated to a "second-rate status"—since she was created from Adam's rib—Eve was also depicted as guilty of committing humankind's "original sin." But this story of "original sin," Villoldo informs us, is more accurately described as a story of "original wounding," the injury and pain of disconnection and separation from grace and from the garden.[29]

The biblical narrative, Villoldo continues, "teaches us that it's the fault of the feminine that we're banished from Eden," as Eve represents both the feminine and Eden, and both had been disparaged and denigrated. "This loss of the sacred feminine that Eden and Eve represent in our culture, whether it's reflected in our disrespect for women or our denigration of Mother Earth, is our *collective* soul loss as human beings. And when we demonize the feminine, we live in a world devoid of the sacred."[30]

Villoldo explains further that the biblical story of expulsion is unique among creation stories. "In fact, other belief systems don't embrace this Judeo-Christian idea of being cast out of Eden":

Aboriginal peoples of Australia weren't cast out; nor were the sub-Saharan [African] peoples, Native Americans, rain forest-dwelling tribes in Brazil, or Pacific Islanders. All of these peoples still perceive themselves as continuing to live in Eden as they speak to the rivers, the trees, and God. In fact, native mythologies go so far as to state that we humans were created to serve and be the stewards of the garden.[31]

The illogic that Earth could or even should be owned and possessed is the same illogic that sanctions the practice of exploiting the labor and lives of the many in harvesting Earth's bounties for the benefit and privilege of the few. The objectification and exploitation of the land is the same objectification and exploitation of a Black woman's body. The theft of the fruits of the land from the people who labored in the fields is the same theft of the fruit from Black women's wombs that they labored to yield.

It is often said that America was built on the backs of enslaved Black people. It is also true that America was built, literally, on the backs of enslaved Black women. All of the Black bodies standing and stooping in all of the fields and working in big houses and small houses and commercial and domestic enterprises, all of those bodies were made of her blood and flesh and bone and came into the world through her.

The same arrogant authority that dictated the mode of production on a given portion of land in colonial America on a given plantation in a given season was the same arrogant, patriarchal authority that presumed to dictate the uses of a Black woman's body, divine her productive capacity, or, in the season of the pseudoscience of eugenics, determine whether she would produce or reproduce at all.

"Slavery is," said the collective voice of African Americans during the Savannah Colloquy, "receiving by *irresistible power* the work of another man, and not by his *consent*."[32] Dominating "by *irresistible power*" the womb of the Black woman, desecrating her procreative power, and terminating her capacity to reproduce "and not by [her] *consent*" was probably the most elemental formulation of the institution of "slavery" and the re-enslavement and colonization of African Americans post-emancipation. For the Black woman was still perceived collectively by the racialized patriarchy as property. The hysterectomies the doctors performed were among the badges and incidents of slavery she would be forced to suffer.

The racialized patriarchy in Sunflower County would deny Fannie Lou Hamer authority over her own body, her reproductive prerogative, and her procreative capacity as a linguistic being. When Mrs. Hamer insisted on her right to vow and to wish, her right to vote and to voice her vision, the thing that always happens when a woman tells the truth about her life happened: the world split open.[33] To speak is to assume subjectivity. To speak directly to someone who assumes himself superior is to assert one's equality. For a woman to speak directly to a man who assumes himself her lord is to assert her equality and her own sovereign power. Here, "the rebel" finds herself unwilling to tolerate the conditions of servitude. Here, the dynamic between "master" and "slave," and white and Black, between landlord and tenant, and dominant man and submissive woman, is upturned. "The rebel" redraws the boundaries and sets limits—on her terms.

This choice shook the foundations of the white, patriarchal establishment, from the plantation house to the White House, where even President Lyndon Baines Johnson was in a dither about how to contain and silence Fannie Lou Hamer. When she could not be bribed or threatened into abandoning the objectives of the MFDP, the president had Mrs. Hamer's televised testimony preempted. He then contrived an impromptu press conference to distract the television cameras and the national audience away from the history unfolding at the convention and away from Mrs. Hamer's mesmerizing speech.

Frustrated with his impotence to control events, Johnson directed his advisers to "fix 'the Mississippi problem.'" But hadn't Fannie Lou Hamer already been "fixed"? Lyndon Johnson did not want to hear from "that illiterate woman."[34] But Hamer's thirteen-minute testimony was broadcast on the evening news. Prime time. America had an opportunity also to bear witness to the treatment of Black citizens in general and Black female citizens in particular, in the state of Mississippi where the highway patrolman, purportedly bound to "the rule of law," declared that there "ain't no damn law."

All of America had an opportunity to ponder the question that concluded Hamer's testimony—the question that was also a plea:

Is this America, the land of the free and the home of the brave, where we have to sleep with our telephones off the hooks because our lives be threatened daily because we want to live as decent human beings, in America?[35]

Hamer's impassioned appeal touched and resonated with American humanity, propelling her to the forefront among leaders and guardians of the national Civil Rights Movement.

The three law enforcement officers who orchestrated her beating weren't different from the doctors who performed the hysterectomy without her permission. They were not different from Marlow, who demanded her submission or her suffering. And he, Marlow, was not different from the president, all the president's men, and all other men enthralled by the status quo, men who upheld the white, patriarchal power structure that sought to desecrate the feminine principle while also attempting to emasculate men of color.

Strong, resilient, and determined, Fannie Lou Hamer acquiesced neither to "a woman's place" nor "a Negro's place." She would neither lie nor stoop down. So the white and patriarchal establishment in Ruleville, in Indianola, in Winona, all throughout Sunflower County and counties left and right of the meridians of Mississippi had converged to hush or crush Mrs. Hamer. The planter W. D. Marlow would be compelled to demand Mrs. Hamer's submission and her silence: "If you don't go down and withdraw your registration, you will have to leave."[36]

Withdrawing her registration, however, was no guarantee that she would be allowed to remain in her shack on his plantation. Hamer and her family's tenancy on Marlow's land was in jeopardy—*irregardless*. Hadn't it always been? He was "the lord" of the land, and as such, he sensed the slightest threat to his absolutist reign. Even if Hamer had conceded to withdraw her application, "you still might have to go because we are not ready for that in Mississippi," Marlow acknowledged.[37]

Planter Marlow was inclined to evict Mrs. Hamer and her family willy-nilly, as he had divined in her act of applying to register a "gesture of rebellion."[38] And her refusal to withdraw her application stirred that age-old fear that had haunted enslavers and the white population of slave societies during America's antebellum years: the chronic fear of "slave insurrection."

Marlow sensed within Hamer that movement of rebellion that arises when someone who has been subjugated begins to see through and beyond the absurd world in which they had been forced to live. He intuited that stirring of a sense of self-worth and personal sovereignty that contradicted the lies told, dispelling the exaggerated sense of self of tyrannical landlords, lawless lawmen, and the unprincipled politicians and policymakers who upheld and empowered them.

Hamer's application for voter registration was perceived by county courthouse officials in Indianola as evidence of a "plot," a revolt. Even before entering the courthouse, Hamer and her cohorts had been set upon in Sunflower County by highway patrolmen. In the manner of antebellum patrollers or "pattyrollers," whose official duty was to keep a constant watch for escapees and for signs of planned "slave insurrections," Indianola patrolmen held Hamer suspect, as Hamer had neither a pass from Marlow to be off the plantation, nor his permission to be in Indianola—registering to vote. As Hamer and all her cohorts were all considered suspect, the highway patrolmen harassed the group and fined their bus driver for "driving a bus the wrong color," a fine which they, collectively, paid.[39]

Having gleaned her place of residence from her application, Indianola city officials alerted Marlow of Hamer's audacity as a potential "runaway." So, as Hamer told her story to the committee, Marlow had been "raising Cain" all the while she was returning to the Marlow plantation, where he awaited her arrival. As if to second Marlow's emotion, white mobs in Ruleville, in the manner of antebellum citizen slave patrollers, went on the hunt for Hamer once she stepped foot off the Marlow plantation. A little over a week later, as she told the Credentials Committee, a mob fired sixteen assassins' bullets into the home of one of her friends, believing that Hamer was staying there. The same night, vigilantes shot two random girls and shot into the home of another resident.

In perceiving Fannie Lou Hamer's continued tenure or eviction as a consequence of her wish to vote and thereby evoke a certain reality for herself, Planter Marlow, said, in effect, that Hamer's residency and her registration were one and the same thing. His threat suggested that to evict Mrs. Hamer would be tantamount to annihilating her presumed authority to speak, to vow, to wish for anything but what thus saith "the lord" and "master" of all.

For only white men in Mississippi were to exercise the right to speak, to voice, to vote; that is, only white men in Mississippi were to have the right of creation. Only they were to activate the power of "the Word" and bring a world into being. Hamer's insistence on voting, to Marlow, signaled something beyond an exercise of American citizenship. For Marlow, Hamer's intention to vote signaled something for which the collective *he* was "not ready."

Were the threats and intimidation and impending eviction all "on account of we want to register"? What about a Black woman's self-assertion triggered such visceral reaction and vindictiveness? Did it have something to do with white men's fear of losing exclusive access to the power of the spoken word and thus losing the sense of security inherent in the pretense of a white man's "total authority"? To undermine her constitutionally empowered right to vote would ensure the "master class's" continued political and economic domination.

To forcibly terminate Hamer's reproductive capacity was to usurp her natural power and prerogative as a woman, which would serve to further entrench the notion of racialized white, patriarchal men as *the* gatekeepers of life, as avenging destroyers of generations, and as unnatural regulators who presume the authority to control birth.

To stop Hamer's procreative power of speech would protect the upside-down world white patriarchs created with themselves at the center. To muffle her screams was to deny her social power to protest the injustices and to make true the lie that there was no law—at least none that would hold white men accountable, as Black women also had no rights that white men were bound to respect.

The would-be gods of Ruleville and Indianola sensed the going of an age in Mississippi. They feared a toppling of an order of things, a threat to their illegitimate privilege. Unwilling to accept their common humanity, unwilling to evolve to an understanding of limits, a respect of equanimity, an honor of balance, the Marlows of Mississippi resisted vigorously and violently.

But for as much as their anger and rage were directed outward toward quelling perceived external rebellions, the din of it really only served to superficially silence and quell their own internal war. Still, in the midst of the clash of wills was an emptiness. Mute beneath the clamor of vociferous protest was that age-old question that avaricious and malicious patriarchs are compelled to answer, too: Who am I? A question that those under the spell of greed and glory never believe they must answer because they believe that their accumulations and their privileged positions *are* the answer.

But of course they are not. The men who refuse to be what they are also refuse to engage in this basic human question on their own. But when external circumstances force a response, such men will slaughter anyone whose behavior and attitude evoked the question within them. The codependent world manufactured by the self-appointed "master class" can only exist to the extent that those relegated to subservient roles continue to identify with those roles. The Marlows of the world are confounded by a codependency of their own making. They are confused by a sense of self so tenuous and empty that the sound of a woman who is full of herself will echo and vibrate throughout the collective void of their existence. The Marlows of the world find this unforgivable.

And so the men of Mississippi unleashed their force on Mrs. Hamer. The insecurity that Marlow himself felt must be felt by Fannie Lou Hamer—thus the unceremonious eviction and the ending of eighteen years of tenancy and usurious "employment." In order that the men of Mississippi arrest their fears, they must arrest her. And so the state highway patrolmen tracked her and their contingent of citizen patrollers hunted her. To regain a feeling of control over their splitting world, they must seize, detain, contain, and physically overpower her.

※ ※ ※

Entangled in the racialized roots of America's Peculiar Institution are the misogynist roots of pathological patriarchy. Encoded in the judicial processes of colonial law were the excesses of the white male in relation to race, sex, and class. The law reflected his privileges and sanctioned his oppression of peoples of color and white women. "Thus the colonial legal system," Higginbotham instructs, "can be better evaluated by recognizing that it was a system controlled by a white male-dominated culture, a society generally antagonistic toward blacks, a society wherein white males wanted to maintain their domination over *both* white and black females."[40]

The legacy of colonial jurisprudence has continued to reverberate into the twenty-first century in both the dismantling of voting rights legislation and the Supreme Court's 2022 *Dobbs v. Jackson Women's Health Organization* that overturned *Roe v. Wade*, undermining women's rights to their own bodies and authority over their reproductive health. Inarguably, women have realized empowerment under patriarchy in the public domain of "politics, corporations, or the professions"; however, as Johnson has pointed out, patriarchy can accommodate the presence of women as long as women embrace core patriarchal values and "the society retains its essential patriarchal character."[41]

Where women's movements, like the more recent #MeToo and TIME'S UP movements, are demanding *fundamental, transformative* change—that is, change that goes beyond the politics of representation to an evolved worldview—the patriarchy has moved to neutralize the perceived threat. With the *Dobbs* decision, for example, women and their support communities and healthcare providers are now subject to the same kind of criminalization that re-enslaved and colonized Black citizens have suffered. "The law" has been weaponized to bring women back under due subjection to their "masters."

## NOTES

1. Bobby D. Plant, letter to author, June 15, 2022.
2. Bobby D. Plant, letter to author, June 15, 2022.
3. *Sister I'm Sorry* is a 1998 social documentary directed by Frank Underwood, Jr., hosted by Margaret Avery and starring Blair Underwood, Michael Beach,

Thomas Mikal Ford, Steven Williams, and Tico Wells. The film exams African American male-female, heterosexual relationships. The film serves as a platform from which Black men acknowledge and apologize for the physical, mental, and emotional abuse that Black women have suffered at their hands.

4. Bobby D. Plant, letter to author, May 19, 2022.

5. Bobby D. Plant, letter to author, October 1, 2022.

6. "Inside Todd Kohlhepp's Storage Container Used for Torture," *CBS News*, June 23, 2018, https://www.cbsnews.com/pictures/inside-todd-kohlhepps-south -carolina-storage-container-used-to-torture-kala-brown/6/.

7. Bill Whitaker, "'Know My Name': Author and Sexual Assault Survivor Chanel Millers's Full '60 Minutes' Interview," *CBS News*, August 9, 2020, https://www .cbsnews.com/news/chanel-miller-full-60-minutes-interview-know-my-name -author-brock-turner-sexual-assault-survivor-2020-08-09/.

8. Allan G. Johnson, *The Gender Knot: Unraveling Our Patriarchal Legacy*, third edition (Philadelphia: Temple University Press: 1997; Philadelphia: Temple University Press, 2014), 146.

9. Johnson, *The Gender Knot*, 147.

10. Johnson, *The Gender Knot*, 147.

11. Johnson, *The Gender Knot*, 5.

12. Johnson, *The Gender Knot*, 5, 18.

13. Johnson, *The Gender Knot*, 50.

14. Johnson, *The Gender Knot*, 50.

15. Daniel Patrick Moynihan, *The Moynihan Report: The Negro Family—The Case for National Action* (1965; New York: Cosimo Reports, 2018), 29.

16. Moynihan, *The Moynihan Report*, 47.

17. Daniel Patrick Moynihan, "Employment, Income, and the Ordeal of the Negro Family," *Daedalus* 94, no. 4 (1965): 745–70, http://www.jstor.com/stable /20026945.

18. Moynihan, "Employment, Income, and the Ordeal of the Negro Family."

19. Alison Lefkovitz, "Men in the House: Race, Welfare, and the Regulation of Men's Sexuality in the United States, 1961–1972," *Journal of the History of Sexuality* 20, no. 3 (2011): 594–614, https://www.jstor.org/stable/41305886.

20. Moynihan, *The Moynihan Report*, PAGE TK.

21. DeNeen L. Brown, "Civil Rights Crusader Fannie Lou Hamer Defied Men—and Presidents—Who Tried to Silence Her," *The Washington Post*, October 6, 2017, https://www.washingtonpost.com/news/retropolis/wp/2017/10/06/civil-rights -crusader-fannie-lou-hamer-defied-men-and-presidents-who-tried-to-silence-her/.

22. Zora Neale Hurston, *Their Eyes Were Watching God*, in *Zora Neale Hurston: Novels and Stories*, ed. Cheryl A. Wall (New York: Library of America, 1995), 175.

23. Fannie Lou Hamer, "Testimony Before the Credentials Committee, Democratic National Convention," American Public Media, August 22, 1964, https:// americanradioworks.publicradio.org/features/sayitplain/flhamer.html.

24. Hamer, "Testimony Before the Credentials Committee."

25. Hamer, "Testimony Before the Credentials Committee."

26. Hamer, "Testimony Before the Credentials Committee."

27. Hamer, "Testimony Before the Credentials Committee."

28. "Prest. Johnson's Amnesty Proclamation . . . Done at the City of Washington, the Twenty-Ninth Day of May, in the Year of Our Lord One Thousand Eight Hundred and Sixty-Five . . . Andrew Johnson," Library of Congress, May 29, 1865, https://tile.loc.gov/storage-services/service/rbc/rbpe/rbpe23/rbpe235 /23502500/23502500.pdf.

29. Alberto Villoldo, *Mending the Past and Healing the Future with Soul Retrieval* (Carlsbad, California: Hay House, 2005), 47.

30. Villoldo, *Mending the Past and Healing the Future*, 48.

31. Villoldo, *Mending the Past and Healing the Future*, 52.

32. "Minutes of an Interview Between the Colored Ministers and Church Officers at Savannah with the Secretary of War and Major-Gen. Sherman," Freedmen and Southern Society Project (New York, New York, February 13, 1865), http:// www.freedmen.umd.edu/savmtg.htm.

33. Muriel Rukeyser, "Käthe Kollwitz," in *The Collected Poems of Muriel Rukeyser*, eds. Janet E. Kaufman and Anne F. Herzog (Pittsburgh, PA: University of Pittsburgh Press, 2005), 463.

34. Brown, "Civil Rights Crusader Fannie Lou Hamer Defied Men."

35. Hamer, "Testimony Before the Credentials Committee."

36. Hamer, "Testimony Before the Credentials Committee."

37. Hamer, "Testimony Before the Credentials Committee."

38. Camus, *The Rebel*, 13.

39. Hamer, "Testimony Before the Credentials Committee."

40. Higginbotham, *In the Matter of Color*, 42.

41. Johnson, *The Gender Knot*, 8.

# CHAPTER 9

# *BARRACOON* REVISITED

*Welcome to the world of constant yelling, bad language, cursing, and fussing. A place of depression and aggravation. This is a place where you are to live with total strangers. Survival is the name of the game, but its not a game. Even if you keep to yourself trouble will come to you. We live in a dorm that was meant for 68 people Now its 96. There are 5 sinks in the bathroom, maybe 2 works as also the showers. We have to share 5 toilet for 96 people. We have a TV room for 17 people. Wow! There have been many many fights over the TV and a place to set. One computer 96 people. 2 water fountain 1 works. We live in a dorm all day and night where we are locked in by our selves. If something happen to Anyone, Some body might go to the window and holler for help if not that person can get killed. Sometime there is no security around for periods of time here. Now these days and time we will sometime have one security officer to watch over 4 dorm of 96 people, 4 separate dorms. Wow!! Lots of fights have happen without security even knowing, they will see the results of the fight the next day or so on the inmate face.*[1]

THE CROWDED, DYSFUNCTIONAL, HAZARDOUS, and ominous space in which my brother lives recalls the conditions endured by Africans jailed in *barracoons*, imprisoned in the belly of "slavers," those ships used to transport Africans to the so-called New World. Trafficking vessels were originally merchant ships or warships that were refitted to accommodate the African bodies "exported" across the Atlantic during the Middle Passage of "the triangular slave trade."[2]

They were named *Jésus*, *Espéranza*, and *Mercy*. The *Vergenoegen*, the *Progresso*, and the *Desire*. The *Brookes*, the *Amistad*, the *Henrietta Marie*, the *White Lion*, and the *Clotilda*. They came from Portugal, Holland, Sweden, Germany, and the United States. They anchored offshore, along the West and Southeast African coastal waters, and awaited the embarkation of African women, men, and children. These trafficking vessels were the means of the largest transoceanic, forced migration of people in the history of humankind.

At the outset, Europeans ferried their "black cargo" across the Atlantic "in the most dense configurations" possible.[3] African peoples were "packed body to body, often with less than eighteen inches between ceiling and floor, of which there were layers upon layers," many dying from the foul air in the ships' holds. Others were "forced to crouch, with their knees up to their chins, in areas that were no more than four feet high."[4]

"Tight packing" was the common method used in ferrying Africans across the Atlantic. In order to maximize "inventory" in spite of high mortality rates, captains had their crew "cram as many people into a hold as they could. Barely room to turn over, none to walk, and no allowance for latrine buckets." On some ships, Africans were "stacked like logs, literally lying on top of one another."[5] The African captives forced aboard these ships experienced shock or melancholia, knowing neither their destiny nor their fate. The darkness and closeness in the hold reflected the fear and gloom in their hearts. In the words of Beloved in Toni Morrison's novel *Beloved*, *"it was a hot thing."*[6]

In the late eighteenth century, European shipbuilders— influenced by experience, technology, acts of legislation, and interest in their financial bottom lines and profit margins— developed ships specifically designed for their trafficking enterprises. Regulations dictated that the number of captives aboard a ship was to be determined by the ship's tonnage. Usually half the size of a normal cargo ship of the same period, the vessels were "outfitted with decks and platforms in the space below the main deck and above the second or 'tween deck.'" Copper sheathing increased their speed and longevity in tropical waters.[7]

The *Clotilda*, built by William Foster in Mobile, Alabama, in 1855, was one of these ships "built for speed." Though intended for use in the lumber industry, Foster, in collaboration with businessman and enslaver Timothy Meaher, refitted the ship for use in the industry of trafficking. In defiance of the 1808 US prohibition against the importation of Africans into the country, the two conspired to undertake a trafficking venture.

Folklore had it that while he was traveling aboard the *Roger B. Taney*, in April of 1858, Timothy Meaher boasted that he could not only smuggle Africans into Alabama in spite of the ban against transatlantic trafficking, but he would do so and not pay the penalty. Meaher had bet "any amount of money that he would 'import a cargo in less than two years, and no one would be hanged for it.'"[8]

When William Foster returned from the Bight of Benin with 110 African captives in 1860, his ship was towed up the Mobile River near Twelve-Mile Island, where Foster transferred his "contraband" from the *Clotilda* to the *Czar*, the steamship owned by Timothy Meaher's brother Burns Meaher. With the captives hidden below in the bowels of the steamship, Burns had other items loaded onto the steamer to make it appear that the ship was making a regular delivery run.

Traveling farther upriver, the "last black cargo" would be disembarked at a friend's plantation and secreted among the canebrakes. For his part, William Foster had sailed the *Clotilda* into Bayou Canot near Twelve-Mile Island, where he scuttled the ship. With seven cords of lightwood strategically placed, Foster set his ship ablaze in an effort to hide their crime and his guilt, and to erase history.[9]

⌘ ⌘ ⌘

Despite his efforts to obliterate the evidence, the hull of the sunken *Clotilda* was still quite visible at low tide. Nonetheless, Timothy Meaher had won his bet, as the case against him and Foster was dismissed. But as the cultural anthropologist and writer Zora Neale Hurston has stated, Timothy Meaher's bet was not a mere prank. Indoctrinated with the pseudoscientific tenets of biological racism espoused by those like Josiah Nott, Timothy Meaher believed it was his birthright as a white man and his citizenship right as a white, male American to build his wealth out of the bodies of Black people.

Timothy Meaher, along with his three brothers, owned plantations, timberlands, sawmills, and steamboats. And they exploited the labor of enslaved African people who were the "human machinery" on which their processes of production depended. Timothy Meaher's voyage to Dahomey was undertaken as much to augment their "human stock" as it was for Meaher to defy abolitionists and assert his white supremacist, elitist, and patriarchal power.

Timothy Meaher sold some of the Africans from the *Clotilda* voyage to waiting buyers, used some of them to pay his debt to Foster, and divvied up the remainder among the brothers. As the Confederate states lost the war, the Africans smuggled into the country aboard the *Clotilda* would not have to endure enslavement for the rest of their lives. They would, however, like all newly freed Blacks, have to evolve into new identities as American citizens and suffer the backlash of resentful whites who would do everything in their power to thwart their efforts.

Zora Neale Hurston's *Barracoon: The Story of the Last "Black Cargo"* documents this epic moment in national and world history. In this work, she captures the first-person narrative of Oluale Kossola (Cudjo Lewis), one of the 110 aboard the *Clotilda*, who survived capture, the Middle Passage, enslavement, the war, and Jim Crow. His life in Africatown-Plateau, Alabama, was a microcosm of the world of Black America and something of a portent of things to come. Similar to the experiences described by my brother, Kossola and his family and associates who remained in Africatown experienced a hostile environment, a place of "total strangers." The injustices suffered from a "white supremacist," Jim Crow America were compounded by the ostracism and aggression suffered by African Americans. In this inimical, post-emancipation milieu, survival was not a given.

There is no issue in contemporary Black America that has been debated and addressed or protested that was not foreshadowed in *Barracoon*. Reparations, racial disparities, voter suppression, economic inequities, workplace abuse, wage theft, convict leasing, police brutality, mass incarceration, health disparities, environmental injustice, social injustice are all issues that Kossola and his family contended with and are issues consistent with the concerns of African Americans in the twenty-first century.

Kossola along with other men from the *Clotilda* who had been enslaved by the Meaher brothers had remained in Plateau and worked in their employ. Kossola made shingles at the Meahers' sawmill. Like other employers who used their position to reestablish the "master-slave" order of things, the Meahers would also tyrannize and cheat their employees. At the mill, Kossola and others "were paid a dollar a day for ten hours of work, and . . . the Meahers had demanded that they work an extra hour daily for free."[10]

We can only imagine what it took for Oluale Kossola to approach Timothy Meaher and ask for reparations: "Cap'n Tim, you brought us from our country where we had lan'. You made us slave. Now dey make us free but we ain' got no country and we ain' got no lan'! Why doan you give us piece dis land so we kin buildee ourself a home?"[11]

Enraged and indignant, Meaher no doubt wondered at the audacity of Kossola. Jumping to his feet, he exclaimed, "Fool do you think I goin' give you property on top of property? I tookee good keer my slaves in slavery and derefo' I doan owe dem nothin'. You doan belong to me now, why must I give you my lan'?"[12] The idea that someone he considered property would come to him with a claim about property incensed him. Kossola, who was speaking on behalf of his community, was undaunted.

As the Africans from the *Clotilda* could not accumulate a sufficient sum to cover the cost of a voyage back home to "Affica," they had resolved to stay in America. As Timothy Meaher had refused to assist those whose labor built his wealth, they had resolved to "buy de land from de Meaher. Dey doan take off one five cent from de price for us. But we pay it all and take de lan'," said Kossola. They couldn't return to Africa. "Derefo' we make de Affica where dey fetch us." They built homes for one another on the land they bought and called their village "Affican Town."[13]

Because he was not born in America, Kossola, like his compatriots, had to become citizens through the naturalization process. As citizens they were keen to exercise their right to vote, though they knew voting to be a perilous affair for Black men. During the 1874 state elections, Timothy Meaher had given his African employees a speech about voting and told them that they must give their votes to the Democrats. Unconvinced that Kossola and coworkers Charlie and Pollee would do as told, Timothy Meaher intended to stop them from voting. "See those Africans?" he said to an official at one voting station. "Don't let them vote—they are not of this country." Meaher repeated this scenario at two more stations. Undeterred, Kossola, Charlie, and Pollee walked farther to a distant polling station that Meaher had not anticipated and cast their vote for Republicans. They were given a piece of paper as proof that they had voted. "They kept it for decades."[14]

Debates and discussions about racial health disparities and the impact of racialism on healthcare access and on the physical and mental health, life expectancy, and mortality rates of African Americans are longstanding. These issues and concerns were forefront in the national effort to address both the COVID-19 pandemic and the grief and anger surrounding the police murder of George Perry Floyd, Jr. These same issues and concerns are captured in the text and contexts of *Barracoon*. Kossola and his wife Abile (called Seely) lost all of their six children, one by one, to illness, violence, or heartbreak, or combinations thereof.

The girlchild Ebeossi, called Seely, after her mother, "tookee sick in de bed." She was fifteen years old, the only daughter, and the first child to die, despite following a doctor's protocol. As Kossola recounted, "Dat de first time in de Americky soil dat death find where my door is."[15] The baby boy Feïchitan, called Cudjo, after Kossola, was fatally shot by the local deputy sheriff. This same son had been convicted of manslaughter and condemned to five years in the Jefferson County state penitentiary. Once the prison's physician determined him to be able-bodied, Cudjo Lewis, Jr., was dispatched to provide forced labor in the Pratt Mines of the Tennessee Coal and Iron Railroad Company. He was "leased for $10 a month," another black body delivered into Alabama's convict-leasing system.[16]

Kossola and Abile learned through whispers and hushed talk of the mysterious death of their son David (Adeniah). His decapitated body was discovered at the railroad tracks in Plateau. Kossola, himself, had been badly injured in an accident involving a train, in Mobile. He was fourteen days in bed with three broken ribs. Though he survived his wounds, the accident left him unable to continue working at the sawmill. In 1903, Kossola won a lawsuit against the railroad company for $650 (worth $22,000 in 2023).[17] "De railroad lawyer say, 'We ain' goin' to give him nothin'.'" And they didn't. "De people see I ain' able to work no mo', so dey make me de sexton of de church."[18] Later on, Kossola would be forced to sell pieces of his land in order to survive, economically.

Son Pollee (Pollee Dahoo) wanted to sue the railroad company for compensation in David's death. Kossola asked, "Whut for? We doan know de white folks law. Dey say dey doan pay you when dey hurtee you. De court say dey got to pay you de money. But dey ain' done it."[19] Outdone, enraged, aggrieved, and demoralized Pollee no longer laughed. Then he disappeared: "one day he say he go ketchee some fish. . . . He never come back."[20] Shortly after, son James (Ahnonotoe) came home from work feeling not so good. His parents put him to bed, watched over him, and followed doctor's orders—to no avail. According to the coroner, James "died of paralysis."[21]

Abile followed her five children to the family grave plot. Chronic kidney disease was reported as cause of death.[22] But, "Cudjo doan know. She ain' been sick, but she die. She doan want to leave me. . . . But she leave me and go where her chillum." A month later, the oldest child and last son, Aleck (Iyadjemi), too, died unexpectedly. This death left Kossola with a heartrending pain that reverberated across three generations and two continents. Death, said Kossola, "come in de ship wid us."[23] So did injustice.

The story of Oluale Kossola and his companions, like the story of the Angolan Africans of Florida, has only recently been recovered. Completed in 1931, the narrative Kossola entrusted to Zora Neale Hurston was published eighty-seven years later, in 2018. Since *Barracoon*'s publication, the firsthand accounts of Sally Redoshi Smith and Matilda McCrear, who had been aboard the *Clotilda* and had also survived slavery and its aftermath, have been recovered. Positively identified in 2019, America's last known "slave ship," the *Clotilda*, is also being recovered. Archaeologists studying the remains of the ship state that not only is it more intact than anticipated, but "this is the most intact slave ship known to exist in the archeological record anywhere."[24]

America is being called to reckon with our history. To do that, we must be willing to remember. *Barracoon* and the *Clotilda*, like *The Ark of Return*, can inspire and guide our journey.

## NOTES

1. Bobby D. Plant, letter to author, May 16, 2022.
2. Ships anchored offshore along the West and Southeast African coastline were laden with refined and manufactured commodities that would be used in the exchange for African women, men, and children. These ships hailed from various parts of Europe, such as Portugal, France, England, and the Netherlands. Once the hold was filled with African peoples, they sailed to the Caribbean islands and the Americas. This voyage across the Atlantic is called the Middle Passage. In the Caribbean and the Americas, the "human cargo" would be exchanged for raw materials, such as sugar, molasses, cotton, tobacco, and rice. These raw materials would then be shipped to England or elsewhere in Europe to feed their industries. The products

from these industries, along with guns and ammunitions, were then taken to Africa for more "human cargo." This circular, three-point exchange of human beings, raw materials, and refined and manufactured commodities, which began in the mid-fifteenth century and continued into the latter part of the nineteenth century, has been designated by scholars as the "triangular slave trade."

3.  Herbert Klein, *The Atlantic Slave Trade* (Cambridge, UK: Cambridge University Press, 1999), 132.

4.  Molefi K. Asante and Mark T. Mattson, *The African-American Atlas: Black History and Culture—An Illustrated Reference* (New York: Macmillan, 1998), 40.

5.  Asante and Mattson, *The African-American Atlas*, 122.

6.  Toni Morrison, *Beloved* (New York: Alfred A. Knopf, 1987), 211.

7.  Klein, *The Atlantic Slave Trade*, 132–33.

8.  Deborah G. Plant, "Afterword," in *Barracoon: The Story of the Last "Black Cargo,"* by Zora Neale Hurston, ed. Deborah G. Plant (New York: Amistad, 2018), 134.

9.  Sylviane A. Diouf, *Dreams of Africa in Alabama: The Slave Ship* Clotilda *and the Story of the Last Africans Brought to America* (New York: Oxford University Press, 2007), 73–75.

10. Diouf, *Dreams of Africa in Alabama*, 131.

11. Hurston, *Barracoon*, 67.

12. Hurston, *Barracoon*, 67.

13. Hurston, *Barracoon*, 68.

14. Diouf, *Dreams of Africa in Alabama*, 175–76.

15. Hurston, *Barracoon*, 74.

16. Diouf, *Dreams of Africa in Alabama*, 192, 194.

17. Inflation Calculator, U.S. Official Inflation Data, Alioth Finance, December 28, 2022, accessed January 12, 2023, https://www.officialdata.org/.

18. Hurston, *Barracoon*, 80–81.

19. Not only did Kossola not know the white folks' law, the white folks weren't keen on having him know it or even on having him be aware of the state of his own legal affairs. Kossola had been left uninformed that the 1903 verdict of $650 in damages had been overturned. The Louisville and Nashville Railroad Company (the L & N) had appealed the verdict all the way up to the Alabama Supreme Court. Court officials informed Kossola neither of the appeal, nor of the order to pay court costs. Kossola's lawyer, who filed the initial suit, died shortly after, as a consequence of the yellow fever epidemic that hit Mobile that year. (Diouf, *Dreams of Africa in Alabama*, 214.)

20. Diouf, *Dreams of Africa in Alabama*, 87.

21. Diouf, *Dreams of Africa in Alabama*, 217.

22. Diouf, *Dreams of Africa in Alabama*, 217.

23. Hurston, *Barracoon*, 74.

24. Chelsea Brasted, "America's Last Slave Ship Is More Intact than Anyone Thought," *National Geographic*, December 21, 2021, https://www.nationalgeographic.com/history/article/americas-last-slave-ship-is-more-intact-than-anyone-thought.

# CHAPTER 10

# RE-MEMBERING, RE-ROOTING

## Ain't We All Got a Right to
## the Tree of Life?

### "ON EITHER SIDE OF THE RIVER,
### WAS THERE THE TREE OF LIFE"[1]

*Speaking about life in prison, you said 75% of the [Angola] prison population will do life in prison. But even a percentage of the 25 will also do life, see some of those numbers mean prisoners with 10, 15, 25 and so on . . . letters mean L I F E, so some of those numbers will fight some one and kill someone, so the number turn into letters. If a [prisoner] kill someone in prison he can get a life sentence. His number turn into letters.*

*Now this is what the court system does to a person who only crime was robbery. But the 3 strike law gave him 30 yrs. with parole, but in 10 years he has learned all kinds of new stuff. This person was only a robber but now when he gets out he may do a new crime because he has spent years around other real harden [criminals]. This same person can get out on parole in about 20 years. Only to do a new thing that he learned in prison.*

*Now that person when he get caught will get a life sen-*
*tence. Being in prison will turn a good man bad. Some rap-*
*ist commit rape after they have done time in prison. Well if*
*not most a percentage of them will commit rape. And when*
*caught, come back with a life sentence.*
   *It's not the men in here it's the court system.*
   *I just thought you should know.*[2]

## TREES OF FORGETFULNESS

In some vicinities on the west coast of Africa, like the kingdom
of Dahomey, before captured Africans were allowed to be taken
onto trafficking vessels, they were forced to circle the tree of
forgetfulness. The men were to go around the tree nine times,
the women seven. The intention of the ritual was to have those
who had been sold to forget their former lives—their family,
their culture, their homeland. "From that moment on they
would have no identity or memories of their past life."[3] But
as Oluale Kossola's narrative might suggest, the past is not so
easily forgotten. And as African cultural retentions around the
globe might suggest, our African cultural heritage is resilient
and transformative.

   This resiliency is even more amazing in face of the hostility,
animosity, and sheer hatred that people of African descent have
been forced to endure. Characters in Haile Gerima's *Ashes and
Embers* dramatize the ramifying dimensions of this struggle in
America:

Ned Charles, you see this? You see this branch? It comes
from the main tree. And when you take this branch from its

homeland and you plant it in a foreign country, the whole struggle is to try to grow its roots.[4]

Ned Charles is the main character in Haile Gerima's 1982 film *Ashes and Embers*. He is a Vietnam veteran, just home from a war that continues to rage inside him. He is disillusioned, angry, and lost. His fractured memory exposes a dismembered life. Internal anguish and externalized rage disconnect him from "the main tree"—his grandmother. She has been his comfort and his champion. She, for Ned Charles, is the embodiment of home, community, heritage, and mythic memory. She represents the land he left. She reflects his essential Self.

But there is a crack in Ned Charles's conception of self that threatens to shatter his identity. His mind is split, and his conscience is haunted. His soul recoils from the atrocities he witnessed and those he committed as a soldier in Vietnam. And such memories vie with recollections of his young self in rural Virginia and his adult self in Los Angeles and Washington, DC, after the war—a marginalized existence of low-wage jobs, police harassment, and limited options. His optimism dulls. He discerns that his tour of duty returned him to an America still steeped in hostile indifference toward Black life.

On his grandmother's land in Virginia, working the family garden alongside his girlfriend, Liza Jane, and her son, Kimathi, Ned Charles, called Nay, experiences calm and peace. His grandmother has managed to hold on to some portion of her land by selling her property piecemeal, "bit by bit," in order to prevent losing the whole of it to tax collectors or vulturistic real estate developers. Balancing her stance with a walking cane in her right hand, she plants herself in front of her grandson and holds up before him, in her left hand, a tree branch, weighted with leaves.

"Ned Charles, you see this? You see this branch? It comes from the main tree. . . ." But Ned Charles, distracted, is busy reprimanding Kimathi for trampling on the plants. Her words seem to fall on deaf ears.

But Grandma continues her talk-fuss about having her land taken from her and the threat of being uprooted after a lifelong struggle of trying to put down some roots in America. "Trying to uproot me," she tells Liza Jane, who *is* listening. "Trying to uproot me." And she is bone-tired from this struggle: "My legs, and my hands, my whole body. The senses failing, and they become more numb and numb!" But Grandma declares that she will hold herself together, carry the weight and burden of the body until the Lord calls her. "And you know what's keeping me together?" She pauses, looking at Liza Jane. "It's my fighting soul."

The heady elation of again being in the warm embrace of his grandmother and enjoying the sense of well-being inherent in the land of his childhood is, eventually, dispelled by a growing paranoia, belligerence, and disconnection—from Liza Jane and Kimathi, his grandmother and everything she represents—from his heritage. "Now, I love you, Grandmama," Ned Charles states as he struggles to separate what he knows to be true out from that which confounds him. "But I don't think that this place, or this land, nor this house, nor the memories here gonna contain me no more."

He fears that who he was, the Ned Charles she raised, had been undone: "I ain't that innocent little boy that left the country." And he warns her against his woundedness and perceived brokenness: "I can't even begin to explain to you the things that been done to me and the things that I done," he tells her, as though those things would be unforgivable and must necessarily

cut him off from love and relationships, forgiveness and restoration, and justifiably annul his sense of belonging to the circles
of family, community, and culture that have been his grounding
and that continue to claim him.

In his nightmare of alienation, Ned Charles becomes the branch
that is torn from the main tree. He feels that his perceived brokenness renders him incapable of being accountable to anyone,
to join with anyone, including his grandmother, who expects him
to assume stewardship of the land. "Now, don't you count on me,
Grandma," he protests. Then, from a pained place, he tells her
what she already knows: "Grandmama, I'm not back home. Now
I know, I know I done come home. I come home, and yet I'm not."

She had prayed and she had awaited Ned Charles's return
from the war. She believed her prayers had kept him alive, just as
his imminent return kept her alive. She would wait another eight
years. She would be the space for his full return—in mind and
spirit, as well as body; she would await his "second coming."

Grandma's fighting spirit is buoyed up by her church community and the collective African American cultural legacies that it
represents. And she awaits the time when she can pass on to her
grandson what is left of the land—her earthly stores—and her
stores of knowledge and wisdom. As she waits, Grandma continues
her work as elder, as the mother tree of her family and community.
While waiting for Nay Charles, she imparts her collective wisdom
to the ready receivers of the next generation. Like the knees about
a great cypress, Liza Jane (an "everydaughter") and Kimathi (an
"everygrandchild"), sit by the fireside listening to Grandma's stories. She is at once griot and raconteur, time and eternity, history
and prophecy. "I got my mind on Denmark Vesey." She captivates
her rapt audience. "He was such a wonderful man."

## A TALE OF TWO TREES

In 2018, the city of Boston celebrated the reopening of Liberty Tree Plaza. A commemorative elm tree was planted there to recall and honor the original Boston "Liberty Tree." Recognized as the site where American colonists gathered to talk about liberty and natural rights and to protest the Stamp Act and other tyrannical acts by the British government, the Liberty Tree symbolized the spirit of freedom and democracy. But the tree that was a rallying site for the cause of justice also became a rallying site for the cause of violence and mayhem, where the "Sons of Liberty" would terrorize British officials and loyalists, humiliate them, and, with a noose around someone's neck, threaten to lynch them. It became a gathering point for violent mobs that dispersed to break into, vandalize, and loot the homes and properties of "Tories."

Perceiving the Liberty Tree as "an Idol for the Mob to Worship," British soldiers cut the tree down in 1775. The tree was around 120 years old. Not accidentally, some historians say, the Boston Liberty Tree had been "lost to history." Perhaps "a willful forgetting" was fostered by Boston's "Brahmin elite" who decried "the violent, mob-uprising, tar-and-feathers side of the American Revolution—a side of our history that's still too radical for comfort."[5]

Quiet as it's kept, the Boston Liberty Tree was not colonial America's only "Liberty Tree." In towns from Boston to Charles Town (Charleston), South Carolina, disgruntled colonists found their own liberty trees to rally around. South Carolina's ruling "elite" had harangued crowds of artisans and laborers in the shadow of the Charles Town Liberty Tree. While manipulating the political moment to advance their elitist agenda, these leaders also massaged the discontent the masses felt over their economic marginalization within the provincial political economy and redirected their rage toward the British.

The rallying cry of "Liberty and Property" was put on their tongues, though the greater portion of them had no property of which to speak. The self-interested oligarchs of Charles Town gave lip service to revolution while rousing the passions of the masses to a riotous pitch. They incited their followers to stage Charles Town's own version of the Boston Tea Party and aided and abetted mobs in their destructive and brutal acts.

Disregarding the emerging class struggle between the oligarchy and white laborers, the more radical members of the ruling class formed alliances with the extreme factions among "the People." Rather than categorically denounce the violence and lawlessness of the mobs, the "wealthy elite" sought to harness their power and incorporate it within a "new, emerging political machinery."[6]

This structured alliance between the political leaders of the gentry and those of the "Rank and File" or "the Herd" was intended both to secure the oligarchy's leadership over Charles Town and the Carolina colony and to garner clout against the imposing British. Although the "Men of Property" pretended to deplore violence and disorder, they weren't above instigating it to stabilize their social position and to advance their economic and political ambition. They used their authoritative position in manipulative collaborations with the working middle class to assert their presumed right to a "deferential society" under their "aristocratic" rule. They redirected the anger and aggression of the masses—born of years of struggling within an economy based on enslaved labor—toward the British and used it "as a political weapon" to extort more political prerogatives from the British Parliament.[7]

This emerging "political machinery" entailed the deft manipulation of the laboring classes for the benefit of the wealthy. It was designed to harness the destructive force of a perceived inferior and subordinate class of people for the purpose of protecting a "superior" status quo. From the point of view of South Carolina's ruling "elite," "the use of violence in the name of the social order was no crime."[8] The order to be preserved, however, was the hierarchical order enjoyed by the colony's "aristocratic" oligarchy. The peace and harmonious order of *their* lives was all-important.

As stated earlier, James Baldwin reminds us that to the extent that we do not become consciously aware of our "past," of our "history," it continues to control us and to assert itself as our present-moment reality. In planting a commemorative elm in the Boston Liberty Tree Plaza, will we open to the whole truth that the tree, which represents liberty, has to teach us? Are we courageous enough to re-root ourselves in the original ideals of freedom, equality, and democracy? Could we be strong and resilient enough to examine and contemplate the politics at the root of the variety of trees that sprang up in imitation of and in the disguise of the original Boston Liberty Tree?

Are we not at that point of reckoning wherein we might allow the full knowledge of the elements of "dawn and doom" that danced in the branches of America's liberty trees to evolve us and move us toward our more perfect union?[9] Did silencing certain parts of the cacophony of voices that make up our early American history prevent contemporary public officials from hearing the rumblings of discontent that manifested on January 6, 2021? Did the tradition of hiding, simplifying, ignoring, and sanitizing the complex, difficult, and repugnant truths about our developing democracy make it difficult for witnesses to the January 6 event to discern sedition from peaceful protest, a mob from a crowd?

Might it be somehow useful to know that the political fault lines that run through our Constitution were reflected in the bifurcated philosophical mind of the philosopher John Locke, who consulted with and advised the framers of the Constitution? For, as Locke had assisted the framers of the US Constitution, Locke had also assisted the framers of the Fundamental Constitutions of Carolina.

For South Carolina oligarchs, "enough" was not a concept they entertained. Limits were ideally imposed on others, the better to give themselves limitless and unbounded license. For these oligarchs, compromise also was for others, for they were never appeased by any effort to address their "aristocratic" aspirations, claims, and demands. No concession made by the more liberal framers of the Constitution met with their incontrovertible approval or contentment.

The claims and demands of the oligarchy, as represented by General Charles Cotesworth Pinckney, were rooted in the constitution that governed the Carolina colony, especially their supposed "aristocratic" right to keep Black people in bondage forever. Even before the colony was populated and "settled," the lords proprietors of Carolina had already classed African peoples as "slaves" in the colony's founding governance document: the Fundamental Constitutions of Carolina.

During the debates at the Constitutional Convention, delegates referenced John Locke's political theories and his treatises on liberty and "the natural rights of man." Locke's categorization of the natural rights of "property, liberty and estate" were broadened to "life, liberty and the pursuit of happiness" by Jefferson. Armed with the natural rights arguments asserted by Locke and the earlier declared "liberties of Englishmen," it was but an "easy step" for these men to move "to the universalist assertion that all men had a right to be free.'"[10]

Paradoxically, just as John Locke's political science upheld the

ideals of liberty and natural rights in support of the colonists' bid
for freedom, his political science also buttressed the "racially bifurcated construction of slavery" in support of pro-slavery delegates'
rights in the oppression of Blacks.[11] For just as Locke had influenced the composition of the US Constitution, he had influenced
the composition of the Fundamental Constitutions of Carolina.

"The authors of that document, the so-called Fundamental Constitution of 1669," writes the historian A. Leon Higginbotham, Jr.,
"were John Locke and the first Earl of Shaftesbury. In matters of
race, it seems, the understanding even of John Locke, to whom is
attributed the whole concept of man's inalienable rights, was more
a product of his time than of his conscience."[12] And Mark Goldie,
editor of *Locke: Political Essays*, makes it clear that John Locke's
contribution to the governance document was not limited to dic-
tation and editing:

> There is no mystery about the type of polity that Locke
> thought it prudent to adopt. . . . It is the regime elaborately
> reproduced for export to North America in The Funda-
> mental Constitutions of Carolina, which, under a nominal
> monarchy, envisaged rule by an hereditary nobility and
> landed gentlemen, "that we may avoid erecting a numer-
> ous democracy."[13]

Goldie describes Locke's contribution to the Fundamental
Constitutions as "a vexed matter." For Locke associated himself
with Carolina and its constitutions for the rest of his life. In a
letter to Locke, the Lord Proprietor Peter Colleton had remarked
on "that excellent form of government in the composure of which
you had so great a hand." Locke had purchased a hundred copies
of the Fundamental Constitutions of Carolina and loaned copies

of it to his friends.[14] It would seem that, for John Locke, this document that elevated "aristocrats," subordinated the masses, and sanctioned enslavement was a source of pride.

If we are revolutionary enough to remember what has been forgotten, to see what has been hidden, to become aware of what has been submerged in our historical unconscious, to take an accounting of and develop an appreciation for human contradiction, then might we have the wherewithal to embrace the evolutionary phase of our revolution?

## RE-MEMBERING

The African Burial Ground National Monument in New York City acknowledges and commemorates the presence of "some 15,000" enslaved Africans who had been trafficked to New York in the 1700s. They built the infrastructure, buildings, and facilities of a burgeoning metropolis that would become a world capital. These "African New Yorkers" lived, worked, and died there. A 6.6-acre cemetery, "the 'Negroes Buriel [sic] Ground,'" was their final resting place.[15] The entire area had been built over.

Only an intent to build over the cemetery once again resurrected this dimension of New York's colonial history. Human remains were unearthed during a 1991 construction project in Lower Manhattan. Outrage and protest halted construction. Excavations of 419 burials, "a small portion of the actual burial ground," had been removed. Study of their bones told the story of a horrific existence, a life of "overwork, painful injuries, and disease." Study of the artifacts at the site also spoke of a sense of the sacred, a spiritual knowledge that was reflected in "a persistent collective memory of how to address death."[16]

In 2003, the remains were reinterred in an elaborate cere-
mony of community members and local and visiting dignitaries.
On the site of the memorial grounds, more than twenty trees
stood sentinel, honoring the ancestral spirits and applauding
our re-memory.

☒   ☒   ☒

A few blocks south of the African Burial Ground is the National
9/11 Memorial and Museum. Erstwhile referred to as "Ground
Zero," it is the site of the 2001 attack on the World Trade Center
that resulted in the collapse of the Twin Towers and, with it, the
terrible and tragic devastation of nearly three thousand expressions of humanity. In the process of rescue and recovery, some
workers also managed to save some damaged trees. Among those
pulled from rubbish heaps was a Callery pear tree:

> The little tree had been severely burnt, a number of its limbs
> were reduced to stumps, and its bark was charred from the
> intense fires at the site. Yet somehow, it continued to sprout
> leaves from beneath the rubble.[17]

To support the tree's struggle for survival, city workers transported the tree to a nursery, where it was replanted and given
"watchful care." "The transplanted tree slowly took root in its
new home" and began to overcome its violent deracination and
heal its traumatic history. Seven years later, this witness to history still carried scars from that fateful day, but the Callery pear
thrived nonetheless. Only eight feet tall when violently uprooted,
it had stretched thirty feet upwards. The tree's "burned and

gnarled stumps now extended into long branches, each sprouting white blossoms in the spring."[18]

In 2010, after having survived additional storms, the Callery pear would be replanted once again. It would "return to its 'roots.'" Resuming its position at the 9/11 Memorial site as a witnessing presence, it would become renown as "The Survivor Tree." It would signify our capacity to persevere and to remember that we have the innate capacity to hold and carry our entire history. It would become a "symbol of resilience and renewal, an emblem of rebirth."[19]

✘ ✘ ✘

## BRANCHES[20]
"They see men only as trees walking."[21]

George Perry Floyd, Jr. • Breonna Taylor • Ahmaud M. Arbery • Atatiana K. Jefferson • Michael O. D. Brown, Jr. • Sandra A. Bland • Freddie C. Gray • Eleanor Bumpurs • Eric Garner

Philando D. Castile • Michael Griffith • India J. Kager • Tamir E. Rice • Quawan "Bobby" Charles • Korryn S. Gaines • Jonathan Price • Walter L. Scott • Dijon Kizzee • Tanisha N. Anderson • Shantel Davis • Sean E. Bell • Yusef K. Hawkins • Kayla Moore • LaQuan J. McDonald • Alberta Spruill • James E. Chaney • Shelly M. Frey • James Byrd, Jr. • Emmett Louis Till

Laura Nelson • L. D. Nelson • Denmark Vesey • Ned Bennett • Rolla Bennett • "Gullah" Jack Pritchard • Monday Gell • Celia • Octavius Catto

## LEAVES: CORONA CIVICA

"And the leaves of the tree were for the healing of the nations."[22]

Foley Gibson • Wynta-Amor Rogers • Monica Brady-Barnard
• Josie Landau • Boaz Garrett • Aaron Burriss • Avis Burriss •
Emma Kazanski • Cameron Radcliff

Kamryn Johnson • Nolan Davis • Mikhail Ali • Yolanda Renee
King • Ethan Goldsmith • Brayden Harrington • Abdel-Rahman
Al-Shantti • Tybre Faw • Amaya Harris • Greta T. E. E.
Thunberg • Keedron Bryant • Maya Adams • Cameron Adams •
Zerah Simeon Jones • Darnella Frazier • Amanda S. C. Gorman
• Gwen Berry • Emily Bernstein • Isaac Harris • Marilyn Watts

Simone A. Biles • Alicia Garza • Patrisse Cullors • Ayǫ Tometi
• Megan A. Rapinoe • Naomi Osaka • Rashad Robinson •
Tarana J. Burke • Shawn M. Dromgoole

## SEEDLINGS

"And he shewed me a pure river of water of life."[23]

Chanel Miller • Chelsea J. Handler • Peggy McIntosh •
Melvyn R. Leventhal • Howard Zinn • Alec Karakatsanis
• S. Arundhati Roy • Debra A. Haaland • Ethan G. Hawke

Angela Y. Davis • Alice M. T-K. Walker • Joni Mitchell •
A. Philip Randolph • Dorothy "Mama Dot" Bailey • César
Chávez • Jonathan Myrick Daniels • Viola Liuzzo • Benjamin B.
Ferencz • Fannie Lou Hamer • Zora Neale Hurston • María
Sabina Magdalena García • Flo Kennedy • Marjory Stoneman

Douglas • Black Elk • MaVynee "Beach Lady" Betsch • Anna
Eleanor Roosevelt • Lillian Smith • John Marshall Harlan •
Charles Sumner

Frederick Douglass • Abraham Lincoln • William Lloyd
Garrison • Elizabeth Heyrick • John Brown • Angelina Grimké
Weld • Sarah Moore Grimké • John Woolman •
William Wilberforce

## NOTES

1. Revelation 22:2 (KJV).
2. Bobby D. Plant, letter to author, December 26, 2021.
3. Laura Samsom Rous and Hans Samsom, *Tree of Forgetfulness* (Amsterdam: KIT Publishers, 2004).
4. *Ashes and Embers*, directed and written by Haile Gerima (Washington, DC: Mypheduh Films, 1982). Transcription by the author.
5. Erick Trickey, "The Story Behind a Forgotten Symbol of the American Revolution: The Liberty Tree," *Smithsonian Magazine*, May 19, 2016, https://www.smithsonianmag.com/history/story-behind-forgotten-symbol-american-revilution-liberty-tree-180959162.
6. Walter J. Fraser, Jr., *Charleston! Charleston!: The History of a Southern City* (Columbia, South Carolina: University of South Carolina Press, 1991), 147.
7. Fraser, *Charleston! Charleston!*, 109, 125, 139, 150.
8. Fraser, *Charleston! Charleston!*, 187.
9. Zora Neale Hurston, *Their Eyes Were Watching God*, in *Zora Neale Hurston: Novels and Stories*, ed. Cheryl A. Wall (New York: Library of America, 1995), 181.
10. A. Leon Higginbotham, Jr., *In the Matter of Color: Race and the American Legal Process: The Colonial Period*, (New York: Oxford, 1978), 374.
11. Higginbotham, *In the Matter of Color*, 376.
12. Higginbotham, *In the Matter of Color*, 163.
13. Mark Goldie, "Introduction," in *Locke: Political Essays*, by John Locke, ed. Mark Goldie (Cambridge, UK: Cambridge University Press, 1997), xxiv.
14. Goldie, "Introduction," 60–61.
15. Martia G. Goodson, *New York's African Burial Ground* (Fort Washington, Pennsylvania: Eastern National, 2012), 3–4.
16. Goodson, *New York's African Burial Ground*, 3, 19.
17. Allie Skayne, *The Survivor Tree: A Story of Hope and Healing* (New York: 9/11 Memorial and Museum, n.d.), 11.

18. Skayne, *The Survivor Tree*, 12, 15.
19. Skayne, *The Survivor Tree*, 22, 24.
20. "BRANCHES" honors the lives of uprooted African Americans. "LEAVES" celebrates the youth and young adults, youthful activists, and upcoming generations who symbolize the leafing of branches yet rooted or re-rooted and the leaves that spiral out of even fallen trees. "SEEDLINGS" recognizes and applauds allyship, collaborative politics, possibility, those committed to transformative change, social justice, environmental justice. All names listed are symbolic, as the number of names in each section also symbolizes and commemorates the length of time, officially, that Officer Derek Chauvin kneeled on the neck of Mr. George Perry Floyd, Jr.: Nine Minutes • Twenty • Nine Seconds.
21. Frederick Douglass, "The Future of the Negro People of the Slave States, Speech Delivered Before the Emancipation League in Tremont Temple, Boston, February 5, 1862," in *Frederick Douglass: Selected Speeches and Writings*, 479.

    In his speech, Frederick Douglass expressed his dismay with the new converts to the abolitionist cause. Though convinced that slavery was the cause of treason and war and would continue to be a threat to the republic, they were hesitant about adopting a policy to abolish slavery. They were confounded by the question of what was to be done "with the four million slaves if emancipated." As the blind man in the parable who saw men as trees walking would eventually see "every man clearly," Douglass argued that the new converts should recognize their blurred vision when it came to Black humanity and to see clearly that Black people, who are part of a common humanity, were not exceptions to the "principles and maxims" that governed human life. Four million emancipated human beings, Douglass assured them, would strive like any other people and would "bear the responsibility of our own existence." ("The Future of the Negro People of the Slave States," 480.)

    As with pro-slavery advocates and diffident abolitionists of the nineteenth century, there are those in contemporary society who are likewise confounded by the questions that have arisen in relation to the 2020 Abolition Amendment that seeks to close the criminal-exception loophole and end slavery in America once and for all. Equally confounding is the prospect of dismantling the prison-industrial complex that practices slavery and involuntary servitude. Yet as Douglass protested, "But why, O why should we not abolish slavery now? All admit that it must be abolished at some time. What better time than now can be assigned for that great work?" ("The Future of the Negro People of the Slave States," 477–78.)
22. Rev. 22:2 (KJV).
23. Rev. 22:1 (KJV).

# AND JUSTICE FOR ALL

*Hey Lil Sister,*

*Well I'm alright, just setting in this prison wasting time.
I think a lot about what I could be doing if I was at home.
All my days are being wasted, and I feel like I could be doing
something with my life. I'm smart and I learn fast, but I
have nothing to do here. Life here is a drag. I wonder a lot
why am I here. I never raped nobody but I'm still here, what
is my purpose of living? I'm not helping any one or doing
anyone any good. I feel like my life should have meaning.
It's bad when 12 people decide if you live or die. The thing
is these 12 people don't know the law. All they do is listen to
the D. A. and go home eat and sleep not knowing what they
just done to a person that day. Anyway I know everybody
has their own cross to bear. But I wont mind it so much if
I deserved this. I'm not a bad person. I'm grateful for you.
You are always thinking about me. You know me better than
anybody. Sometime I don't know what I would have done
without you. Everyday is a challenge for me, I try hard to
do the right things here. Sometime I don't want to do right
because of the way I feel some days, but I think about what*

*would it change (Nothing). I would still be here wasting
time.*

*I feel like I could have been anything I wanted to be if I
had my mind in the right places. That's why I'm proud of
you. You did what none of us could have done with what we
had. I'm really tired of prison. I would like to be free once
more before I die. I'm closer to death than life right now. I'm
almost 60 years old. I would like to see the house again or
maybe our childhood church or even just the hood one more
time. Do you think God still has a plan for my life? Maybe
he do, but I don't like this part of his plan. Well I wont hold
you too long, keep on keeping on you are the best. If you see
Jean or talk to her tell her I said hello.*

*Love ya,*
*Bro Bobby*

*p.s. Still looking for the movie.* ☺[1]

T HE FIRST FILM THAT MADE an impression upon me, an impression that has lasted all these years of my life since I first
saw it, in 1979, was . . . *And Justice for All.* Al Pacino was featured
as the main character, Arthur Kirkland. He was a lawyer, a public defender who figuratively and literally fights for his clients. In
the opening of the film, Kirkland is in jail, himself, on contempt
charges. Outraged that Judge Fleming (played by John Forsythe)
refused to look at the evidence that could clear an innocent man,
because of a technicality, Kirkland takes a swing at the judge. This
"letter-of-the-law" judge is disinterested in the spirit of justice. He
is more interested in quoting discrete legal scripture and enforcing
"the law" than in serving justice, and Kirkland can't seem to wrap
his mind around that kind of judicial disposition.

Kirkland is perplexed that so many court officials and staff see his economically marginalized clients as worthless and undeserving of the protection of the law or their respect. He believes that justice ought to be about finding the truth, but he finds that truth, justice, guilt, innocence, fairness, and mercy are irrelevant in the court of law. Winning is everything. "It's just a show!" he yells out at the beginning of his opening statement during a pivotal trial. "It's a show! It's *Let's Make a Deal*!" When he refuses to play the game, when he chooses to speak the truth and not be bought and blackmailed by his "prestigious" client, who is Fleming himself, the judge who is overseeing the trial declares Kirkland out of order. "You're out of order!" Kirkland fires back. "You're out of order. The whole trial is out of order!" Chaos erupts.[2]

I am always struck by the truth captured in this film and the honest, heartfelt passion of Pacino's performance. The absurdity inherent in our legal system, as revealed in . . . *And Justice for All*, is made less overwhelming only to the degree that what is also revealed in the film is the power in choosing to confront this absurd reality rather than resigning ourselves to it.

How many public officials and private citizens have been indoctrinated and socialized to think, as Fleming did, that people who are criminalized and delivered into the system deserve to fester in the prison hellholes that, according to Fleming, the prisoners themselves created? Except, of course, imprisoned persons don't create the harsh and violent environments that they are thrown into. Decisions made by callous and disconnected criminal-punishment bureaucrats who see innocence and guilt as irrelevant, and rehabilitation and restoration as a farce, engender the inhumane conditions that millions of American citizens endure and that some, like the character Ralph Agee, cannot survive.

Any number of judges and lawyers, like those in . . . *And Justice for All*, manipulate the system and the loopholes in the law to protect their "elite" clients as well as to protect themselves and avoid taking responsibility for their own crimes. They are seldom found guilty of the criminal acts they commit, and thus, they seldom experience the hellholes they construct and maintain as shining manifestations of Lady Justice. In this system, those who cannot afford private, high-powered corporate lawyers or are not lucky enough to have public defenders who have professional integrity and heart are looked at and treated as "scum" by criminal-punishment bureaucrats and those who have been indoctrinated to believe that the system works and that the system is just.

As Attorney Warren Fresnell tells Kirkland point-blank, he doesn't care about *"them"*—those citizens with "penny-ante" cases who cannot afford to scrub their corrupted images clean and pay for or extort the privilege of living above the law. "It's nickel and dime, Arthur!" Fresnell shouts. "It's all nickel and dime." Distracted by a meeting with another client from whom he stands to collect a $7,000 fee, Fresnell forgets his promise to represent Kirkland's client Ralph Agee, while Kirkland sees to his partner, who has suffered a mental breakdown. Fresnell rushes in late for Agee's sentencing hearing and is unprepared to communicate certain particulars of the case to the judge. Consequently, instead of being released on probation, Agee is sentenced to three years in jail.

Ralph Agee is thus remanded to an environment populated by poor and impoverished othered human beings, guilty and innocent alike, who, like Agee, have been subject to the violence of the criminal-punishment system and treated by criminal justice bureaucrats as though they are "scum" and mere brutes. Agee would have been in jail sooner or later, Fresnell reasons. Fresnell's brand of legal profiteering and his rationalized indifference toward those who cannot pay are pervasive in the halls of justice and ensure that the bodies of the socially marginalized and the poor fill American jails and prisons.

Knowing how the system works, how it sustains itself on the predictable caging of Black and brown bodies, Fresnell excuses his negligence with the fatalistic conclusion that if Ralph Agee "is not in jail this week, he'll be in jail next week." Fresnell resolves that, in any case, Agee will be out on probation in ten months, as though ten months in jail are just "numbers." He then advises an inconsolable Kirkland to appeal the verdict. Appeals always generate more money for the system, but they don't guarantee a fairer hearing or a changed outcome, and they can be filed, but they are not always granted. And there is no accounting for what happens to a person in the meantime.

As my brother states, numbers oftentimes mutate into letters, meaning "L I F E." In the case of Ralph Agee, his life sentence was death at his own hands. Any appeal would have come much too late for him. A poor, African American, gay male, cross-dresser, Agee is terrified of being subjected to more of the violence he has already experienced in jail. "Half hour after they put him in the lockup," an aggrieved Kirkland rails at Fresnell, "he hanged himself." Such events are simply proof for insensate bureaucrats of the ilk of Fleming that not only do "criminals create their own hellhole" but that those perceived as "criminals" *should* be subject, also, to "unjust punishment"—as though this is not already the case.

✖ ✖ ✖

State and federal abolition amendments seek to end the mass caging of American citizens who are disproportionately African

American, persons of color, the socially stigmatized, and the poor. Policymakers want to amend the criminal-exception loophole that sanctions slavery as a punishment for crime and that fuels the mass incarceration era that has given rise to an ever-expanding criminal-punishment bureaucracy. Their stated objective is to end slavery, in any and all forms, *once and for all*. To do that, it is necessary to not only recognize *all* the forms that slavery takes but to also realize the essence of this process termed "slavery" and its core "master-slave" dynamic and see and acknowledge the controlling hand of Western patriarchy.

The reforms that have been advocated for are welcome steps in the processes we must undertake in regaining our individual and collective freedom. But reforms maintain the status quo, and history has shown us that slavery cannot be reformed. The ending of *slavery* requires personal and societal transformation. The beginning of those steps in the process of gaining freedom and experiencing personal sovereignty include understanding the ways in which we are bound, discerning what incidents of slavery look like in the twenty-first century, and determining how the badges of slavery are imposed on us and how we impose them on others.

This involves, but is not limited to, the following actions:

- Learn how to identify the interlocking systems of oppression, examine their processes of reproduction and reformulation, and assess and redress how we ourselves reinforce and maintain these systems
- Understand the patriarchal social system as fundamental to other systems of "privilege" and oppression
- Practice the theorist Mari Matsuda's method (quoted in Davis et al. 2022) called "ask the other question" to assist in peeling back the interlocking layers of oppression: "When I

see something that looks racist, I ask, 'Where is the patriarchy in this?' When I see something that looks sexist, I ask, 'Where is the heterosexism in this?' When I see something that looks homophobic, I ask, 'Where are the class interests in this?'[3]

- Refuse to remain complacent, transfixed by, and dutiful to politicians who willfully sacrifice democratic principles and smother the sovereign voice of the people for career ambitions and personal gain and glory
- Seek the nonhierarchical wisdom of the land, flora, and fauna of geographical America
- Develop an appreciation of the history, culture, and wisdom of the Indigenous stewards of this land
- Realize that so-called anti-woke legislation is designed to keep you asleep, isolated in a self-righteous silo, separated from family and community, and to make of you a stumbling block in the path toward a more perfect union
- Give yourself permission to have an informed, critical, creative, and constructive intelligence
- Reactivate your curiosity and desire to know, to learn, to explore, to evolve
- Cultivate the courage to question fiats and mandates, court decisions and legislated policies, and tradition and custom that defraud us of our constitutional right to our bodies, the bodies of our loved ones, and to our sovereign humanity
- Dare to be strong and bold enough to be vulnerable and humble and present to challenging conversations and difficult dialogues
- Open to the possibility of possibility

Ultimately, we want to become consciously aware human beings and citizens. It is essential that we commit to doing the

alchemical, transformative "Work" of moving out of unconscious stasis to evolve ourselves and our society. So much has
been hidden from us, dismissed, rendered unimportant, cloaked
in invisibility, erased, buried, burned, obscured, whitewashed,
obfuscated, and concealed in lies that are wrapped in our American flag. And this is by design.

We cannot overestimate the challenges of effectively addressing social disparities, structural inequities, imposed starvation
(euphemized as "food insecurity"), uprooted individuals and
families who are unhoused and cast out of doors (euphemized as
"homelessness"); or the bravery it will take to throw off the har-
nesses and chains of patriarchy and the tyranny of corporate oligarchs; or the compassion and creativity that will be demanded
of us as we face the complexities and surmount the psychological, political, and social obstacles related to the decarceration of
America, the dismantling of a duplicitous and corrupt criminal-
punishment system, and the ending of slavery in every form, once
and for all.

We also cannot underestimate the will of people who believe
in freedom, the spirit of "the people" in their ongoing pursuit of
liberty and justice, and the soul's own longing for the experience
of expressed sovereignty. We cannot underestimate our capacity
to think, act, and evolve ourselves, our collective humanity, and
our nation. Just because the questions are big doesn't mean they
can't be answered. Because a mountain is rough-backed and tall
doesn't mean it can't be scaled. And so we cannot underestimate
the power of our capacity for self-empowerment. What happens
when we ourselves begin to remove the scales from our own eyes?

The interlocking systems of oppression are no doubt daunt-
ing. And given that particular forms of oppression are embedded

within and entangled among the roots and limbs of the others, these systems must seem unassailable. One form of oppression overlaps, hides, and camouflages another—but only to the extent that we are distracted from recognizing it and to the extent that we are actively advised and taught to *not see* the conditions of our lives. Being oblivious, willfully or naïvely, we are easily baffled, manipulated, and disempowered in ways that have us be complicit in our own oppression. Our very blindness, unawareness, and unconsciousness keep these systems wrapped in a mystique of invincibility. These systems of oppression that enthrall and enslave us may be interlocking, but each of us is a key, and individually and collectively, we can open any and all locks.

Our capacity to free ourselves, our loved ones, and the revolutionary spirit of America will be commensurate with our capacity to imagine and to dream. This, too, cannot be underestimated. We must be able to imagine a better future and prepare to engage the questions and issues that will allow us to pierce obfuscations and see past the clouded lens of oppressions. Within our capacity to unlock the interlocked is our power to perceive and the power to shift our perception, reimagine our possibilities, and consciously direct our actions.

We have to imagine and to "act as if it were possible to radically transform the world," exhorts Angela Davis. "And [we] have to do it all the time."[4] In 1862, Frederick Douglass pondered the question, "What shall be done with the four million slaves if emancipated?"[5] In 2003, almost a century and a half later, the professor-activist Angela Davis pondered the question of "dealing with the more than two million people who are currently being held in the country's jails, prisons, youth facilities, and immigration detention centers."[6] As there is no one, singular answer or solution to the multifaceted problem of the prison-industrial complex, Davis counsels a multifaceted response that entails life-affirming, democratic approaches and processes that include responsive education, physical and mental healthcare, restorative justice, and reconciliation.

Such an approach requires us to comprehend the various relationships embedded within the prison-industrial complex. It requires us to "imagine a system in which punishment is not allowed to become the source of corporate profit . . . a society in which race and class are not primary determinants of punishment . . . one in which punishment itself is no longer the central concern in the making of justice." Importantly, given how the "master-slave" dynamic reproduces, disguises, and re-forms itself and has engendered an oppressive society that enthralls us all, we must be mindful of this caveat: "Alternatives that fail to address racism, male dominance, homophobia, class bias, and other structures of domination will not, in the final analysis, lead to decarceration and will not advance the goal of abolition."[7]

Prison-industrial complex abolitionist and transformative justice practitioner Mariame Kaba, too, calls for "a jailbreak of the imagination," a radical "vision of the world we want to inhabit."[8] And we must dream more deeply and expansively and dream a dream that is bigger than our precious prejudices and one that covers those of us who no longer can dream or whose dreams have mutated into nightmares. My brother tells me, "I only have prison dream. Everybody in my dream is inmates. Every now and then I have a outside dream. But now all my dream are a waste of my sleep time. Half the time I can't even remember what they were about."[9]

As we embody the evolutionary phase of the American Revolution, we must keep the American Dream alive, and we must hold up the dreams of our brothers and sisters and those whose imaginations have been dulled within institutions of oppression. We must pursue our common American birthright and exercise our creative intelligence in realizing the principles of democracy in every sector of American society, in an America where slavery is abolished, period, where "greed and glory" are no longer major strands in the American Dream, and where justice, freedom, and sovereignty are the experience of us all.

## NOTES

1. Bobby D. Plant, letter to author, circa April 2019.

2. . . . *And Justice for All*, directed by Norman Jewison, written by Valerie Curtin and Barry Levinson (Culver City, California: Columbia Pictures, 1979). Transcriptions by the author.

3. Angela Y. Davis et al., *Abolition. Feminism. Now.* (Chicago: Haymarket Books, 2022), 3.

4. Angela Davis, "Angela Davis Talk at SIUC on Feb. 13, 2014," James Anderson, posted February 16, 2014, YouTube video, youtube.com/watch?v=6s8QCucFADc.

5. Frederick Douglass, "The Future of the Negro People of the Slave States," speech delivered before the Emancipation League in Tremont Temple, Boston, February 5, 1862," in *Frederick Douglass: Selected Speeches and Writings*, ed. Philip S. Foner (Chicago: Lawrence Hill Books, 1999), 480.

6. Angela Y. Davis, *Are Prisons Obsolete?* (New York: Seven Stories Press, 2003), 106.

7. Davis, *Are Prisons Obsolete?*, 107–8.

8. Mariame Kaba, *We Do This 'Til We Free Us: Abolitionist Organizing and Transforming Justice* (Chicago: Haymarket Books, 2021), 18, 25.

9. Bobby D. Plant, letter to author, September 8, 2020.

# ACKNOWLEDGMENTS

I N HOMAGE TO THE SPIRIT of Freedom and Sovereignty that is the birthright of all Beings. May we live this Truth.

*Of Greed and Glory* was birthed in the cradle of conversations with my former editor Tracy Sherrod. I am grateful for her vision, insights, and collaborative spirit. I thank Tracy Sherrod and my agent, Joy Harris, for their constant encouragement, support, and patience in the process of the manuscript's many iterations. I am particularly appreciative of their recommendation to anchor the contemplations of this book in the poignant story of my brother Bobby Darrin Plant. And I have immense gratitude for my brother's willingness to confide his story of incarceration to me and his unabashed courage in permitting me to share it with the world.

For her warm humanity and editorial guidance, I thank my current editor, Gabriella Page-Fort. I especially value her capacity to make perceptive inquiries and her keen ability to hear that ultimate statement, definitive detail, or concluding idea that has been left unstated, a capacity which is matched only by her equally keen ability to finesse such culminations from the writer. Warm appreciation for my proficient and personable copyeditor Kaitlyn San Miguel and the team of unnamed assistants who contributed to the production of this work.

To my family members and relatives, who in one way or another have supported our beloved Bobby and who have assisted me in the rememory of our family's journey through the ongoing injustice of a sentence of life at hard labor in Angola prison without parole, I thank you for your contributions: Gloria J. Plant-Gilbert and Jerry C. Gilbert, Alfred and Jacquelyn Plant, Erick and Catherine Plant, Dennis and Dawn Plant (who accompanied me in my travel to several research sites in Louisiana, assisted me in my research, and allowed me the use of their kitchen table to sort and type up the data gathered), Denise Elaine Plant, Frederick Demico and Kim Plant, Kersuze Simeon, Zerah Simeon Jones, G. Yvonne Carter, Catherine Omisade John, Von Erick "Blue" Plant, Geraldine Harris-Whitfield, Bobby Plant, Jr., Robby, Kaileigh, and Andros Plant.

Thank you to my community of friends, who have championed my efforts, heartened my resolve, and whose ideas and conversations have inspired my thought and sharpened my perspective in this work: "Queen" Phyllis McEwen (who generously shared her profound knowledge, wisdom, and experience in discussing with me the ideas in the manuscript throughout all its phases), Mary Wendelken, Alice Malsenior Tallulah-Kate Walker (for her gracious and poignant observations and recommendations), Laura Tohe, Gwendolyn Lucy Mary Bailey Evans, Lois Hurston Gaston, Dr. Leyun Shao, Gomati and Vasistha Ishaya, Diane D. Turner, Shekinah Me'chelle Burson, Reginald Eldridge, Loretta McBride, and "President" Glenda Johnson.

Deep gratitude for the collective spirit of all those, across the globe, across cultures and climes, and throughout time, who believe in freedom.

# APPENDIX

| (EXCERPTS FROM) THE 1740 SLAVE CODE OF SOUTH CAROLINA: An Act for the Better Ordering and Governing Negroes and Other Slaves in This Province | COMPARATIVE MODERN-DAY POLICING OF AFRICAN AMERICANS AND COMPARABLE POLICING POLICIES AND PRACTICES |
|---|---|
| "*And be it enacted . . .* that all Negroes and Indians [excepting those now free and in amity with the government] mulattoes, or mustizoes, who now are, or shall hereafter be, in this Province, and all their issue and offspring, born or to be born, shall be, and they are hereby declared to be, and remain forever hereafter, absolute slaves, and shall follow the condition of the mother." (Act I) | Racial profiling. Racialized sentencing of "duly convicted" African Americans to maximum sentences of hard labor and to life sentences of hard labor without the possibility of parole. |
| "The slave may be kept in due subjection and obedience." (Preamble) | Police officers' and white civilians' demands of submission and compliance from African Americans. |
| "*Be it further enacted . . .* that no person whatsoever shall permit or suffer any slave under his or their care or management . . . to go out of the limits of [Charlestown], or . . . to go out of the plantation . . . without a letter . . . or a ticket." (Act III) | Constant surveillance of African American persons. 911 calls to police to report Black presence in presumed white-only spaces, vicinities, or locales. Continued circumscription of Black freedom and denial of Black personal sovereignty. |
| "Without such letter or ticket . . . or without a white person in his company, [such slave] shall be punished with whipping on the bare back, not exceeding twenty lashes." (Act III) | Black persons are subject to demands, beating, choking, shooting, and killing by white civilians. Black persons reported to police are subject to questioning, arrest, beating, choking, tasing, shooting, and killing by the police. |

| | |
|---|---|
| *"And it shall be further enacted . . .* That if any slave who . . . shall refuse to submit or undergo the examination of any white person, it shall be lawful for any such white person to pursue, apprehend, and moderately correct such slave; and if any such slave shall assault and strike such white person, such slave may be lawfully killed." (Act V) | Authorized use of chokeholds, tasing, drugs, and lethal force by officers disproportionately against Black persons resisting or perceived to be resisting arrest, failing to comply, or "disrespecting" officers. Legalized use of lethal force by self-deputized white neighborhood watch patrollers or white citizens, citizen-activists/vigilantes whose violence is made acceptable and legitimate through stand-your-ground laws. |
| *"And be it further enacted . . .* That it shall and may be lawful for every justice assigned to keep the peace in this Province . . . to command to their assistance any number of persons as they shall see convenient, to disperse any assembly or meeting of slaves which disturb the peace or endanger the safety of his Majesty's subjects, and to search all suspected places for arms, ammunition or stolen goods, and to apprehend and secure all such slaves as they shall suspect to be guilty of any crimes or offences whatsoever." (Act VII) | Criminalization of Black persons underlie the inclination to presume them guilty until proven innocent. Antidemocratic politicians, lawmakers, and law enforcers trample the rights of African Americans to freely assemble. Stop and frisk laws. No-knock warrants. Arbitrary application of "probable cause" in search-and-seize procedures. |
| "And *whereas,* natural justice forbids that any person, of what condition soever, should be condemned unheard . . . *be it therefore enacted . . .* That all crimes and offences which shall be committed by slaves in this Province, and for which capital punishment shall or lawfully may be inflicted, shall be heard, examined, tried, adjudged and finally determined by any two justices [and three to five freeholders]." (Act IX) | Unnatural justice allowed for two sets of criminal codes in colonial America—one for enslaved and nominally free Blacks, "Indians," "mulattoes," and "mustizoes," and the other for whites. "Justice," then, was necessarily disparate, and those disparities continue in today's Criminal Injustice System with the consequence of mass incarceration of Black and brown peoples and a multibillion-dollar prison industry. |

| | |
|---|---|
| "*And be it further enacted* . . . That any slave who shall . . . raise or attempt to raise an insurrection . . . shall, upon conviction . . . suffer death." (Act XVII) | African Americans' exercising of their constitutional rights of free speech, the right to assemble peacefully, the right to peaceful protest, and the right to vote is perceived by antidemocratic politicians, lawmakers, and law enforcers as "insurrection" or, in today's political parlance, "domestic terrorism." The result is the suppression of human and constitutional rights through repressive legislation and police intimidation. |
| "*And be it further enacted* . . . That it shall not be lawful for any slave, unless in the presence of some white person, to carry or make use of fire arms, or any offensive weapons whatsoever, unless such Negro or slave shall have a ticket or license . . . from his master, mistress or overseer, to hunt and kill game . . ." (Act XXIII) | African Americans with permits to own and/or carry guns and who have declared such to a police officer have been killed by the police officer. |
| "*And be it further enacted* . . . That it shall and may be lawful for every person in this Province, to take, apprehend and secure any runaway or fugitive slave, and they are hereby directed to send such slave to the master or other person having the care or government of such slave. . . . [If slave is unknown,] then such slave shall be sent . . . into the custody of the warden of the work-house . . . [who] as soon as conveniently it may be, [shall] publish, in the weekly gazette, such slave, with the best descriptions he shall be able to give." (Act XXV) | Stereotyped images of African Americans that reflect and reinforce the single-story narrative of African Americans as criminals and as socially marginalized and residentially restricted second-class citizens persist. Use of flawed, racialized police facial-recognition software. Use of 911 police calls as the colonial, provincial "hue and cry" to report "unknown" Blacks. |

| | |
|---|---|
| "*Be it enacted* . . . That if any person or persons whosoever, shall willfully murder his own slave, or the slave of any other person, every such person, shall, upon conviction thereof, forfeit and pay the sum of seven hundred pounds . . . and is hereby declared . . . incapable of . . . receiving the profits of any office." (Act XXXVII) | Police officer–related shooting, maiming, killing, or murdering of unarmed African Americans sometimes results in settlements, and less frequently in dismissals, criminal charges, or convictions. |
| "*And be it further enacted* . . . That if any person shall be at any time sued for putting in execution any of the powers contained in this Act, such person shall and may plead the general issue and give the special matter and this Act in evidence." (Act LII) | Immunity or qualified immunity for law enforcers. Racialized stand-your-ground laws for the legal protection of white civilians. |
| "*And be it further enacted* . . . That his Majesty's part of the fines, penalties and forfeitures which shall be recovered by the virtue of this Act, shall be paid into the hands of the justices, or in the court where the same shall be recovered, who shall make a memorial and record of the payment of the same, and shall, without delay, send a transcript of such memorial or record to the public treasurer of this Province." (Act LV) | Policing for profit. Establishment of a criminal-punishment bureaucracy that has generated a multibillion-dollar mass incarceration industry by virtue of corrupting the ideals of justice, subverting the principles of democracy, and waging a stealth insurrection against freedom. |

# INDEX

discouragement, 251–52, 260
financial dependency, 44
funeral and burial arrangements
   for, 92–93
gunshot incident, 198–99
on hard labor, 101–2, 105–6
identity, 89, 93
letters from, 42
patriarchal mindset, 201
plea-deal process, 59, 65, 89, 135
on prison conditions, 225
regret, 198, 200–201, 251–52
relationships, 87, 127, 200
trial and sentencing, 16, 75, 78,
   103, 201
wrongly convicted for rape, 59,
   76, 81, 85, 135
Plant, Deborah, 2–4, 16, 40–42,
   72–75, 87
Plant, Elouise Porter, 74
plea-deal process, 59, 75–76, 90n5, 118
Plessy v. Ferguson, 37n7, 46, 148–49
Point Lookout cemeteries, 93
"Politics of the Convict Lease System
   in Louisiana" (Carleton), 116n71
poverty, 1, 62, 67n39, 128, 132n40,
   155, 205
prison-industrial complex, 42,
   60–61, 83, 117, 250n21, 260. See
   also criminal-punishment system
privilege, 153–55
prosecuting attorneys, 75–76, 90n5,
   134, 135, 136, 169, 190
public defenders, 81–82
"Punishment Bureaucracy, The"
   (Karakatsanis), 11n5

racism
   in American economic systems,
      194n20
   in criminal-exception loophole, 17
   in criminal justice system, 14,
      77–79, 139
   in criminal-punishment system,
      1, 15, 43, 77, 109, 111, 119,
      142–43, 150–51, 175

greed and, 22, 52–53, 121
   patriarchy and, 62, 201–2
railroading, 137–138
rebellion, fear of, 215–16, 217–18,
   220, 221
Reconstruction era
   Black Codes, 44–47, 54, 66n6, 77,
      109, 149, 212
   convict leasing, 106
   false narratives in, 32, 58
   "forty acres," 54–55
   "lost" property, 194n20
   lynchings, 15, 56–58, 78
   mass incarceration, 55–56
   patriarchy and, 19
   racial categories, 53–54
Reese, Elizabeth Anne, 54
"refusal" vs. "resistance," 11n13
Richardson, Edmund, 115n57
Romanus Pontifex, 119–20
Roosevelt, Theodore, 53
Rosenthal, Caitlin, 162–63, 164, 165,
   193, 194
Routh, Francis, 95
Rucker, Edward, 179–80

school policies, 128–29
"school-to-prison pipeline," 128
Scott, Dred, 87
"seasoning" of slaves, 102–3, 105–6
separate-but-equal doctrine, 37n7,
   46, 148–49
shame, 84, 87–89, 191
sharecropping, 19, 99, 208, 212
"silent profit," 191–92
Sister I'm Sorry (1998), 222n3
Sites of Conscience, 66n12
slavery
   in antebellum America (See slavery
      in America, antebellum)
   defined, 215
   global, 27, 47–48, 49, 107–8, 119–21
   in modern America (See modern-
      day slavery)
   in postbellum America (See
      Reconstruction era)